# Discover Carp Fishing

# Discover Carp Fishing

*Simon Crow & Rob Hughes*

The Crowood Press

First published in 2002 by
The Crowood Press Ltd
Ramsbury, Marlborough
Wiltshire SN8 2HR

**www.crowood.com**

This impression 2007

**British Library Cataloguing-in-Publication Data**
A catalogue record for this book is available from the British Library.

ISBN 978 1 86126 556 2

Line illustrations by Helen Crow and Carp Fishing News Ltd.

Photographs by the authors and contributors.

**Dedication**
For Cath and my beautiful daughter Elly.
*Rob*

For my two gorgeous girls Bethany and Sharna.
*Simon*

Typeset and designed by Helen Crow.

Printed and bound in Great Britain by Cromwell Press Ltd., Trowbridge, Wiltshire

# CONTENTS

# ACKNOWLEDGEMENTS

This book would never have been completed without the efforts of many of our friends and family. First and foremost, our thanks must go to Crowy's wife, Helen, for her design and layout skills. The book looks fabulous and this is due to her work and efforts alone. Thanks also to Kev Clifford at Carp Fishing News Ltd for allowing us to use his computers at times of need. Thanks to Cath, simply for being so understanding of Rob's work commitments, and to both of our families for helping us wherever they have: especially the little ones – Bethany, Sharna and Elly. Oh, let's not forget Digby, Rob's dog! Thanks to the anglers who have inspired us over the years. Especially to Tim and Hutchy who are both true legends of our sport. Thanks to Briggsy just for being such a superb mate, and to Martin and Gilly down in South Africa who are the biggest pair of plonkers going (only joking lads!). Lastly, thanks to everyone who's helped us along the way especially Jon 'Shoes' Jones and Derek Fell. We owe you all a beer. And guess what? For once Crowy's paying!

# INTRODUCTION

As we write this, it is almost five years since we released our first book to the British market – *Strategic Carp Fishing*, another of Crowood's titles under the carp fishing banner. Since then, the sport has changed a great deal and consequently so has our approach to fishing. *Strategic Carp Fishing* was a rather technical book more suited to the experienced carper. Although there is some overlap with this title, we like to think this is at the opposite end of the spectrum and has an updated feel to it. *Discover Carp Fishing* is, as the title suggests, basically a book for the newcomer to the sport. We've tried to be as thorough as possible in the design of the chapters, trying to include as much as we think is relevant to the beginner. At the same time, we've also tried to exclude the sort of advice that we think may lose you along the way. There are many books about carp fishing. There are also many videos and other media sources available today, but many of these, we feel, don't get down to the 'grass-roots' level we are trying to achieve with this title. In today's carp fishing world, we are both still considered young anglers. We like to think that we have benefited from working our way through the trade because this has given us the privileged position of having been at both ends of the scale. There is nothing that will ever replace the all-important 'experience it for yourself' lessons, but we know that this book will teach newcomers some of the valuable lessons necessary to achieve those target dreams. The book was originally published for the French market in 1999 and has since, we are proud to say, been applauded by many anglers the world over. We are proud that The Crowood Press has recognized this too, and that you have decided to delve into its depths for some carp-catching tips. We just hope that we can provide you with the goods you are after. We're confident that we can, but at the end of the day, just remember the most valuable piece of advice we can offer – like waters, all angling situations differ. There are no hard and fast rules to catching carp. The angler has to think for him/herself, he/she has to work for him/herself and only then will the rewards be there for the taking. Whatever your dreams are when it comes to catching carp, make sure that you enjoy yourselves along the way. We certainly have!

Simon Crow & Rob Hughes

# 1  KNOW YOUR QUARRY

In our minds, one of the topics most overlooked by modern-day carp anglers is knowledge of the species they are angling for. It's all well and good possessing a developed mind for bait, rigs, and tackle, but fundamentally, the angler will fail in many ways if he doesn't fully understand the target fish. A fish is not just a fish, as all will differ in many ways. This chapter seeks to address some of the important characteristics of the carp and how it survives in its favoured habitat of the freshwater rivers and stillwaters. Use the information wisely to plan your tactics for your chosen venue. Before we look at the fish themselves, however, it is important to know a little about the world in which they live. Remember that freshwater fish have a very simple existence in that all they require for a happy life is food, oxygen and a mate with whom to reproduce.

## SIMPLE FRESHWATER BIOLOGY

Many of you will have heard of the food chain in past biology classes at school, but if you were anything like us, you will have spent most of the lesson time daydreaming of being out on the banks instead of inside a stuffy classroom. Basically, the food chain is the name given to the way superior animals feed upon lesser animals lower down the chain. Man is said to be at the top of the food chain, but each and every link is important as, if one were missing, a natural balance would not be reached so animals higher up the chain would suffer. So where does the animal at the bottom of the chain get its food? The answer to this question is that light and heat energy from the sun together with various chemicals, such as phosphates and nitrates in the water, create the part of the chain known as photosynthesis, which allows plants to grow. Once plant life is established, animals will also be able to survive. The carp, in common with all other fish, takes oxygen from the water through its gills in order to breath. The gills are situated just behind the head of the fish and are protected by

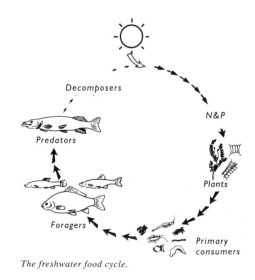

The freshwater food cycle.

bony plates called gill covers. The fish breathes by taking water into its mouth with its gill covers closed. Then it closes its mouth, opens its gill covers and raises the floor of the mouth, forcing water out over the gills. The gills themselves contain very fine blood vessels which allow oxygen to pass through their outer membrane and into the blood stream. As an illustration of how effective this system is, consider that the air we breathe has an oxygen content of approximately 21 per cent, whereas water contains only 0.001 per cent oxygen at 8°C. Photosynthesis is another word you may recall from biology lessons. Basically, this is the process whereby green plants take in carbon dioxide and sunlight and produce simple sugars, releasing oxygen into the water in the process. This is obviously useful to know, as it is only during the daylight hours that the green plants are oxygenating the water. At night the opposite is the case, with the plants taking oxygen out of the water and releasing carbon dioxide back in. Furthermore, the water temperature also makes a difference to the amount of oxygen it contains – the warmer the water, the lower the dissolved oxygen content. So what does all of this mean? Well, we know that carp require a certain amount of oxygen to survive and we also know that oxygen gets into the water via a number of different ways (wind action, pressure changes, etc), but we can also draw the conclusion that, at certain times of the year (for example summertime), certain parts of the lake will have more dissolved oxygen than others. The shallows, where the water is warmer, will have less dissolved oxygen than the cooler parts of the lake. Also, the weed beds at night will be taking oxygen out of the water and replacing it with carbon dioxide. The shallow margins, especially those with reedbeds and weed, may therefore become depleted of oxygen during a warm summer night, so fishing in these areas during this time may not be productive. It is vitally important to note here that if you intend to sack a fish for the night in summer, from a fish welfare point of view, it must be away from weed and reedbeds in a reasonable depth of water. In the daytime, it is best to sack fish in the shade if possible, but really there should be no need to sack a fish during the day.

## THE CARP FAMILY

### Background
Although a very popular sporting fish, the carp accounts for a huge percentage of the annual aquaculture production around the world. The carp is a native of the Caspian Sea and its distribution is widely associated with the Romans. It is a hardy fish, and tolerant of a wide variety of environmental conditions – it

*A carp illustrating the body conformation of the wild carp.*

can survive pH levels as low as 5 and as high as 10. It is classed as a warm-water fish and begins feeding reasonably well at a water temperature of 10°C, with its optimum growth occurring at around 25°C. *Cyprinus carpio* is found in five main genetic varieties, namely the wild, common, mirror, linear and leather carp.

## Wild Carp

The wild carp is the original form of carp and its distribution around the world can be traced back thousands of years. All of the carp mentioned below are mutations of this fish and have evolved through the continued cross-breeding practices of fish farmers. The wild carp is very long and streamlined in appearance and very rarely grows above the weight of 10lb. It is distinguished by its slender flanks and the lack of a 'hump' towards the top of the head. The fish is stronger, possesses 20 per cent more red blood cells and has a higher blood sugar level than the domesticated carp. Although originally widely distributed, the fish is not commonly found in our waters today.

## Common Carp

The common carp, as we know it, is the nearest descendant of the wild carp. Fundamentally speaking, the common carp is genetically different to the 'wildie' through the possession of an inherited recessive trait connected to growth. When compared with the mirror, leather and linear types of carp, depending on the environment it is

*Simon with a Horseshoe Lake common of 27¾lb.*

subjected to, the common carp has been scientifically proven to have the best growth rate (rate meaning increase and not potential size). All of the other types are mutations of the common and this is the main reason why most common carp live longer, are hardier and have very few deformities when compared with the others.

## Mirror Carp

The mirror carp was the first mutation of the common carp and its formation is related to two alternative forms of genes,

*Gilbert Foxcroft with a stunning South African mirror.*

known as the 'S' and the 'N' alleles. Both alleles are paired and may possess a major and a minor version (the minor is recessive). The genetic term for the mirror carp is 'ssnn' (all minor). The actions of the 's' (minor) and the 'N' (major) genes in carp have an effect on a wide scope of traits besides scaling and this is the reason why the mirror carp often has fewer soft rays in the dorsal, ventral and pelvic fins than the common and wild carp. As with all carp, the mirror possesses a number of other genes which account for the fish's body length, mouth positioning, scale pattern and so on, and this is where the terms 'race' and 'strain' have become widely intertwined. Certain mirror carp have been scientifically proven to be capable of attaining higher weights than commons, leathers and linears, and once again, this is related to genetics.

## Leather Carp

If you look very carefully at the picture of the leather carp it possesses a few scales and some people may think this makes it a mirror carp. Scientifically, however, a leather carp can possess a few scales, with the principal difference being that the dorsal row of scales is either absent or, if it is present, it is not continuous, showing breaks. Scales are small and absent altogether from the head up to the start of the dorsal fin. Leathers have reduced growth when compared with the commons and mirrors because they have fewer red blood cells. This means the fish also requires a higher volume of oxygen to fill itself up when feeding. The true leather carp is not as hardy as the other varieties and, as well as having fewer dorsal spines than the other types, it frequently shows genetic kink/ deformities in its fins.

## Linear Carp

True linear carp have a single row of scales along the lateral line – any variance to this signifies another genetic classification of carp. Like leather carp, linears have restricted maximum growth potential. Generally, both types also

*Christian Finkelde with a French leather carp.*

*The classic linear scaling.*

grow more slowly than the mirrors and commons (when from the same strain). Another classic feature of the linear and leather carp is their more intensive fat metabolism. Fat amasses more quickly in both types during the summer time and is also utilized in greater amounts during the winter. The delayed growth of the linear and leather carps is often related to the reduced amount of gill organs/rakers in the fish as well as the decreased number of pharyngeal teeth they possess – both types have two rows (sometimes only one) compared with the three rows of the common and mirror types.

## THE CARP'S EXTERNAL FEATURES

*More food please!*

### Fins

The carp possesses a number of fins to help it to yaw, pitch, or roll. There are two sets of paired fins known as the pectoral and pelvic fins, whilst all others are singular. Both paired sets assist with vertical and horizontal control, whilst the dorsal and anal fins help with balance. The tail fin is the most important fin of a fish as this helps with sudden bursts of speed so it can avoid danger and thus survive within the aquatic environment. However, a carp can survive without the use of its fins, and it is not uncommon to come across healthy fish that do not possess a full set.

### Olfactory Senses

Situated on the dorsal surface of the snout are the olfactory sensors (the nose). The nostril opening is double, and the water enters via the anterior opening and leaves via the posterior opening; the flow of currents is generated by the swimming action of the fish. Inside the organ there are millions of tiny hairs that assist with chemoreception. There is very little scientific data about chemoreception in king carp, but in the case of the goldfish (*Carassius auratus*), a close relative, recordings of activity carried out by electro-olfactograms show that the fish can detect four definite olfactory stimulants: bile salts, steroids amino acids and prostaglandins. Amino acids will function as feeding stimulants, whereas prostaglandins and steroids will act as sex pheromones in the breeding season. Chemoreception in king carp is thought to be very similar to the goldfish.

### The Gustatory System

The gustatory system is basically the taste organ of the fish. Within carp, the mouth is said to be the main gustatory organ. The main taste buds known as the palatal organ, are located in the roof of the mouth. However, the lips, barbels, gill rakers and pectoral fins all carry taste buds of some sort. The gustatory organ is sensitive to sour, sweet, saline and savoury substances, and is incredibly sensitive compared to that of the human. There is a limited gustatory response to amino acids or nucleotides in carp, but in particular orders both can be excellent feeding stimulants.

### The Eyes

The carp's eyes are located on either side of the head to give an excellent field of vision; they are very sensitive to movement. However, they do not offer the fish a good binocular vision. The carp's eye operates very much like a camera, and rays of light are focused onto the retina by the lens. According to scientists, fish see within an angle of 97.6 degrees and can see in a circular window when looking above the water.

Outside the window, images are reflected off the water surface onto the bottom, which is why fish have difficulty viewing items on the bottom during strong winds. Carp are thought to possess photoreceptors which have enhanced sensitivity to capture photons (solar radiation components) at low light levels, but in the main, they are said to have trichromatic vision with visual pigments absorption peaks of approximately 455nm (blue), 530nm (green), and 625nm (red) – this means that the fish sees better in depths of less than 25m. Deeper than this, the carp is thought to see in the blue light spectrum, although biotic and abiotic factors can influence this.

### Mechanoreceptors

All carp possess an acoustic-lateralis system. The mechanoreceptors are located in this system, comprising the ear and lateral line, which work in co-ordination with one another. The neuromast is the basic mechanoreceptor and this consists of a group of sensory hair cells which help the fish to locate water movements and direction, as well

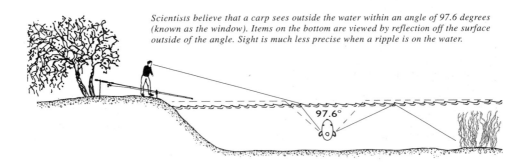

*Scientists believe that a carp sees outside the water within an angle of 97.6 degrees (known as the window). Items on the bottom are viewed by reflection off the surface outside of the angle. Sight is much less precise when a ripple is on the water.*

97.6°

as to co-ordinate balance. It basically operates by causing vibrations in the fish which allow it to detect sound as well as potential dangers – such as those projected by outboard motors or echo sounders. Although the ears of carp are hidden, the lateral line is often very distinct on mirrors, leathers and linear carp.

### Scales

The carp's skin comprises two different layers – an inner (dermis) and an outer (epidermis). All scales grow from within the inner layer and are protected by a layer of mucus. Both layers act as major defences for the carp against infection. It is possible for fish to lose scales naturally or through bad handling by anglers, and they will normally grow back. However, anglers should try to minimize any possible damage by wetting weighing equipment prior to use and having a bottle of antiseptic solution, such as Klin-ik, handy.

## THE CARP'S INTERNAL FEATURES

### The Skeletal Structure

The carp is a member of the teleosts, a sub-group of the bony fish, and it possesses a skeletal structure throughout its whole body. The most obvious parts of the internal skeleton are the dorsal and central vertebrae, and it is to the latter of these that some of the most important internal organs are attached. Surrounding the internal organs are ribs; very often, protruding ribs on the sides

of the fish are incorrectly claimed to have been caused by anglers, when in actual fact most are genetically evolved. Nevertheless, the shape of the skeletal structure may be down to any one of a number of reasons (very often you will come across fish that have developed deformities at the egg-hatching stage).

### The Swim Bladder

Aside from the use of the fins, carp, and indeed all bony fish, can regulate their depth in the water column by using their swim bladder. The swim bladder is basically a gas-filled sack above the intestine. It helps the fish to reduce the amount of energy it expends, and is filled with air from the surface in the first few weeks of the fish's life (known as the swim-up stage). Carp have been known to survive perfectly well without the assistance of the swim bladder.

### The Kidney

The carp has a number of internal organs to help it to survive in the aquatic environment. It is a cold-blooded creature, so its internal temperature is always in balance with that of the surrounding water. Internally, the carp's

*The skeletal structure of the carp with the dorsal and central vertebrae clearly visible.*

bodily fluids contain large amounts of salt, so the kidney, its most vital organ, is continually flushing out water which has travelled via osmosis into the fish. If you make your own boiled baits always watch the amount of salt you use – any exertion of the carp's kidney may lead to possible damage, resulting in the fish swelling or bursting through taking in too much water.

## The Heart

The carp's heart lies just below the gill cover (known as the operculum) and pumps blood around the body. The blood is pumped in a single circulation and absorbs oxygen from the water in the gills. Here, the blood passes through capillaries (fine blood cells) which have a very thin wall. As the water is drawn over the gill capillaries, oxygen is drawn from the water. Smaller fish breathe (so to speak) at a quicker rate than larger fish, and this is one reason why the smaller inhabitants of a water are normally the first to be lost during times of pollution.

## The Intestine

The carp does not have a stomach but instead has a very long intestine, where its food is broken down by enzymes. The carp's diet is very varied (it is omnivorous) so the intestine needs to cope with both meat and weed products. Weed generally requires more mastication by the fish and takes longer to digest (due to the large number of cells it possesses), and this is why the intestine is so long. Within the intestine, which starts directly behind the oesophagus, powerful digestive juices assist with the passage of food. The reaction caused by digestion is usually alkaline (pH 7–7.7); recent experiments have shown that the pH level fluctuates depending on the temperature of the water. Pepsin (an essential protein-digesting enzyme) is not found naturally in the carp, but has to be gained by the fish through its food sources.

## The Central Nervous System

Decisions and movement are triggered by the central nervous system, which, in

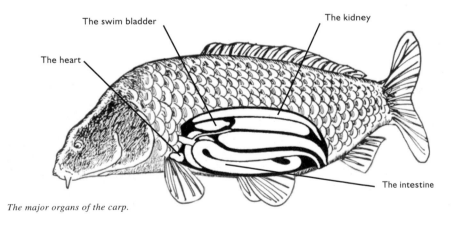

*The major organs of the carp.*

its simplest form, consists of sensory nerve paths, brain nerve paths and motor nerve paths (it is these pathways that are disrupted by electricity when electric fishing). The spinal cord runs along the back of the fish and is supported by the dorsal vertebral column, whilst the brain, which lies at the top of the head, is surrounded by the cranium box. Automatic responses in carp are governed by the memory division of the brain, and, simply put, this can be split into the two areas of interpretation and long-term memory. The latter of the two is said to be the most developed in fish; for example, carp have the basic intelligence to know that there will be a hookbait amongst a bed of free offerings, but they have difficulty in working out which one it is. Nevertheless, the carp can learn to modify its behaviour through experience, and this can be a very difficult area to crack for the carp man even on the easiest of waters.

# FOOD AND FEEDING

### The Food Selection Process (FSP)

| Phase 1 | Detection | ► Ignore |
| Phase 2 | Approach | ► Avoid |
| Phase 3 | Select | ► Reject |
| Phase 4 | Sample | ► Eject |
| Phase | Ingestion | |

All fish feed on food items by following a selection process. This is never changed in any way and a simple diagram outlines the main stages. In order to progress from phase 1 to phase 5, carp are required to utilize a number of different sensory organs, including the chemoreceptors, taste receptors, sight, mouth and the pharyngeal teeth. Studying the FSP shows that everything needs to fit into place within your overall angling strategy. Here we have provided a breakdown of tactical considerations in order of importance:

1. Bait attraction properties.
2. Bait and rig positioning.
3. Bait abundance.
4. Rig appearance.
5. Rig efficiency.
6. Bait taste.

### Feeding
The carp will sample most food items with its lips, which are equipped with minute receptors. If the item is found attractive, it will pass to the carp's throat teeth before ingestion. The pharyngeal teeth are located behind the mouth proper and comprise between one and three rows of teeth, depending on the type of carp. These will crush food items with the assistance of a pad in the palate of the mouth, and these do wear out with time and excessive use. Besides the lips and teeth, the carp also possesses a bronchial system which filters out minute particles from the water (comprised of branchiospines, branchial arches and bronchial apertures). Generally speaking, small young fish

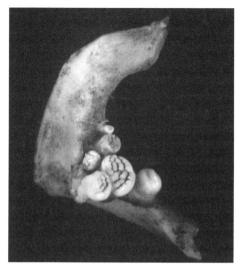

*A close-up on the pharyngeal teeth of the carp.*

be another ruling factor here as well as water quality and type. The natural diet of carp is a difficult topic to address because it is site-specific, but generally speaking, it will range from minute particles such as water fleas (Copepoda) to larger items like molluscs (Gastropoda). Where anglers are present in large numbers, there is scientific evidence available to suggest that over 70 per cent of the carp's diet may consist of artificial feed. It is our opinion that all carp, regardless of the venue, will feed on natural food items throughout the year. The only difference is that the percentage of artificials in the diet will vary from venue to venue depending on a wide range of influences such as angler numbers, stocking density, available habitat and so on. Nevertheless, during the calendar year, the natural food cycle (NFC) in all aquatic ecosystems undergoes a number of important changes that all carp anglers should be aware of if they wish to be successful time and time again. At the onset of winter much of the natural aquatic food stock decreases in one way or another. Cold fronts of high pressure cause water temperatures to plummet, and with this, the abundance and variety of natural food available to the fish also drops. In Europe the most distinct NFC fall normally occurs somewhere around the end of October/early November but, such is the unreliability of the weather, it can be earlier or later than this (depending on where you live). The supply of natural food in water bodies may be altered by any one of a number of factors at any time (for example, freak weather conditions, pollution, stocking

have a finer and better developed bronchial system than larger carp, but both are capable of feeding on suspended particles like branchiopods (such as *Daphnia hyalina*, *Simocephalus vetalus*, and so on), ostracods (such as *Cyprus*), and copepods (for example *Cyclops*, *Diaptomus castor*).

**Seasonal Diet Variations**

In the main, carp are bethivorous fish (that is, bottom feeders), but they can feed at all levels of the water column when the need arises. The natural diet of carp will shift with seasonal variations depending on a number of important factors – that is, some food items (such as chironomids) are profusely available in the spring, whilst others are more abundant in the cooler periods of the annual calendar (for example *Asellus*). Favouritism will also

or introductions), but, generally speaking, it falls towards its lowest level in December/January. Scientific studies and field experiments show that certain natural food items that carp in most waters become dependent on for healthy living, such as Chironomus (a large family of midge larvae otherwise known as bloodworm), molluscs and crustaceans, fall to their lowest levels towards the beginning of winter and don't begin to multiply until the water temperature starts to rise in the early part of spring. Many other natural foods of fish display a similar cycle, and the carp will recognize this and feed selectively on its favourite or most readily available item throughout the year. Basically, as one particular food item begins to decrease, the carp will cleverly shift its diet towards another source (for example, in August it may be mollusc, whilst in September it may be the Chironomus). The table below shows a typical breakdown of the seasonal variation in natural carp diet during a twelve-month period. This information was gained from a study carried out on three large lakes in southeastern France. Although a similar experiment carried out at your local lake may well yield different results, it nevertheless gives us something to work off. To obtain the information, fish were taken from the lakes continually throughout the year. Once taken from the waters, the fish were killed immediately and their stomachs sampled to identify what they had been feeding on. To cut a long and potentially boring story short, the result was that the diet of the carp alters with the availability of food items within the annual cycle. Towards the beginning of winter, the carp has very little natural food to turn to in order to fulfil its requirements, so anglers' baits frequently become the main focus. With some fish this is normal as they have a

|  | J | F | M | A | M | J | J | A | S | O | N | D |
|---|---|---|---|---|---|---|---|---|---|---|---|---|
| Chironomid | 6.2 | 11.3 | 4.6 | 10.2 | 8.4 | 39.2 | 39 | 56 | 19 | 1.6 | 6 | 2.3 |
| Coleoptera (beetles) | 2.8 | 2.6 |  | 10.8 | 1.2 |  | 1.1 |  | 10.6 | 4.2 | 11 |  |
| Diptera (flies) |  |  | 0.8 | 0.5 | . | 1.8 |  |  | 3.1 | 0.3 | 0.6 |  |
| Mollusca (snails etc.) | 63 | 48.3 | 33.6 | 26.5 | 38.3 | 13 | 18 | 2.3 | 19 | 13.6 | 31 | 45 |
| Tubifex (worms) |  | 3.3 | 14.2 | 20.3 | 0.9 |  |  |  | 6 | 14.2 | 24.2 | 10.7 |
| Small crustacea |  | 0.3 | 2.9 | 3.4 | 13.2 | 31.4 | 36 | 28.6 | 9 | 3.4 | 0.1 |  |
| Large crustacea | 13.2 | 9 | 6 | 3.8 | 0.3 | 1.1 | 2.2 | 1.3 | 18.3 | 16.1 | 13.2 | 11 |
| Vegetable material |  |  |  |  |  |  | 1.2 |  | 0.3 |  |  |  |
| Unidentified | 6.3 | 19 | 19.9 | 4.3 | 18 | 6 |  | 0.5 | 4.3 | 25 | 2.1 | 24 |
| Leech |  | 0.3 |  | 2.1 | 6.7 |  |  |  | 4.3 | 2.1 | 7.8 |  |
| Terrestrial | 8.5 | 6 | 8 | 18.1 | 13 | 7.2 | 2.5 | 11.3 | 6.1 | 9.5 | 4 | 7 |
| Total | 100 | 100 | 100 | 100 | 100 | 100 | 100 | 100 | 100 | 100 | 100 | 100 |

*Seasonal diet variation in carp from three south-eastern French lakes in 1975 (figures expressed in percentages).*

preference for such items, but others, which are shy to anglers, do so only because they have no other option. Furthermore, being a cold-blooded creature, the carp needs to feed heavily at the start of winter to prepare for its dormant winter period. As a result, the late autumn months are one of the best periods of the year for carp fishing. The first signs of dropping water temperatures usually excite the carp into a big intensive feeding frenzy. Strong winds often assist here as they provide excellent feeding conditions by stirring up the bottom and oxygenating the water well, but at venues where the carp's diet is mainly comprised of natural food, it is the decrease in its availability and the onset of the long cold winter months that chiefly explain why this is the best time of the year for angling – especially if you are using artificial baits, like the majority of carp anglers these days.

### Single Sitting Satisfaction (SSS)

As the carp begins to fill itself up with food, oxygen demand is greater than when it started feeding on an empty stomach. During the summer, when oxygen levels in the water are lower, fish physically have difficulty filling themselves up to a maximum in one sitting (known as Single Sitting Satisfaction). Leather carp are an excellent example here, as genetically they are different to commons, mirrors and linears in that they require greater levels of oxygen when feeding (they possess fewer red blood cells). Where low levels of oxygen are present in a water, leather carp cannot eat as much food in a single sitting as the other varieties and this is one reason why true leathers have restricted growth potential. Where SSS is not possible in the summer months in a water, all varieties of carp will more than likely feed regularly throughout the day in a little and often manner. In the winter, however, the higher levels of oxygen present in water bodies makes it increasingly possible for all varieties of carp to gain SSS, which may be reflected in the low number of repeat captures that occur in some fisheries during the cooler months.

### Digestion

The carp does not have a stomach but digests its food in the intestine. This is an important matter in itself as the absence of a stomach means that the fish secretes acids or the enzymes responsible for gastric digestion. Furthermore, there is the loss of storage

*Simon with one of two English thirties caught during below zero temperatures in a half-hour feeding spell.*

function. The intestine in a carp is fairly long (ratio of 2:3 when compared with its body length), and digestion is carried out by enzymes which are present in the intestinal wall and through the presence of gut microflora. The predominant protein-digesting enzyme is trypsin – an endopeptidase which requires residues from either lysine (amino acid) or arginine (amino acid) to assist with protein digestion. The passage of protein is also assisted by the alkaline conditions present in the carp's intestine (approximately pH 7–7.7), but is inhibited by substances such as soya or zinc. Soya inhibits the action of trypsin and therefore the passage of food items within the intestine. Zinc, on the other hand, tends to activate trypsin but decrease assimilation for some reason not yet clearly understood by scientists.

*A massive Romanian female carp of 70lb.*

increases in weight, but these fish are often in a stressed state due to ovulation. It is the males that have the solid but steady growth potential, and it is these fish that often live the longest.

### Growth

The genetic make-up of a carp and its available resources determine how big a fish will grow. The current accepted world record for a rod-caught king carp (*Cyprinus carpio*) is a reported 37kg (two fish of this weight), but it is very likely that the species will grow to above this size. There is a traditional saying amongst fish breeders that a 'quality food source results in a quality fish'. Fed the correct diet in a relaxed environment, three-year-old carp can reach a weight of well over 5lb. The carp's optimum growth rate is reached at approximately 25°C, with potential size decreasing progressively from 20°C, virtually ceasing at 5°C. Female carp usually show the greater sudden

## HABITAT

Carp can adapt to both relaxed and stressed river and lake environments. They are widely regarded as a territorial species, but within river networks it is not unusual for them to travel long distances to feed or spawn. The type of habitat a fish is subjected to usually dictates its physical characteristics. Very often fish in rivers become long and lean to accommodate the water currents, whereas in the lakes and stillwaters they are often fatter and deeper in body section. Habitat also has a huge influence on the growth potential of a carp, as its availability is very much associated with water quality and stocking densities, which in turn, are connected to available food.

# 2 MODERN CARP GEAR

The amount of tackle available to catch carp successfully is growing annually. There are now literally hundreds, if not thousands, of different companies in the market place advertising equipment for sale. This has both its good and bad points, but it is worth pointing out that one of the most difficult things for any newcomer to the sport is avoiding being drawn into buying everything that is financially possible. It is our experience that you do not need every single item of tackle, and a lot of the time you can get away with making some of the simpler items for yourself, thus saving more money.

Many of you may find yourselves lost amongst the large array of modern carp fishing tackle, and indeed many of you will find it a very tedious job  deciding what tackle best suits your needs. Although the majority of tackle shops are excellent at advising you when purchasing the right tackle for your first

steps in carp fishing, one cannot help thinking that in some cases beginners are seen as easy pickings for a good sale. In this chapter we take an in-depth look at the kind of tackle  required for modern carp fishing, from the more complicated aspects such as rod choice right through to the technicalities of bait boats.

## THE CARP ROD

### Terminology

What is a carp rod? Fundamentally speaking, it is a tool used for playing a fish, but it also has the secondary function of casting a bait. Advancements in technology have delivered to today's angler a vast range of carp rods. A simple browse through the adverts reveals a maze of pictures and words of how all are far superior to one another. Try not to lose yourself amongst such marketing hype, as it is a safe bet that

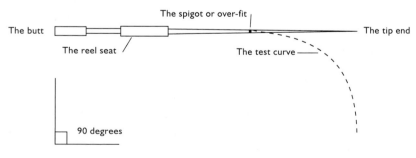

The components of the carp rod.

many of those advertised are way above the price range you actually need to spend to fulfil your needs. Don't be too disheartened by this, as we can assure you that the Rod Hutchinsons of the world all started with very basic tackle. Before we take a look at selecting a rod and its functions, we will begin with a brief glossary of terms:

**Action** Describes the performance of a carp rod with regard to its flexibility or stiffness.

**Blank** Used to describe the carp rod before the reel fittings, rings and final varnish (known as the finish) are added.

**Butt end** The thickest end of the rod (the handle).

**Tip end** The thinnest end of the rod (the top eye).

**Test curve** The weight needed to pull the tip end of the rod down till it is at right angles to the butt end. The heavier the weight needed, the stiffer the rod.

**Tip action or stiff rod** A rod that is more flexible towards the tip end and better for casting long distances.

**Through action or soft rod** A rod that is very flexible throughout and better for playing fish.

## Construction

*The Blank*

Most carp rods consist of two parts – the butt section (lower part) and the tip section (upper part). However, it is possible to purchase some that are divided into three or four parts (for storage purposes), and even ones that are telescopic. Two-part rods are usually the preferred option for general angling by most anglers as they are said to have less weaknesses in the blank than those with more sections. Wherever a section joins another, you will come across either a spigot or over-fit connection. Both types are suitable for carp rods, but we prefer the spigot fitting. Before purchasing a rod, always check this area for any damage as it is a sure thing that it will crack if it is not 100 per cent sound.

A carp rod can be made from a number of different materials, the most successful being cane, fibreglass and carbon fibre. A number of other materials can be added to these to aid with strength and to reduce thickness and weight. To minimize confusion we will stick to the simple terms listed above. As far as cost is concerned, fibreglass rods are the cheapest. Although you might think cane would be a very cheap material, rods made from it have recently become very few and far between and so the price of some cane rods has risen accordingly. Carbon fibre is a moderately cheap and extremely versatile material. Understandably it has dominated the carp rod field since its discovery, and is widely regarded as the best foundation for carp rod blanks.

A good carp rod will be made from a relatively thin blank, measuring from as little as just over half an inch (12mm) thick at the butt end and tapering down to the tip.

*Reel Fittings, Grips and Rod Rings*

Once you have chosen your blank, you can start adding the reel fittings, grips and rings. The type and the positioning of these are just as important as the type and length of the blank itself. Always look to purchase a rod equipped with what is termed a screw-lock reel fitting (the part that holds the reel). Most modern carp rods have this type of fitting, but pay close attention to the standard of this area when purchasing a rod. The last thing you want to happen is for your reel to come loose when the all-important 'take' occurs. Our favourite reel fittings are those that have aluminium or stainless sleeves over the top, but to be honest, there are plenty of good makes available on the market. Those with metal sleeves not only perform well, but also enhance the attractiveness of the rod.

Moving onto handles and grips, these usually consist of cork or sponge (Duplon) attachments, and should be chosen to suit your personal preference. There is no real difference from an angling perspective between the two varieties other than that Duplon is soft, doesn't become brittle with time and, unlike cork, won't be nibbled by mice! It doesn't really matter which type you

*Good rod rings make all the difference.*

choose, but do make sure that it provides you with enough grip when you decide to put the rod through its paces. Although it may sound obvious, it is worth stressing here that you should always pick up a rod and ensure that the positioning and distance between each grip feels comfortable. If the distance is too short or too long, your casting ability will be severely restricted. The same can be said for incorrect positioning, as this will make the rod feel unbalanced.

As far as the rings are concerned, carp rods usually have anything between six and ten rings. These come in a range of different sizes, with the largest at the butt section, tapering down to the smallest at the tip end. Rods designed for long-range casting have larger and fewer rings to help reduce friction, while soft through-action rods have more and smaller eyes to help with control when playing fish under the tip. The type, quality, and position of the rod rings is important for a number of reasons. Single-leg eyes are more suited to long-range casting as they can be positioned to allow a fluent pathway for the line, whilst the quality and make of the rings can also have an impact on the distance you cast and the risk of line damage occurring. For obvious reasons, incorrect positioning of the eyes can affect the performance of a rod in a big way, so always check the whipping and whether or not the location of the eyes provides a flowing pathway. Their distribution along the blank also needs careful consideration as the rod will not perform well when put through the test curve if the rings are incorrectly spaced. The rings should be spaced more widely towards the butt end of the rod, tapering down to the tip. There is no use in giving precise spacing distances for the rings, as not only is rod technology a complicated science, but the suggested distancing will differ depending on the type and make of the blank. If you wish to get that knowledge in-depth, may we suggest you consult a rod manufacturer like Alistair Bond.

Modern rods tend to have SIC (silicon carbide) rings because they reduce friction on the line and thus enhance casting. However, such rings add greatly to the price of the rod, so always consider the type of fishing you are going to be doing before you buy. We must point out, though, that SIC rings are a must if you tend to use braided lines, as the friction applied to the rings when playing a fish on this material is so great that it frequently cuts into and damages standard/ cheap rings.

## Carp Rod Selection

Now that we have taken a brief look at what a carp rod comprises, we can finish off with a brief summary of what to look for and what to avoid when deciding to purchase. Remember that the carp rod is the angler's main piece of kit and it will not come cheap.

- The width of the handle should be such that you feel comfortable and in control of the rod.
- The reel seat should have a screw lock mechanism.
- A two-piece rod between 1½lb and 2lb in test curve is ideal for close-range casting (up to 70yd).

*Simon puts a through-action rod through its paces at Llyn-y-Gors.*

- A rod between 2lb and 2¾lb in test curve would be ideal for multi-range casting.
- A rod 2¾lb and over in test curve would be ideal for casting at long range.
- Check rods for scratches and loose fittings, and examine the join to ensure it is a comfortable fit and has been made to suit.
- You do not need to buy matching pairs of rods; it won't make you a better angler if all your rods are the same.
- Look out for second-hand rods that are in good condition, or discontinued ranges of rods.
- Choose a rod with a height and weight suited to your abilities, technique and physique; it may be a good idea to try to have a cast with one of your friends rods

before you buy your own. Other than this, try to get a 'feel' for the rod and make sure that it is not too heavy, short, long, or uncomfortable.

- Don't get drawn into buying the first rod you see.
- You do not need to buy top-of-the-range rods to be successful.
- We would always advise the complete novice to opt for a through-action rod first in order to get the feel of a carp rod and its use. It is useless trying to start off with a stiff rod, as these are really designed for casting rather than playing fish.

For the record, we both use 13ft 3½lb Rod Hutchinson Dream Maker rods for all of our fishing (apart from stalking in restricted areas), which in our opinion are the nearest you will get to the ultimate universal carp rod. They are excellent for both casting and playing fish at both short and extreme range, and believe it or not, we have heard plenty of people comment on how they have improved their fishing in several ways. The rod has a through-action blank built by master rod-builder Alister Bond. The rod can provide both sensitivity and power whenever necessary, and really does need to be used before the effect can be felt.

The only time we decide against the Dream Maker is when we have limited space, for instance when we are stalking fish in restricted areas. We both possess 6ft fibreglass rods that have been custom made for this type of fishing. These have a very through action so that they can cope with the powerful lunge of a carp hooked under the rod tip. They are also

painted matt black so that the sun does not reflect off the blank and spook any fish.

## REELS

Before buying a reel, the first thing you should do is consider what you want it for. You may have read a lot about Shimano Big Pit Long Cast reels, but if you are only fishing a 2-acre lake where the margins are the most productive areas then the asking price may be a bit steep, especially if you can get away with something a lot cheaper and much more practical. The moral is, always buy the correct tools for the job. Reels are expensive; try to use a bit of foresight and consider where you will be fishing over the next few seasons before you buy. It would be a waste of your hard-earned cash to buy something that will do for now, but may be woefully inadequate in twelve months' time. A good all-round reel is the best bet both practically and financially.

Not only should you consider what you want the reel for, you should also

*Standard fixed-spool reel.*

take into account the rod it will be matched to. We don't mean looks here, we mean balance. A large-spooled big pit reel would be completely out of balance on an 11ft 1½lb test curve fibreglass rod – as indeed would a small baitrunner reel, such as a Shimano GT 5010, on a 13ft 3½lb test curve rod. The best way to make sure you don't make a mistake is to buy your rod and reel at the same time, or, if you already have a satisfactory rod and just want to upgrade your reel, take the rod along with you to the tackle shop and ask them to attach it to the reel so you can check that you are happy with its feel. This can also save further disappointment if you get your new reel home only to find it won't go into the rod's fittings, which can happen.

**Terminology**
**Spool** The part of the reel that holds the line.
**Coned spool** A spool where the front of the spool is narrower than the back to assist long-range casting.
**Clutch/drag** Tensioning mechanism on a reel which puts pressure on the spool to stop line being pulled from it.
**Anti-reverse** Switch/gear on the reel that stops the handle going backwards.
**Bale arm** The metal bar on the front of the reel that collects and lays the line when the handle is turned.

**Standard Fixed-Spool Reels**
These are a slightly bigger version of the average reel used by everyday coarse/match fishermen. They have an anti-

*Shimano's excellent Baitrunner.*

reverse button on them to stop the reel handle from turning backwards and also a drag control known as the clutch. This allows line to be pulled from the reel without the bale arm being open, but the clutch has to be tightened up before reeling in. These reels are fine for standard, relatively close-in work such as stalking, but are somewhat outdated for modern style static carp fishing as well as tricky to come to terms with if you are a beginner. Although they are relatively cheap, we both prefer to opt for the baitrunner or big pit-type reel.

**Baitrunners**
These are almost identical in shape to fixed-spool reels, but have a mechanism on them which allows a fish to take line without the bale arm open – known as the baitrunner. This can be engaged immediately by the flick of a button or can be turned off by reeling in line or flicking a lever. Baitrunners have been designed for modern specimen hunting, and therefore some models are larger than the standard fixed-spool reels and much more suited to the carp angler. They are by far the most practical for all-round carp fishing, as, loaded with the correct line and matched with a

*The Big Pit reel.*

decent rod, the larger models will allow the angler to cast in excess of 120yd. To boot, they are also suitable for soft rods and margin fishing.

Besides baitrunners, such reels are also commonly known as free-spool or bite 'n' run reels. Our preference is for the Shimano GT Baitrunner, which comes in a variety of sizes, but, as with most items of tackle these days, it isn't exactly cheap. Don't worry if you don't have or can't afford one of the purpose-designed Baitrunners, though, as a standard reel will do the trick just as well: they just aren't quite so easy to use.

### Big Pit Reels

Although these reels can be used at a variety of distances, they are ideally suited for the angler whose fishing is usually done at a range in excess of 150yd. They are very small-bodied, large-spooled reels that carry a huge amount of line. The clutch/drag is adjusted at the front of the reel to play fish, and the spool is shaped like a cone with the front narrower than the back so that line can easily pour off on the cast

or when boating the baits out. These reels are best avoided by beginners, as it is unlikely they will be fishing at a distance where one is required. The best advice we can give to the starter is to learn the trade on the much easier-to-handle reels mentioned above rather than on the tricky big pit reels. These reels are designed for a specific purpose and will set you back at least £100 each. If you're going to be fishing the big French reservoirs, though, such as Chantecoq, Orient, then you will need a full set to fish effectively. Our favourites are Shimano's Big Pit Long Cast reels.

There's not a great deal more to say about reels other than that there is more to a reel than just casting out and reeling fish in. You have a clutch to control the tension of the line as it is pulled off the reel, something which you should always check before you start fishing. Do this by closing the bale arm and pulling the line. If you cannot pull any line off the spool try turning the clutch setting half a turn (it will be located on the front or back of the reel), until you

*The correct way to fill a spool with line (left). Always fill right to the lip of the spool. Too much and line will spill off; too little will restrict the distance you can cast (right).*

can pull line off the spool using reasonable pressure. If you can pull it off too easily tighten the clutch setting up a bit. You don't want it too slack or you'll never reel in and almost certainly give the fish you may be playing an all-important advantage. By setting the drag on your reel correctly you will be less at risk of losing a fish if it makes a fast, powerful run. As with many things associated with carp fishing, this is where experience plays a vital role.

At this point it is worth mentioning quickly the subject of line twist. This is something that has come to light in recent years through the overuse/ misuse of baitrunners and the clutch. Simply put, line pulled from the reel under the tension of the baitrunner/ clutch causes it to twist and coil when retrieved. The worst twist is created when boating baits out long distance with the baitrunner/clutch engaged. Whilst the tension on the line created in this way does somewhat help boating baits out, it is much better to open the bale arm and get a friend to hold the line under tension with his hand. Line leaving the spool with the bale arm open does not create line twist. Some of you may be wondering what the problem is with line twist. The answer is that the line can coil around the rings during casting, as well as become weakened when put under heavy tension. Avoid it.

## ALARMS AND INDICATORS

### Alarms
In the good old days at the beginning of carp fishing, bite indication was no more

complicated than the movement of a piece of silver paper, a twig, or a washing-up bottle top on the line near the reel. There is nothing to say that these methods will not work today, but as with everything else, technology advances and there have been a number of improvements which the angler today would be stupid not to take advantage of. The main breakthrough is that of the electronic bite alarm or buzzer, which, in its youth, was no more than an antenna around which the line was placed and which buzzed when a fish pulled the line. Nowadays, most electronic bite alarms work on a roller/ sensor principle: the line is placed across a roller/sensor, which, when moved, breaks an electric circuit and bleeps when the line is pulled. Some of the more traditional anglers refuse to accept electronic buzzers as part of their kit, but we believe buzzers serve an important dual purpose for the modern carp angler. Not only do they let you know when a fish has picked up your bait, they also allow you to watch the water instead of your indicator.

Here's a look at some of the different types of alarms on the market today (roughly in order of price).

**Bitech Viper** An economy alarm with tone, volume and on/off switch. In our opinion this model can be too sensitive in wind and gives plenty of false indications.

**Bitech Micro** Another alarm from Bitech with volume, tone and sensitivity controls. Very small and effective, and our favourite of the two models from

Bitech. Works on a roller principle. Highly recommended.

**Optonic XL** A very good roller wheel alarm which is moderately priced. It is equipped with an on/off button, both a run and delay LED, as well as a tone and volume control. The only problem with this alarm is that you need to take it apart to change the battery as well as the sensitivity, which is a bit awkward. Although it is reasonably priced, it requires extra additions to upgrade it to those below.

**Fox Micron SX** One of the new wave of alarms, with volume, tone and sensitivity controls. Although we haven't used this alarm ourselves we have heard plenty of good reports about it. It is another of the many roller-wheel types. There is a mini version of this alarm available which is proving to be very popular due to its budget price.

**Fox Micron RX Digital** The top of the range from the Fox stable, and certainly an alarm that comes well recommended. It works on the same principle as the Micron SX, but has the added advantage of a remote receiver facility (not to be abused by wandering too far away from your rods). This alarm also distinguishes between lifts and drop-backs, which can be very useful in some situations.

**Delkim** The new alarm from Delkim has the same features as the other modern alarms above as well as a line diameter control for when you use thick or thin lines. It can be used with a remote if necessary as well as adjusted to suit both windy and calm conditions. It possesses a sensor board which indicates both line movement and vibration. Another excellent choice.

## Indicators

As well as an alarm, you will need something which creates tension on the line to indicate which way the fish is running. We think that the best way to approach the topic of indicators in a book of this sort would be to take a look at their history, their specific uses, and also some of the more up-to-date versions. It is worth pointing out here that it is important to know *why* you need something and exactly what it is designed to do before you use it. Far too many anglers buy and use an item of tackle purely for the sake of keeping up with the latest trends rather than because it is the correct tool for the job. Besides, it's very easy to get confused between the various different types of indicators on the market, such as swingers and springers, hangers and wangers, wisps and wasps – they all sound very similar, but are in fact quite different and each is suited to different angling situations.

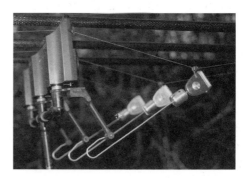

*Fox Swingers.*

## Hanger-Style Bobbins

In the age-old days of the sixties, when carp fishing was in its infancy, anglers used to use washing-up bottle tops, which were hung onto the line between the butt ring and the reel. These were the first hanger-style indicators and, of course, came free with a bottle of washing-up liquid. They were lightweight and served the purpose of indicating a bite when the line was pulled tight by the carp. In those days, before the bolt rig was widely used, anglers fished for twitches or slow, steady takes. They wanted as little restriction on their lines as possible and bottle tops were ideal.

As the carp became wise to the rigs of the day, a new indicator was needed. Things progressed rapidly and the 'monkey climber' was born. This was a heavier bobbin indicator that was threaded onto a metal pin on which it slid up and down. The main advantage of a monkey climber over a simple bobbin was that it did not swing around in the wind as much as a light bobbin and thus reduced false indications. Later on, bobbins became bigger and heavier so that they were able to register drop-backs more easily. There was a problem with monkeys, though, as they were not as free-running as a hanging bobbin. There was a lot of friction between the so-called 'monkey' and the pin, especially when it had been raining and grit had found its way onto the pin. In winter they even used to freeze to the pin! Monkeys were subsequently dispensed with and other, more modern methods of indicator used.

As far as the standard hanging bobbins are concerned, Gardner do an excellent model called the Rangemaster, which has removable weights for adjustment between long- and short-range fishing. Fox sell a Lightweight Hanger, a Carp Hanger and an Adjusta Hanger, all fairly cheap. Solar also sell a decent one called a Dangler, which is a little cheaper than the others. In our opinion hanging bobbins are the best types of indicator to use at short to medium range when the weather isn't too windy. They are not restricted to moving vertically, nor in an arc (as a swinger has to), and so are much more sensitive if set up correctly.

## Swinging-Arm Indicators

The most popular indicators today, swingers, are very versatile systems. Swingers consist of a bobbin attached to a swinging arm equipped with a sliding counterweight to enable you to adjust the weight of the bobbin, depending upon the style of fishing you are doing. Probably the most popular swinging arm indicator is the Fox Mk2 Swinger. Fox also have a Mk1 Swinger and a Euro Swinger for extreme range, but in our opinion the Mk2s are the best for all round fishing.

The advantage of swingers over bobbins is that they are very stable in the wind and, if you set them up correctly, they do not normally swing to give false indications. One of the most important points when it comes to setting up your swinger is to make sure that the counterweight on the arm is in the correct place for the style of fishing you are doing. The closer the weight is to the

*Tension arm indicators are a popular choice.*

bobbin, the heavier the bobbin will be. We know it sounds obvious but we have frequently seen anglers fishing in the margins with the weight right up against the bobbin, or at long range with the weight at the other end of the arm and the indicator too light to do its job properly. If you think you are likely to get a drop-back instead of a screaming run, make the indicator as heavy as possible so that it will fall easily when the line falls slack. If you are expecting full-blooded takes then move the weight along the arm so that the bobbin has only a bit of weight to it. It's a case of trial and error, but it is important for you to think about your style of fishing and change your tactics according to that style. Never just use the same indicator on the same setting every session you fish, or your indication sensitivity will certainly suffer.

**Tension-Arm and Combination Indicators**

There used to be two tension-arm indicators on the market: the MCF Wanger and the Fox Springer. The Wanger may no longer be available, but the Springer is. Both of these indicators are basically a bobbin on the end of a quiver tip. When it comes to setting up a tension-arm indicator there is very little you can do to change the sensitivity – it is governed by the stiffness of the tension arm.

Tension-arm indicators are ideally suited to long-range fishing or tight-to-island margins, where they will keep the line tight and under pressure, helping to stop any bowing of the line. However, they are not so good in the margins as they tend to create a bowstring-tight line, which can spook fish.

Nash Tackle's two bite indicators, the Wisp and the Wasp, both have a swinging-arm facility on them, as do Solar's Quiver-Loc and Fox's Swing Spring; and all double up as tension-arm indicators to boot. These are what is known as combination indicators. They have sliding weights to vary the loading in swinging-arm mode. The Wisp and the Quiver-Loc come with two different strengths of spring arm, for short- or long-range fishing, but as far as adjustment goes there is little further room for movement. The Wasp has a tension dial to vary the power of the spring, which allows the loading of this model to as much as 12oz (useful for fishing ultra long distance). We don't use this model, since we prefer the swingers for all our fishing, but we do know several successful anglers who do. The legendary Tim Paisley is one example.

# ROD RESTS, BUZZER BARS AND PODS

## Rod Rests

Many carp anglers fish primarily with what is known as 'static baits', whereby long hours are spent sitting behind rods that are specifically positioned in areas where carp may feed. In such circumstances long hours of holding the rod will soon become tiresome – and this is where the rod rest comes in. Rod rests are also used to assist with indication by keeping the rod off the ground and clear of any debris that may interfere with line movement. They can be made from a wide range of materials, from a simple tree branch to a machine-turned piece of steel. They come in many different designs and shapes, with some already complete and others with adjustable heads and lengths. Those with adjustable heads are usuallytermed banksticks and are normally preferred by the carp angler as they can accommodate the widely used bite alarm. Banksticks also have a multitude of other uses – including the support of the buzzer bar, which is covered below.

*You'll need a sturdy rod pod on some banks.*

## Buzzer Bars

Buzzer bars are horizontal supports that hold the rods at regular intervals. They always consist of two or more head screws, depending on how many rods you wish to use, and they are designed to keep the bankside rod set-up neat and at hand. As with rod rests and banksticks, buzzer bars come in a number of different designs to suit personal preference. Many carp anglers like to use two sets of buzzer bars for their set-up. These are termed the front and the back bars, and are used to support the alarms and butt rests respectively.

All buzzer bars are supported by bankstick inserts. These give the carp angler excellent rod stability, but they can sometimes be awkward to insert on hard banks. For this reason the infamous rod pod was born.

## Rod Pods

In simple terms a rod pod is a one-piece rod rest that you can move about easily and that you do not have to push into the ground. The original purpose of a rod pod was to create a stable set-up whilst fishing on hard and rocky banks such as those around many of the big reservoirs but, in recent years, convenience and fashion seem to have taken over. Like everything else, rod pods come in many different designs and materials, and therefore the price of them varies greatly. Although most junior anglers are on limited budgets, we recommend that beginners try to purchase a rod pod ahead of buzzer bars and banksticks. This will be of more benefit to you in the long run.

## Butt Grips and Rests

The back bars of any carp rod set-up should include butt grips or butt rests to rest the butt end of the carp rod on. They come in an array of different shapes and sizes, with our choice being the grippers, which almost lock the rod into place.

## Our Preference

We've tried to be very reserved about which pods and banksticks we favour for our fishing. There are so many good models on the market at the moment that it really is a matter of which type you like the look of the most and can afford. We have been using the super-lightweight Nash Titanium range of bar for a while now, but these are very expensive. Because most of our fishing is done in short sessions, we have tried to cut down on the weight of our gear in a big way. Being extremely light, the Titanium range suits this style of fishing very well. Both short and long banksticks are available as well as buzzer bars, so they accommodate plenty of situations. At present, however, it is not possible to purchase a titanium rod pod; we make do with a lightweight KJB model, which is no longer available unless you can find one second-hand. Another good rod pod we can recommend, though, is Solar's Globetrotter.

# LINE

Many anglers pay great attention to rigs, rods and so on, and perhaps do not attach as much importance as they should to line. It's all very nice having the best gear on the bank and the latest super rig, but if your line isn't up to the job then your tackle is worthless as you'll never land fish. You should always buy the best line you can for the type of fishing you do, as not all lines are the same and some are designed with a specific purpose in mind (for example long-distance low-diameter casting lines or thicker abrasion-resistant snag lines).

There are two main types of line and these are braided and mono. In the main, most lines used today are nylon monofilament, but for extra strength and less stretch, braided lines have become popular. Nylon is a man-made substance and monofilament means 'one strand'.

## Pre-Stretched Mono

Nylon line is by its nature very stretchy and therefore some people prefer a line that has had all the stretch taken out of it. This is done by pulling each end of the section of line by machine, thus making the line thinner and at the same time more brittle due to the lack of stretch. An example of a pre-stretched line is Drennan Double Strength. This is favoured for ultra line-shy fish in clear waters or at some of the heavily pressured waters where the fish have become accustomed to angler's lines. It is also excellent for long-range casting as it flies through the rings a lot more easily, but we wouldn't use it for extreme range.

## Unstretched Mono

The direct opposite of a pre-stretched line is line which has not been stretched

*Sabrebraid Dyneema – the best braid by a mile.*

at all. This is a bit thicker in diameter, and when a fish starts to pull the mono will stretch slightly. This has the plus point of acting as a shock absorber when playing fish. An example of such a line is Berkley Big Game, which is also a tough, abrasive line well recommended for using in snags.

## Part-Stretched Mono
In between the two extremes mentioned above is part-stretched line. This has the advantage of being a bit thinner than the unstretched line but still retains a bit of the shock absorbing quality (an example is Sabreline). These lines are favoured for all-round type carping and come in many different breaking strains.

## Braided Lines
Braided lines have become a favourite in recent years for those anglers fishing amongst sunken tree roots such as on the big reservoirs like Chantecoq or Orient in France. Such lines have no stretch whatsoever and are very good for long-range fishing as they enable anglers to be in direct control of fish. Our favourite

braided line is that marketed by Rod Hutchinson Fishing Developments and known as Sabrebraid Dyneema.

## What to Consider when Buying Line
On each spool of line you buy there will be a number indicating its breaking strain. This means that when that amount of pressure is placed on the line it will snap. Most lines, especially unstretched varieties, will take more strain than the stated weight, but always use the breaking strain as a guideline. When buying line you should always consider what type of fishing you will be doing as some lines are made for specific purposes and will not be suitable for general, all-round fishing. If in doubt ask at your tackle shop for advice, telling the assistant what sort of fishing you will be doing.

If you intend to be casting great distances you will want a fairly thin line, which will allow you to cast    further. Use a line of around 10lb breaking strain, which will be strong enough to play fish on but thin enough to be cast long distances. Back this up with a shock leader if you want to cast extra far and also to be safe. This is a length of line of high breaking strain (12–15lb), which is attached to the weaker mainline (10lb) to withstand the punishment of casting a heavy lead a long distance. If you use a shock leader, you must make sure the joining knot (known as the leader knot) can pass through the eye of the lead. If it can't, you will be fishing with what is known as a 'tether rig': any fish that picks up your bait following a crack-off may have to drag your lead and a length of line around with it for a very long time and may even become permanently snagged.

If the type of fishing you do is close in and amongst snags then you will want a line which is very abrasion- resistant and can cope with being pulled back and forth along tree roots or lily pads. For obvious reasons, always use a thick, higher breaking strain line for this type of fishing.

Finally, what you must remember with all lines is that they lose their strength with use and exposure to sunlight/water. As soon as your line shows signs of wear and tear, change it      immediately, as it could cost you fish. If you buy a bulk spool of line you should be able to fill at least three or four spools with it, so even the more expensive lines are quite reasonable if bought in bulk. Be aware of this loss of strength when purchasing lines from tackle shops. If you know for certain that a particular spool of line has been on sale for some time, avoid buying it. Also avoid lines for sale in bargain boxes – it is almost certain that they will not be up to scratch.

*Rod Hutchinson with his choice of overnight shelter.*

# BIVVIES AND SHELTERS

Being comfortable on the bank is of great importance, especially if you are likely to be fishing for long periods of time as most of us tend to do these days.

Your choice of shelter obviously depends on the length of session you are going to be fishing. Based on our experience of fishing all manner of different sessions, ranging from overnight trips where we've had to walk a couple of miles, to two-week sessions out of a swim you can drive to, here are the types of shelter we opt for.

### Overnight Lightweight Shelter

There is nothing as good as a simple oval umbrella for short overnight trips. These are marketed by several of the top-flight companies. Not only are they extremely light and slip easily into the rod bag, they are also very strong and very weatherproof. We have used the oval for a number of years now, in both winter and summer and cannot recommend it enough. Besides the brolly itself, you will need a couple of banksticks to prop it up. For further comfort, again at very little extra weight, you can attach a wrap to the brolly.

### Long-Stay Shelter

It is becoming increasingly necessary to fish for lengthy periods of time on some of the difficult waters. In such instances, it is a real bonus if you are as comfortable as possible, or you may find yourself bored and tired out after only a couple of days – especially in poor weather conditions. Having fished for periods lasting longer than two weeks in the same swim, and having used numerous bivvies and tents, our long-stay fishing is now always done under a Rod Hutchinson 2-Man Apotheosis. This will house one angler together with enough gear for the session and gives excellent comfort when needed. Although a large tent, it can be erected in a very short time and has a large entrance at the front and the rear - ideal for the social gatherings that seem to be the norm amongst long-stay anglers these days. It is suitable for winter fishing as well as summer – the built-in ground sheet and double-skinned liner assist greatly here. And in the summer the mosquito net is invaluable.

## BAITING-UP EQUIPMENT

One of the most important aspects of carping in the 1980s and 90s was the baiting principle – indeed, it still is today. Many beginners will be confused about the whole idea of bait as there are

*Hutchy's Enduro. Home for the week!*

so many companies out there who say theirs is best. Yes, there are some very good baits on the market, but the newcomer should concern himself more with putting a bait in the right place with the correct amount of feed around it, which is far more important. Besides the more obvious ways of placing bait, such as by hand and by manually operated boat, there are many other ways of baiting up your swim. We discuss our favourites below.

### Catapults
The next step up from baiting by hand, a catapult is useful to bait up to about 60yd maximum. Above this distance the accuracy starts to tail off and you would be better off using something else, such as a throwing stick. Apart from the distance aspect, the main disadvantage with catapults is the 'catty slap' from the elastic – when the pouch flaps back and stings the wrist – which can be very painful, especially in winter. Fox sell some very good catapults, as do Drennan and Hutchy. Check to see what you want the catapult to achieve before you purchase. A catapult is not just a catapult these days. You'll find feeder pults, boilie pults, maggot pults and so on. The list is endless.

### Throwing Sticks
If you want to bait up with boilies at a distance and be accurate in the process, a throwing stick is the best thing for you. As far as long-range throwing sticks go there is really only one type to choose – the Jumbo Cobra. This takes a bit of

*The catapult is ideal for 0–60 metres.*

load a strong leader onto your line to accommodate a spod. When fully loaded with boilies, most weigh about 1lb. There are several good brands of rockets on the market, with some of the better ones being produced by Gardner Tackle. Our favourite is the Gardner Pocket Rocket – a great piece of kit.

time to master, but once you have, you should be able to put baits up to 100 yards with ease and be very accurate with it. Besides the Jumbo, the Cobra range includes the Mini Cobra for up to 30yd distance, the Spod for firing out particle-type baits, and various other sizes to assist the type of fishing you are interested in. We use Cobras all of the time when fishing in England because boats are normally not allowed, and we usually favour the Jumbo as it accommodates all types of situation. The one thing worth noting with throwing sticks is that certain tools are designed for certain purposes, so you may lose accuracy if you use a long-range stick at short range and vice versa.

## Bait Rockets

These are small, missile-shaped tubes about 6-10in long, which you fill with bait and cast out to the desired area. They deposit a small amount of bait in a tight little group and, with practice, can be cast distances over 150yd (in the right hands). A heavy rod with a medium action is required to cast Spods and they do make quite a lot of noise when they land on the water, but otherwise they can be very effective. You will also need to

## Bait Boats

Although a very expensive item of fishing tackle, bait boats are a fantastic modern-day angling tool. They can be used to place hookbaits as well as free offerings in the perfect spot and, if necessary, in the most awkward of places such as close to overhanging bushes. Besides helping with hookbait placement, the nice thing about using a bait boat is that it overcomes the

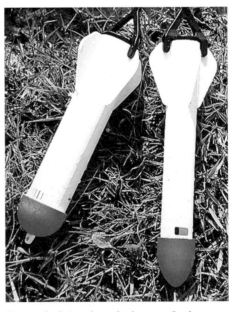

*Two popular bait rockets, also known as Spods.*

problems encountered with seagulls when trying to bait up with a throwing stick. Bait boats appear very awkward to handle, but after a little bit of practice they can be manoeuvred quite easily. We have both been using a wide variety for a few years now and we have found the Angling Technics Microcat to be the best of the bunch. This is purpose-made for anglers and can be used very easily after only half an hour's practice. It has some fantastic little gadgets that can be added to assist with presentation. It can be used effectively at distances over 300yd with the use of a beacon light, and you can even add an echo sounder to the bottom of it to find out the depth beneath. The latter tool really is a gem, which really comes into its own when you are trying to hit a marginal shelf on the far bank at night. Furthermore, a bait boat saves you spooking fish out of your swim via frequent casts with a heavy lead or pottering about in a large boat yourself.

For reasons we cannot understand, and probably never will do, some waters in England do not permit the use

*Phil Fry of Angling Technics displays one of his excellent Baitboats.*

of bait boats on the grounds that they are not ethical. It is, therefore, essential that you enquire about local rules before using one on your venue – the last thing you want is an angling club official on your back because of a minor transgression.

We must mention that if you are about to use a bait boat on a water for the first time, always make sure that you have dragged a lead through your swim beforehand. An area of water may look snag-free from above, but you never know what lies beneath. Use a bait boat professionally and it will catch you fish as well as make you friends. Use one without care and attention and you cause problems not only for yourself, but also for the fish.

## BOATS AND ACCESSORIES

Boats come in all manner of different sizes and shapes, so cost will certainly be the main area to consider here. For the record, the more expensive boats are hard-bottomed and made from fibre glass, while cheaper versions are usually made from PVC or canvas. Better advice on this topic can be obtained at your local boat shop or army-type store, so we advise that you consult these before purchasing. Some traditionalists knock the use of boats for carp fishing, but they really are a necessity for many of the large waters if one wishes to be consistently successful rather than simply lucky. Our fishing on the rivers in France, as well as the large reservoirs (where allowed) is assisted by a Sevylor Fish Hunter 250 boat for transporting gear and a Zodiac hard-bottom inflatable for transporting ourselves. With side safety panels and a double inflatable floor for added stability, these are highly recommended for all manner of different uses. They are not only excellent for transporting gear and rowing your baits out to the desired distance (be it 200 or 400yd), but they can also be used effectively for mapping out the lake bed. For this, many prefer the assistance of an echo sounder, but there are also other methods just as effective, if a little more time-consuming, where the echo sounders are not permitted (*see* below).

On the echo sounder side of things, we both use the Eagle range with the side scan facility. These are excellent for locating such important items as weed, silt, gravel, snags and so on. It is important to point out here that although sounders are excellent for mapping the lake bed, they are virtually useless for locating carp. This is because echo sounders have difficulty in differentiating between groups of small fish/invertebrate life and large fish. This is obviously important to know if you are planning to fish a stretch of river

*Boats are an essential piece of kit for the carp angler.*

which is inundated with what appears to be carp on the screen, but are unfortunately not. Besides this, echo sounders also emit a buzzing sound through the water which the fish can become conditioned to. For obvious reasons, where they have been used extensively, the fish may relate this sound with danger and move off before you have even set up base camp. Used wisely, echo sounders can be efficient, but don't rely solely on them for locating and catching carp.

Many of the large lakes in France have in recent years banned the use of echo sounders for angling purposes. If this is the case on the water you are planning to fish, do not be too disheartened. With a boat and a prodding stick you can still map out the lake bed. Remember that if you are prodding about on the bed of the lake with a stick, you should balance the boat out first (with another person or a heavy rucksack) so that you don't accidentally fall overboard – an obvious point but one that is frequently disregarded. Prodding is also an excellent method for getting a 'feel' of the bottom. If you haven't got a pole long enough to prod, then a simple spool of line with a lead attached can be just as good. With this method, it is a good idea to mark the line at intervals so that you can measure the depth more easily.

Finally, on the fish-locating front, boats give you the opportunity to look beneath the water and see what's going on. To do this, you will need a clear plastic bowl to take away the glare from the water and allow you to look into it. Obviously this practice is almost

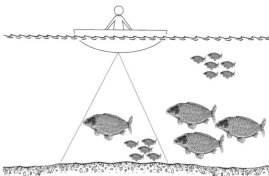

*One of the disadvantages of echo sounders is that they have difficulty distinguishing between shoals of small fish and individual big fish.*

*The Eagle echo sounder.*

useless on turbid waters, but for clear waters it is excellent and avoids the need to dive into the water. A bowl can be effective for snagged fish, as it allows you to see what's going on below before you start pulling for a break and losing that personal best. A cheap plastic goldfish tank with a square bottom is a favourite of ours. These are cheap and can be bought from most aquatic shops.

Two last points worth mentioning on the boat front are the need for a life jacket and the use of outboard motors. Unfortunately some anglers lose their lives every year whilst fishing with a boat because they have not been wearing a life jacket. Remember that your own

life is more important than the sport itself. Fox International make a good model at a reasonable price, but if you look around, you may be able to pick one up from a second-hand shop for even less. An outboard motor will also come in very useful and save you plenty of pain when using oars only. We both use 12v electric motors from Mincota. On the big pits, an outboard will go a long way and will certainly encourage you to make the effort to move when the need arises.

The only other fundamental tackle items are those concerned with tactics and carp care. We will take a look at both of these in the next two chapters.

# 3  CARP CARE

The subject of fish care has been extensively written about in carp magazines for many years now, and it is excellent to see so many anglers taking note of what is being preached. Unhooking mats and antiseptic solutions are now a common sight around many of our fisheries, and although this is great to see, there is still unfortunately a minority of anglers who seem to be lacking a little in some areas of fish care.

In this section, we will take a look at some of the modern carp care products available to the angler as well as some basic codes of practice to follow.

## CARP CARE TACKLE

### Unhooking Mats

An unhooking mat is, as the name suggests, a mat used for unhooking fish on. It should be used every time a fish comes out of the water and should be carried by the carp angler at all times. Every time you catch a fish, rather than bring the fish out of the water and unhook it on hard, rough ground, place it on a soft protective mat, such as those marketed by Rod Hutchinson Developments. The mat will cushion the weight of the fish and protect it from any unnecessary damage such as lost scales or cuts, which may lead to infection. The mat should be the right size to comfortably fit the size of the fish you are trying to catch.

### When Should they be Used ?

As stated above, unhooking mats should always be used when a carp comes out of its natural environment. This could be: when weighing fish, when unhooking fish, when photographing fish or when treating fish. We know for sure that some anglers do not use unhooking mats when weighing and photographing fish. It is vitally important that they are placed underneath the fish when carrying out either of these tasks. The reasons for this are obvious – you never know when the fish is going to flip out of your hands or when the weighing sling will detach itself from the scales hook.

### Why Should we All Have One?

All carp anglers should carry unhooking mats because the welfare of the carp is our main concern. It is as simple as that.

*South African star Gilbert Foxcroft with a stunning forty-plus common. Notice the unhooking mat?*

Every time a carp is caught we inflict stress upon it, and we should therefore try to minimize any damage the fish may cause to itself as it flaps around on the bank. Never rely on someone else to bring a mat – always take your own each and every time you go fishing.

**Making an Unhooking Mat**

Although you can purchase unhooking mats from most suitable angling suppliers, some are heavily priced for what they are. Neither of us are creative types, but we have managed to put stogether a step-by-step guide to how to make a suitable mat for a relatively low cost. This will quite easily protect your fish whilst saving you a bit of cash.

*What you need:*
Two 40 by 30in (100 by 75cm) sections of waterproof-backed nylon fabric.
One 36 by 26in (90 by 65cm) section of thick foam padding.
A needle, thread and thimble or a sewing machine.

It is advisable to use good, strong cotton and a leather needle to sew with, as the fabric can be very tough. The waterproof-backed nylon can be purchased cheaply from most material traders. The foam may also be available from market traders or, if you are lucky (like us), there may be a shop in your local town centre that specializes in selling foam; for details of suppliers refer to your local directory.

*Method:*
1. Lay one piece of the waterproof-backed nylon fabric on the floor with the waterproof side up.
2. Place the piece of foam onto the piece of nylon fabric.
3. Place the second piece of waterproof-backed nylon fabric on top of the foam padding. Make sure that this piece is placed waterproof-face down.
4. With a sewing machine or needle and thread, sew the two pieces of fabric together around the edges.

Once you have carried out the above steps and you are happy that the two pieces of fabric are sewn together well, your unhooking mat is ready to use. If you follow the size guidelines, your mat should be very light and suitable for strapping to rucksacks or bags.

**Forceps, Disgorgers and Pliers**

When unhooking fish, never try to tear the hook from the mouth or jiggle it about and make the wound bigger. It can sometimes be difficult to unhook carp with your fingers, so always have about you a deep pair of forceps as well as a stick disgorger and a pair of pliers – all available from your local tackle shop. All items will assist in one way or another to unhook a fish rather than following the inhumane method of simply cutting the line.

Forceps help to free a hook caught up in all manner of different positions, while a stick disgorger helps with those deeply hooked down the throat and past the barb. We also advise you to carry a pair of pliers with you at all times because fish can sometimes become double hooked. In this case the best thing to do is to cut

*A good pair of forceps are an essential item of tackle.*

the hook itself and slip it through the flesh of the lips rather than risk damaging the fish's feeding utensil. To carry just one of the above items is not sufficient – you need all three.

## Antiseptic Solutions

Fish are prone to what is termed predatory infection by a wide variety of organisms – and at all times of the year. Such infections may be caused by bacteria, fungus, viruses, or pathogens, and are normally the after-effects of superficial damage.

Any open wound on a fish is open to infection at any time, so it is vitally important for anglers to repair any damage that may be present on the fish they catch, or indeed happen to see in distress. As anglers, the most common injury we will see is hook damage; but besides this, it is also possible to notice cuts and abrasions on the flanks of fish which may have been caused naturally (for example spawning marks). As far as infections are concerned, probably the most common one we see around our fisheries is saprolegnia. Saprolegnia, otherwise known as water mould, is a fungus infection which is present in all fresh waters, but is more likely to occur on injured, weakened, or diseased fish than on healthy ones. It is a very common sight at heavily stocked waters and is a possible cause of fish deaths. In its early stages it looks very similar to mould, but as time passes by, and depending on the size of the wound, it becomes progressively worse and begins to eat away at the fish. At this stage it starts to look like cotton wool and, if not treated in time, may lead to the death of the host.

Saprolegnia or any open wound infection can be treated in a number of ways, but certainly the best is to use antiseptic solutions such as Klin-ik, which is available from Kryston. Simple saline solution is also effective. If you come across a fish with saprolegnia, or an open wound, then simply apply

*Look after your carp!*

antiseptic solution to the open or infected area and leave it to dry for a minute. It is important that you allow a whole minute for the solution to be absorbed by the wound, or much of its effectiveness will be wasted – along with your efforts. The fish can then be returned to the water.

All carp anglers should carry a bottle of antiseptic solution with them - there is really no excuse not to. Make sure you are one of the many rather than the minority. Healthy fish may return to fight another day, and possibly at a higher and personal-best weight. Those that are damaged may never return at all.

### Weighing Slings

Although we both prefer to weigh fish in the landing net and later deduct the weight of the net after returning the fish to the water, there are plenty of excellent specialist weighing slings on the market. These are made from a fine mesh material which helps the fish to be more comfortable when being lifted off the floor. There are plenty of different weighing products on the market, including excellent slings from companies like Rod Hutchinson, Kevin Nash, Fox and Daiwa. Hutchy sells an excellent model which also doubles up into a sack (see below), saving the fish more stress. Known as the Big Kipper Sling/Sack, it simply has a zip across the top which you close when you want to retain the fish for photographing.

### Sacks and Fish-Retaining Items

If, like us, you like to keep photographs or slides of your fish captures, then you will require a suitable fish-retaining product to hold the fish following capture. The ideal really is to not retain carp in sacks in the first place because of the stress this causes them, but obviously not all of us are fantastic photographers in the dark, or we prefer to have others assist or we want to keep the fish for a couple of hours just to calm it down.

As with weighing slings, there are numerous sack/retention items on the market. We prefer those sold by the Rod Hutchinson stable, such as the Be-Safe Sack or the Sling Sack.

When purchasing a sack for carp, ensure that it is made from a soft material and has plenty of air holes. Preferably it should be at least 60in (1½m) long and 40in (1m) deep. It should also have a safety zip or fastener, and be supplied with a long main cord so that the fish can swim freely and settle at its preferred depth. This is an important point, especially in summer when waters are depleted of oxygen, as a stressed fish

*An example of a typical carp sack.*

which is sacked up can end up a dead fish if it is not retained in deep, cool water. Basically, never sack a fish in shallow, warm water or anywhere near reeds or weed beds, which draw oxygen from the water at night.

Here's another good tip: ensure that your sack is equipped with a light marker float attachment. This is so that you can locate the fish should it become unattached from the bankstick. Hopefully this won't happen because you will have secured it well first time around! Sadly, there have been plenty of big fish lost to the depths of lakes because anglers have not bothered to attach the main sack cord safely to the bank. Make sure you're not one of them and make sure the length of line attached to the float is deeper than the deepest area of water. It's common sense really.

### Landing Nets

For obvious reasons, all carp anglers should be in possession of a landing net. In our minds, this should measure at least 40in (1m) across the net, as well as in depth, and be capable of landing fish to the size you might find in the water you are fishing. The net should be made from a non-knotted mesh and be as friendly to the fish as possible (for instance, it should not have any gaping holes in it). If the net is damaged in any way, then it should be disposed of as soon as possible. Believe us when we say that we have witnessed an angler lose a 40lb fish because the bottom of his landing net gave way when pressure was applied to a small hole!

For the record, we both favour the Rod Hutchinson Be-Safe Landing Net, which is equipped with a revolutionary Spring Lock catch and carry system. This allows the angler to land the fish, and then easily detach the handle and also fold and roll the net, with the fish enclosed, around the handle. This makes life a lot easier when carrying fish up steep banks or confined areas. This net also has weighing straps which allow the angler to weigh the fish in the net easily. It is a cracking net, and having used plenty of models available on the market, we can safely say it is one of the better products available to the modern carper.

## CARP CARE

Catching a fish will always disturb the protective covering it has on its flanks. We can help to minimize this by wetting our hands, unhooking mats, weigh slings, and sacks prior to use. It is not a matter of just damping the equipment; everything has to be really soaked in water to avoid problems arising. This is a fairly simple operation and should always be carried out before you lift a fish out of the water. It is also important to get into the habit of carrying a container with you at all times (such as a bait bucket). The container can be filled with water, which can then be poured onto the fish quickly when needed. If white foam forms on the flanks of the fish or equipment, this is a sure sign that there is not enough moisture present and that the fish's protective slime is being disturbed. It is impossible for us to give an exact time when the foaming will occur, but

*Keep the carp soaked at all times when it's out of the water.*

soaking the fish and equipment at least every minute during handling will help minimize any problems. Although such a procedure may help to protect the fish, it doesn't mean that its time on the bank can be increased: get it back into the water as soon as possible.

Be careful when you read the dial of the scales when weighing fish. We have seen numerous anglers (not just juniors) reading the dial of the scales incorrectly and giving the fish a false weight. This is especially so with Avon scales, so you must ensure that you count the number of times the finger moves around the dial before reading off the weight. We have witnessed people adding, and even not counting, 10lb of weight through misreading, which can be very embarrassing and disappointing. Always hold your scales by the handle (if it possesses one) at the top rather than at the bottom or sides. This is the most accurate way of

weighing fish. If you weigh something with your scales whilst holding them from the sides or the bottom, the item will weigh at the very least 4oz too much (or too little). Believe it or not, we have come across scales which, when held in these positions, weigh 12oz too heavy.

You have to be very careful when holding your scales at the top because on some makes there is very little to hold onto and you may find yourself dropping the fish. We advise you to get hold of one of the manufactured weighing bars to help or, alternatively, make one yourself from a piece of heavy-duty dowel and some rope. Simply cut some 2in (5cm) dowel to a length of approximately 12in (30cm). Drill a small hole through the centre and thread the rope. Now pass this rope through the top of the scales and attach with a good knot. Before you use it with a fish, however, always test the strength of the handle knot thoroughly by lifting something heavy and bouncing it. If you're a stroke-puller like Rob then you'll probably completely ignore what we've just said, or indeed you may start weighing your fish the incorrect way just to gain a few extra ounces. If you do, just remember that you are only cheating yourself!

When weighing a fish, ensure that all of its fins are comfortably lying against the side of the fish and not sticking out awkwardly and at risk of being damaged in some way. The fins most likely to lie awkwardly are the pectorals, and it is sadly not unusual to come across fish with broken fin rays caused by bad handling by anglers.

# A STEP-BY-STEP GUIDE TO HANDLING CARP

As anglers, we should all try our utmost to ensure that the carp receives the best possible treatment and care whilst it is on the bank. Unfortunately, there are many anglers around who are not aware of the correct way to treat carp once they've been landed. It is for this reason that some carp bear the scars of battle and look as if they have come to the end of the road.

To finish off this chapter, let's take a look at a step by step guide to handling carp and try to give you a few pointers on how to unhook, treat, weigh, photograph and return fish safely.

*Step 1: Landing the Fish*
When landing the fish, you should

*Come to uncle Rob!*

ensure that you bring the fish to the net. Never chase after the fish with the net as all you will do is cause it to panic. Keep your rod held high and try to keep the fish's head up. Once it is wallowing on the surface, gently guide it towards the net and close the mesh around. When the fish is safely in the net, place your rod and landing net in a safe bankside area. Leave the fish in the water, in a comfortable position, with the net closed around it for at least two minutes. This will give it a chance to 'catch its breath' so to speak. You should now be in a position to organize your treatment and photographic equipment.

*Step 2: Lifting the Fish out of the Water*
Make sure tools, such as the unhooking mat, forceps, liquid treatment, scales and camera are all at hand before you bring the fish on land. When you are ready, lift the fish out of the water and place it gently down on the unhooking mat. Do not put the fish down if it is flapping about – hold it above the mat until it has calmed down. Always have a bowl of water at hand to make sure that the fish remains wet at all times. Depending on the weather, the fish will need to be coated with water at least every minute or so.

*Step 3: Unhooking the Fish*
It may be possible for you to unhook the fish using your fingers. If the hook is firmly embedded into the mouth, though, you will need to use forceps. Never try to twist the hook out of the mouth. Try to perform the task in the safest possible way. When using forceps, grasp the part of the hook that is closest to the insertion.

*Make sure the fins are all tucked in.*

Ensure that you do not pinch the carp's skin with the forceps. Once the hook is out, make sure your rig is out of the way of the net and the fish by hooking it to one of the rod rings.

### Step 4: Carp Treatment

Take a good look at the fish on both sides and treat any sores or cuts with liquid treatment. We use Kryston's Klin-ik for this job and thoroughly   recommend it to anyone.

### Step 5: Weighing the Fish

Try to carry out the task of weighing the fish in the simplest way possible. When handling fish that we are not going to sack, we prefer not to use weigh slings as these are awkward to use and mess the fish about too much. Instead, we weigh the fish in the landing net. To do this, simply detach the head of the net from the pole, zero the scales and weigh. The exact weight of the fish can be calculated by weighing the empty net once you have returned the fish to the water. For safety reasons, never lift the fish too far off the ground and always have the unhooking mat underneath. If, for any reason, the fish starts to bleed from the gills, make sure that it is returned to the water immediately. Usually this is roughly the equivalent of

a nose bleed in a human. It will stop shortly after giving the fish a breather and you can continue with the weighing.

### Step 6: Sacking the Fish

If the fish is to be sacked for photographic purposes, weigh it in a sling (we use the Hutchy sling/sack which we mentioned before). Make sure you soak it well and place it at arm's length from the unhooking mat before lifting the fish out of the water. After treating the fish (Step 4), slide the net carefully from underneath. The fish can then be placed inside the sling/sack. After weighing, place the sack carefully in deep water, with the safety cord attached to a solid support, such as a deeply embedded bankstick. Support and watch the fish until it looks comfortable in the sack and able to settle on its own accord.

### Step 7: Preparing the Fish for Photographing

When photographing fish, you should always have the camera ready prepared before lifting the fish from the water. Get yourself in a comfortable position and always hold the fish over the unhooking

*Most modern-day sacks are closed via a zip-fastener.*

mat. Hold the fish firmly and gently lift it off the mat. Don't lift it too high, it only needs to be a few inches off the ground to get a good photo. Always be prepared for the fish to flip. If it does, remember that your main priority is its welfare, not your photo.

*Step 8: Returning the Fish to the Water*
Once the photos are out of the way the fish can be returned to the water. This is easily done by placing the fish on the mat or lifting the landing net around it. Make sure it is comfortable and that there are no gaps in the mat/net for it to fall through. Always keep a firm grip on the net and carry the fish close to the ground.

*Step 9: Stabilizing the Fish*
Place the fish back in the water in an upright position. Hold the fish and support it until it is ready to go. Never throw the fish into the water and never force it to swim off. You should always

*Ready for the off!*

remain with it until it is ready to go on its own accord, even if it takes an hour!

*Step 10: Releasing the Fish*
When the fish wants to go, let it go, and never take your eyes off it until it is out of sight. Carp care is the most important part of carp fishing. You should always treat the carp with the respect they deserve, regardless of their size.

*There she goes.*

# 4 TACTICS

Before we move on to some of the more topical issues connected with successful carp fishing, such as bait, rigs and so on, it is important to consider the necessary skills of the carp angler. With the development of technology and knowledge, tackle, bait and available fishing information has advanced at a rapid rate, so it is now possible for anglers to go out and catch carp instantly without any previous experience. However, modern tackle and information can only get instant carp anglers to a certain level within the sport, as the lack of basic skills leaves many behind the more experienced and knowledgeable foe. This chapter outlines some of the fundamentals the angler will need to catch carp on a consistent basis. Included are such skills as locating carp, choosing the right swim, feature-finding, playing fish, plus much more. We'll kick off right at the start with a simple look at probably the most vital topic – location.

## LOCATING FISH AND FEEDING AREAS

We wouldn't be far off the mark if we said that locating carp, or more importantly their feeding areas, is the fundamental key to successful carp fishing. Very often you hear anglers asking each other about how they would rate bait, rigs, location and tackle in order of preference. Usually you'll hear several

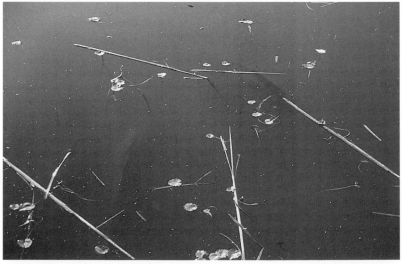

*Find the carp first and you are on the right track.*

different answers, all conflicting with one another, but as this is our book, we will only tell you about our own fishing strategies, and these will almost always be centred first and foremost around locating the carp and their feeding areas. It is no good whatsoever having the best tackle, bait and rigs if there aren't any carp in the lake! The same goes for a swim. We can't put it any more simply than that. Find the fish first, and then find out where they are going to feed and you will make life so much easier. Forget fancy rigs and bait. They don't attract the carp in the way that some of the adverts and articles would have you believe. If they did, you would catch every time you used them!

So where do you start looking for carp? All waters are different and not all carp are the same. This is what makes it sound so difficult. The only way to make it sound easier is to begin with the basics and gradually progress from there. In this chapter we shall do exactly that, so we'll

*A superb big French mirror falls to the rods of Simon.*

begin by considering the four different ways in which we can actually locate the areas that we all set out to discover: visual, aural, mechanical and conversational. These are fairly self-explanatory in that you will either see carp with your eyes, hear carp with your ears, find them with the use of an echo-sounder or feature-finding tool or discover their whereabouts through conversations with other anglers. The one thing that we all like to do is see carp for ourselves, because at least then we are certain of where some are located. The ideal, however, is not just to see carp, but to actually see them feeding in a certain area. That is sure to be the icing on the cake.

We wouldn't just use leaping carp as an indicator here either. Sometimes, especially on the big waters, leaping carp are not always feeding. They may be cleaning themselves of parasites, clearing their gills of unwanted debris, or simply just leaping out of sheer enjoyment. We must say, however, that leaping carp are always going to be a great confidence booster, and wherever they are seen you will always see us casting a bait towards them. The secret here is not to cast right on top of their heads, but rather over the back of them, drawing the rig towards the area where they have shown. This way you are less likely to spook them from the area and they are more likely to inspect the hookbait.

As for aural location of carp, you will hear them topping around the lake both in the dark and during the day. It therefore pays not to have a radio turned up loud or a TV set blasting out for all to hear: you may miss that all-important fish

*Carp love areas with a variety of depth and features.*

location clue. We've both reached a point now where our minds are almost trained into listening for sounds of carp jumping. We may be sleeping at night, in total deep sleep, but come the morning our minds will have registered whether carp have topped in the night or not at all. Sometimes, especially if we are sleeping lightly, we may even rise from bed to try and locate where a particular carp has shown. On still nights, or those where very little wind ripple is present, you may be able to pinpoint exactly where a carp has shown by the splash created on the surface. Obviously this is harder on large waters where the carp are showing at range, but if you wait a short while until the ripples make their way to the shore, you may receive an all-important clue.

Another way of hearing carp is to listen out for the noise they make when sucking items off the surface or from the side of reed stems; they tend to make a clooping sound as they suck in this way. We both remember walking around Patshull Park in Wolverhampton once and stopping at a huge bed of lilies. There were no signs of carp movement around the lily bed, but you could clearly hear them sucking from beneath the pads. On

closer inspection, and after about an hour of hard watching, we finally caught sight of some very cute carp poking their lips less than an inch out of the water underneath the pads. They were obviously sucking at small snails clinging to the undersides of the leaves. We have also witnessed carp sucking at reed stems as well as the drifted pieces of surface bait cast out by other anglers, so the lesson here is never to switch off totally from nature when you are at lakeside.

**Fish-Finding Tools**

As you might expect, there are a number of useful tools available from tackle suppliers to assist in finding carp. The best tool in the world would be a carp-feeding locator but unfortunately these only come through experience and a lot of trial and error. You can, however, purchase such items of tackle as polarizing glasses, pocket-sized binoculars or even echo-sounders. Polarizing glasses are fairly expensive if you purchase them from tackle shops so we advise you to buy them on the high street. Basically, polarizing glasses allow you to look beneath water when glare from the sun would normally make this impossible. The lenses come in all manner of different colours, like orange, red or blue, all of which will suit different users or uses. We both use amber lenses, as these really do tend to make dark shapes such as carp very visible even when they are a couple of feet below the water. A standard pair of sunglasses will not perform the job that a pair of polarizing glasses will, so make sure you spend wisely.

As for binoculars, again these come in all manner of different shapes or forms, with the most expensive being the most powerful. You can even buy polarizing binoculars nowadays. We like the type you can drop into your pocket so they can be carried up trees and around a lake without too much bother. A good pair won't come cheap but will be well worth it.

## Locating Those Carp

It's all well and good having the best fish-locating equipment in the world, but every now and again it won't work in your favour. You'll feel as though your best chance of locating the fish has been completely lost if your echo-sounder hasn't located any big fish or if your best-looking pair of polarizing glasses hasn't enabled you to see any signs of carp. The key success to finding carp and their feeding areas is to look and listen for them. There is no substitute.

You will usually find experienced anglers carrying out a reconnaissance trip of a lake before commencing any fishing. This will involve talking to as many anglers as possible, looking in every swim, checking marginal snags, climbing trees to get a good view of the lake, looking carefully at overhanging bushes or anything that may attract carp. To us, and many other experienced anglers, carp fundamentally love features. Where there are snags or items in the water which will make the carp feel safe, there will usually be carp. The exception to this is waters where there are many features but not enough carp, such as Wraysbury, which is very understocked on the carp front compared to its size.

Carp are relatively simple creatures in that they only have to eat, breathe, spawn and keep themselves safe to live. The only things that interrupt their patterns of behaviour on a day-to-day basis are external factors such as anglers, weather conditions, predators, the nature of the lake, and water quality and flow. We will consider each of these below.

## Weather Conditions

We are both firm believers in the theory that carp like to follow the wind, and from all directions. Like many things, however, this will depend on the lake, carp stock and the pressure the fish are put under from anglers. People in carp-fishing circles do tend to talk about warm winds being better than cold ones, and whilst this is certainly true a lot of the time, it is still never enough to guarantee success. It is our experience that carp in big lakes – of above 10 acres (4ha) - tend to be affected by winds a great deal more than those in smaller waters with lots of islands and weed beds. Food particles get picked up in the 'flow' and can be carried to the windward end of a lake. Usually the water colour here is much more turbid than at the back of a wind, especially at clear waters, and as a result the carp will

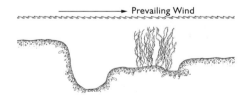

*Food particles will drift along with the direction of the wind and settle in troughs or gullies.*

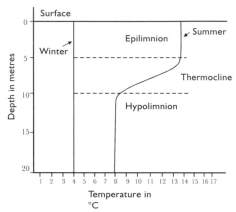

*A typical European lake and its temperature zones.*

not only feel safer and better camouflaged, but will also benefit from an abundance of food. Small plankton items will attract predators which the carp may prefer. The water may also be much more oxygenated, which is another reason why the carp will be in large numbers at that end of the lake.

In the summer months in Europe, westerly winds bring low-pressure clouds, which really are a favourite carp-feeding stimulator, at over 75 per cent of our big waters. Occasionally you will also experience small waters being turned on by winds, but because they are by their very natures 'small', the effects of a wind on the fish are not always as obvious as on bigger venues.

Another advantage of a wind is its effect on the temperature of the water. A warm wind can quickly warm the water at the windward end, whilst a cooler wind will have the opposite effect. How this works for you will depend on the circumstances. In the summer months warm water will make the fish lethargic, so a cooler area may be a good collection

point for food items and a much more comfortable area for the fish to lie up. In winter, on the other hand, a warm wind may attract fish.

We both tend to think that wind does affect the temperature of waters in a big way, especially on deep waters where it can disrupt the thermoclatic layers. To discuss the topic of thermoclines in depth is not necessary in this book, but to put it simply they are zones of rapid temperature change. Thermoclines tend to occur in waters more than 100ft (30m) deep, but there is scientific evidence to suggest that they can occasionally be found in shallower waters that are not affected by wind very much. Below depths of 30ft (10m), areas of a lake can become very anaerobic if big winds don't regularly cause the water to mix. This causes aquatic life to become very scarce in the deeper areas, with the result that the carp will generally only feed in the margins or shallower areas where sunlight has a big effect on the abundance of food. This tends to be the case at waters like Cassien in the south of France, where the deeper areas are only

*The clouds arrive, but where are the fish?*

effective since the carp have become accustomed to being caught in the shallower areas where they would naturally feed.

We've seen it written that colder winds turn carp off, and whilst this may be the case at some venues, in our experience it shouldn't be taken as a generalization. Carp waters are all different. At some venues carp love the back of the wind, even warm ones, whilst at others they prefer to be right in the midst of it. Our advice is always to get to know a water and try to read the signs as much as possible; still, if you are lost for clues, then the windy end of a lake is always a very good starting point, regardless of which direction the wind is coming from.

In the same way that wind can warm or cool water, so can rain and snow. Snow, sleet or hailstones can kill the fishing dead if it has been quite productive over the last few hours or days. It can have the opposite effect if the weather has been very warm and the fish lethargic. Rain can also turn fish on or off, but our findings tend to be more positive with rain than snow, hail or sleet. The number of times we've had good results in the rain is ridiculous. Very light drizzle and no wind is a great booster to our confidence, especially if the fishing has been fairly slow of late.

The last weather feature worth mentioning is air pressure. Air pressure has a massive effect on the carp and, indeed, the weather itself. As the sun's rays warm the atmosphere, fronts of cold and warm air are created. These fronts move up and down and left to right with the movement of the sun, and this movement can be one reason that a wind is blowing from a particular direction. In the northern hemisphere winds are generally drawn towards low-pressure areas. In fact, if you stand with your back to the wind, the low pressure will be on your left.

Warm fronts travel faster than the cooler ones, but both tend to cause a change of wind direction. For obvious reasons, then, air pressure will affect the movements and location of the carp. Air pressure also dictates the amount of oxygen that can be absorbed by the water. High pressure allows more oxygen to be absorbed by water, whilst low pressure has the opposite effect. This pressure/oxygen effect also affects the carp. Carp have a gas-filled sack known as the swim bladder. If you think back to your chemistry and biology lessons, you may recall that when pressure is increased upon a gas, particles in the gas are forced together. This pressure will quite obviously have an effect upon a fish, and usually it will cause carp to become lethargic. A thunderstorm can have the opposite effect. Anglers all tend to talk about thunderstorms being excellent carp-feeding periods, especially once they have passed. One theory behind this is that once the air pressure has decreased the fish become much more comfortable, so they start jumping and preparing for a nice feed.

### The Nature of the Lake Bed

Carp will soon become masters of their own environment once they have been in a particular water for a number of weeks. It is our belief that features are what carp really love the most. Visible features on a lake are always a good starting point. These may come in the form of islands, reedbeds, snags, weed beds, lily beds, sunken cars or similar obstructions, a fall pipe that creates a disturbance on the surface of the water, thus giving the carp some cover, an overhanging bush – the list is endless.

What we can see from the surface, however, isn't always a true indication of what lies below. This is why plumbing and feature-finding are a must for the long-stay carp angler. Below the surface you may discover small weed beds, shelves or drop-offs, plateaux, craters, gravel or sand bars, sunken snags or fallen trees. Carp use features not only as safety, but also as roadways around a water, much as motorists use road signs.

Sometimes features may be very small, such as a tiny gravel patch in a very silty lake, or a tiny silt area in a gravel lake. Some are likely to offer food supplies as well. If a lake is silty all over apart from the odd sandy/gravel area, then try a bait on the sand/gravel. These bars are likely to hold a different type of food supply to the silt. The same can be applied to gravel pits that have the odd

*The warm shallows with a group of carp clearly visible.*

area of silt. Another thing to watch out for is variations in depth. If a lake is fairly flat all over apart from the odd deeper area then try a rod on the latter. A small drop-off may be just what is required to give a carp some security. A small indentation in the silt will also be an obvious area where a carp has been uprooting. Carp are fairly powerful fish and they will know exactly where the food supplies are around a particular water. A crater in the silt or gravel may have been caused through excessive foraging by the carp. It may be a bloodworm larder, so don't overlook it.

In France many of the big water anglers refer to the food larder as the 'crayfish zone'. Crayfish tend to be the natural food of big reservoir carp, but they are wary of light; they prefer to hide under rocks and only tend to be visible to humans during the hours of darkness, when they will visit the margins. Depending on the turbidity of the water, sunlight energy generally only reaches down to depths of 30ft (10m). It is here that a lot of food tends to gather for the crayfish. In the daytime plenty of good catches at crayfish-infested waters are made at this depth, so the best tactic would be to fish the 30ft areas in the day and the margins at night. If you find these spots, then you're onto a winner.

If you wanted to get technical you could apply the same sort of thinking to your fishing at an annual level. If you are aware of what items the carp are feeding on at certain times of the year, you could apply some strategic thinking. Craters in the silt are likely to be areas full of bloodworm, so why not try these in the spring when bloodworm levels are at their highest, and then change to the pads where crustaceans are likely to be in large supply in the summer, and so on. This sort of approach needs a lot of research, but the signs are there if you care to look for yourself. A fish on the bank may helpfully be excreting a particular food source, making it obvious in which parts or depths of the lake it has been feeding recently.

## The Effects of Day and Night

Carp are scientifically considered to be diurnal feeders, which means that both day and night length have an influence on their feeding habits. Whether or not they use day length as a clock no one knows, but it is strange how they frequently seem to know when to start or stop feeding. There are countless venues that we have fished over the years that seem only to switch into gear when a certain hour strikes. Birch Grove in England is a great example here, especially in the winter. Over the four years that we have been in the winter syndicate, only three of our fish have ever been caught in the night. Most have fallen between the hours of 10am and 2pm.

Carp will also use the daily cycle as a trigger to determine when to move to certain areas of the lake. Shallows are a good example here: the warming of the sun's rays may inform the carp of where the most comfortable areas of the lake may be. In the summer, the carp may all head to the shallows at noon where it is much warmer and a good supply of food can be found. As soon as the sun starts to go down the carp may all start to head back into the deeper water. It is all a

matter of trying to fathom out the movements of the carp. If you are targeting a water on a long-term basis then there is no substitute for watching the water. Ask the more successful anglers on the lake and they'll tell you the same.

## The Effects of the Seasons

We cover the effects of the seasons on carp in greater detail in Chapter 10, but there are a few important points worth noting here before we move on. Depending on the water, you may find that the carp are located in different parts of the lake depending on the seasons. There is an old saying that carp go into the deeper water in the winter and, whilst this may be just a saying, it is often the case in England. Deeper water tends to stay at a more constant temperature than shallower water, so always bear this in mind. At Birch Grove we are both convinced that some of the carp spend most of their winter life in the deeper water, and we'd even go so far as to say they spend it stationary in mid-water or at least a few feet off the bottom. This is

*Keeping an eye on other anglers assisted Rob with the capture of this 30lb mirror.*

a very difficult topic to generalize on, because there are also fish in Birch that spend a lot of their time in the snaggy areas of the lake, which are much shallower. Carp have a habit of splitting up into shoals, more so in the warmer months, but you will still find segregated groups in the winter also.

Normally in the winter you will find carp huddled together a lot more, usually for safety, but also perhaps for the comfort of the water. Some people refer to oxygen levels to explain why carp are in a certain area, and whilst this can be a factor, it doesn't tend to apply in the winter as the water is usually much more oxygenated due to the slowing up of the aquatic environment: there is less consumption of the oxygen because everything has slowed down. You the refore tend to find what is known as a saturated oxygen level, when no more oxygen can be absorbed by the water. In the summer the opposite is the case, so locating a fall pipe or a stream inlet may be a fabulous tactic to employ at that time of the year.

Another important seasonal consideration should be the spawning areas of the fish. Carp usually spawn in the same area of the lake/river year after year. If the water is a small venue then you won't have too much difficulty locating the fish. For bigger venues, however, carp will frequently spend days, weeks or even months in a particular area of the lake as the build-up to spawning approaches. They may also stay in the area for weeks afterwards, a good example here being the west arm at Cassien. This area of the famous lake is always a good bet in spring, and each year you will hear about some terrific catches from it.

## Angler Pressure and Other Effects

This is the point at which the general principles outlined above start to become totally irrelevant. Carp tend to become conditioned by anglers and the environment they are subjected to, which means that a lot of the basic rules get totally thrown out when anglers start frequenting a water. If the carp like the wind, then you may find the windward end very difficult for carp if some good catches have been made from there. The same goes for other areas of a lake.

If the carp are very suspicious of anglers then you may find the best areas to try are the snags, but if these too have been pressured a fair bit it may be difficult to receive a pick-up from here. You may find the carp will only venture out of the snags to feed every now and again. This is where pre-baiting can pay dividends. If you are going to be targeting a lake regularly then start to apply bait around all the areas of the lake that you believe they may visit or feed. This will condition the carp into feeling safe when they feed upon a particular food source. This strategy works best if you use a bait with a personalized flavour or base, as this will stop other anglers taking advantage of your efforts. The best time of the year to begin a pre-baiting campaign is in the spring months when the carp are beginning to wake up. They will be very catchable at this time of the year, but if you continue to apply the bait throughout the year, they will eventually recognize which baits are safer. We like to carry on baiting all the way through the winter also, and this sort of effort really can keep the carp on the move in the winter once they are confident of a bait and its availability.

Pre-baiting is also a fabulous way of turning unproductive areas of the lake into very productive ones. Areas that are normally devoid of natural food can be turned into fantastic spots after a few weeks of baiting.

Besides anglers and bait, predation can also have an effect on the way carp behave. If the lake you are targeting only contains small fish of double-figure size and it is a known fact there are some very big catfish in the water, the areas where the cats feed may be very unproductive. We've seen this happen at Fishabil as well as the catfish super-lake in France. The carp in Fishabil tend to move out into the middle of the lake during the night as the cats move into marginal areas to mop up the smaller fish.

Water quality can also influence the location of the carp. Inflows bringing in chemicals that are then diluted into the lake may be devoid of carp. This is also connected to the changing seasons. As autumn moves in, all lakes undergo a natural breaking-down process. Leaves that are deposited on the lake bed will decompose naturally, releasing nutrients into the water which the carp may recognize and take a dislike to. We've seen areas that are very productive in the spring and summer turn totally the opposite as autumn settles in. Such areas are then once again very productive the following year.

We can conclude from all of the above

information that the location of carp and their feeding areas is a complex part of the angler's armoury. Our advice will always be along the lines of: 'Be aware of what can affect the location of the fish, but never rely on only one factor alone.' Angling pressure can turn carp away from windy areas, and so on, so always try to consider every piece of evidence available to you before you decide which swim to target. As an example, consider a lake that is a gravel pit. It may appear to possess very few silt areas. If you start to catch a few carp that are excreting bloodworm then you'll need to put your thinking cap on. The action of the wind may be causing small silt deposits to form in isolated areas of the lake. Consider the direction of the prevailing wind as well as any gravel bars, troughs or gullies. Where are they in line with the winds? You may find that the wind has carried silt particles which have been deposited on the leeward sides of the bars. Are there any more signs? If there is weed growing on one side of a bar then it is likely to be rooted in a silty area. There are thousands of signs like this which the angler needs to notice and piece together, a little like a jigsaw puzzle. Locating carp that you cannot see can be a difficult process, but more often that not the signs will be there. It is just a matter of watching, waiting and thinking.

## SETTING UP YOUR SWIM

### Choosing a Swim

Once you've successfully located the carp and their feeding areas you will be in a position to choose which swim to fish at your venue. Although selecting an area to fish may sound easy, there are nevertheless a number of pitfalls you can fall into if your choice of swim is based solely on aesthetic grounds. Not only can this lead to blank sessions, but it can also be a nuisance to other anglers. Here are a few ideas on what and what not to consider when choosing a swim:

**Car parks** Although on some occasions it may be necessary to select a swim close to a car park, don't get into the habit of selecting a swim just because of its convenience. Easy-access swims are often popular with anglers but not with fish!

**Other anglers** Before considering a swim close to other anglers, establish where they are fishing and if it's OK for you to set up near to them. Don't start slinging out your lead here, there and everywhere or you may find some angry faces around the lake! And if you make yourself unpopular other anglers will not be keen to pass on useful information.

**Swim size** Besides the matter of fish presence, consider the size of a swim before trying to set your gear up in it, and always try to adjust yourself to the area rather than the swim to yourself. If you own a large bivvy, such as a Hutchy Apotheosis, think about the size of the swim before setting up or you may find yourself losing fish because you are hampered for room.

**Overhead trees** Will your casting or

*Are you in the right swim?*

playing of fish be limited? Remember, you need to have enough room overhead so that you can cast your rod in the desired direction. Make sure you are completely familiar with your surroundings if you are night fishing a new swim.

**Bankside cover** If the lake you are fishing is renowned for being more productive when bankside disturbance is minimal and anglers are hidden from view, then always try to select a swim that offers plenty of bankside cover. Remember that you also need to have enough space for comfort.

**Feature fishing** If you wish to fish to a feature such as a snag or a weed bed, always select a swim whose position offers you the best chances of landing fish. Examine all the areas around the feature, especially those lying to the side and between it and the bank. In most cases the best way to approach such features will be to fish directly opposite, so that you have a direct pull against the fish.

*The carp will soon learn which areas of a lake to avoid if certain swims are continually pressured.*

## ORGANIZING YOUR SWIM

After you have selected your swim the next step is setting up your gear and swim. Keeping your swim organized and tidy whilst static session fishing makes life a lot easier than having your tackle thrown down every which way. Not only does it keep things at hand, but it can help you to avoid making silly little mistakes which sometimes cost you fish. The following points outline some of the more important considerations when static bait fishing:

- First erect your shelter. Some questions you should ask yourself are: In which direction is the wind blowing? Can I see the lake to observe fish movement? Is there adequate space to land fish? Is it too close to the water's edge? These simple questions are very often overlooked by anglers.
- Having an organized bivvy is just as important as having an organized swim. Knowing where things are when you need them makes life so much easier. Pay special attention to the small and sharp items of tackle, such as needles and hooks.
- Keep important items of tackle at hand, such as scales, slings, sacks, forceps, Klin-ik, cameras.
- Make sure that your rods are not placed so that you are constantly falling over them. However, do not set them up so that they are too far away. Be sensible with your decision and be aware of the situation you are fishing (close to snags, for example).
- Always have an idea in your mind as to where you are going to land fish. There is nothing worse than spending hour after hour waiting for a pick-up only to lose the fish because you are undecided about where you are going to net it. Make sure the chosen area is free from obstructions or anything else which may hinder the task.
- Ensure that you have an idea of where you are going to unhook fish and that there is sufficient space surrounding the area for you to place the landing net. The unhooking mat should preferably be well back from the water's edge and well away from

*Out go the baits!*

any objects that could injure the fish.

- If you wish to take photographs of any fish you may catch, always decide beforehand on where you're going to do this. To smooth the process it also helps to prepare the camera equipment in advance.
- If the lake you are fishing permits the sacking of fish then decide on a suitable area in advance to minimize any stress put on the fish. Look for an area which has sufficient depth and is well away from any obstructions.

## CASTING

### Accuracy

If you use a boat on a regular basis, accurate hookbait placement is obviously pretty easy and straightforward. However, one of the fundamental skills of the carp angler is to cast a rod, and be accurate with it. 'That'll do!' just isn't good enough these days. The fish are being put under more and more pressure so your casting has to be spot on. If it has to be within 12in (30cm) of a bush on the island then put it there and not 2ft (60cm) away. Whilst the ability to cast comes chiefly through regular practice, below are a few tips:

- The drop between the tip and the lead is important. Find a length that is comfortable for your style of casting. If it's too long or too short your accuracy will suffer; generally 2ft (60cm) suits most people.
- When attempting an accurate cast, we find it best to stand parallel to

the water, holding the rod directly overhead and lining up a mark with the rod. To give you an idea of how the rod should be held, ensure that the reel fittings are directly overhead. If you're right-handed, your right hand should be by the reel, retaining the line with the index finger, while your left hand is stretched out in front of your head, holding the end grip.

- When you are ready to cast, pull down with the left hand whilst at the same time pushing upwards and forward with the right. Try to let the rod rather than brute force do the work. This is where practice makes perfect, as you need to get a 'feel' for the rod and the weight of the lead being used. If it helps, you need to

*The drop between the tip and lead will affect the cast.*

push and pull with the arms, bringing the lead overhead, and letting the curve of the rod do the work. You should look to be letting go of the line with the right index finger when the rod is out in front at approximately 45 degrees.

## A Step-by-Step Guide to Clipping-Up for Added Accuracy

If you are able to hit the hotspot time and time again when casting out your hookbait this will certainly help to improve your catch rate. However, unless you are exceptionally gifted at judging distances, casting can sometimes become a chore if you are unable to hit the desired mark within a few casts. The following guide takes a look at a method known as 'clipping-up'. This improves accuracy by restricting the amount of line that can be cast off the spool, thus ensuring that the hookbait cannot be cast past a certain mark.

1. Cast the hookbait to the desired position. It may take you a few casts. When there, place the line at the reel end in the clip on the side of the spool. Be careful not to crease the line.

2. For reference purposes mark the line at the position of the clip with a permanent marker pen, white correction fluid, or by placing a slither of insulation tape on the line.

3. Line up the direction of the cast with a land mark on the horizon, such as a tree or building. A good tip is to use something which will also stand out at night so you can find the direction easily in the dark.

*A close-up on a line clip.*

4. Now reel in, leaving the line in the clip.

5. Re-cast the rod to check that you are hitting the mark exactly. Try not to overpower the cast or the line will stretch and pull the rig towards you and out of position.

6. When you are happy, unclip the line and place the rod in the rest ready for the action!

Clipping-up is a simple but very effective way of ensuring your hookbait lands in the correct spot. Its use is not only effective in the short term, but if you store specially marked spools they can also be helpful in the long term. You can also use

*Line it up and away you go!*

clipping-up for reaching distant margins which have tricky over-hanging trees, such as those on islands. All you have to do is ensure you cast short of the mark to start with. Then estimate how far short of the mark you are, and take this distance of line off the spool and clip-up. Keep taking line off the spool and clipping-up until you hit the mark exactly.

## Reaching the Distance

Whilst being accurate with your casting proves its worth at catching fish time and time again, it is sometimes necessary to abandon complete accuracy in order to gain a few extra yards. Long-range fishing is becoming increasingly essential on some of the hard-fished waters due to the conditioned behaviour of the carp forcing them further out. Although most of us tend to rely on boats for that extra bit of distance, on some venues these are outlawed by tight regulations, so you have to be able to cast long range.

In reality a 100yd cast is a long way for the majority of beginners without the right tools and method. Below are a few tips on how to gain those vitally important extra yards:

- Try to get as near to the target as possible.
- Obviously the rod is one of the most important factors when it comes to distance casting. A fast-tapered rod with a high test curve is best. This should be equipped with larger and fewer eyes to reduce friction.
- Line friction through the rod eyes will slow down your lead, thus cost-

ing you distance. Lower breaking strain lines have lower diameters which can be cast further – but do not sacrifice safety for distance. If you need to reduce the diameter of your line and therefore its strain, you will have to use a shock leader of a greater breaking strain to withstand the cast of the lead. A shock leader is basically a piece of line which is much heavier in strength than the main line (for example, with a main line of 8lb you may opt for a leader of 15lb, which is thicker and capable of withstanding a heavy cast). We always use a short leader of approximately two rod lengths, and attach it to the main line via a double Grinner knot (section on knots). When casting with a leader, ensure that the

*Going for the big chuck in the south arm at St Cassien.*

knot is at the back of the spool and will fly through the rings easily (so the line coming off the reel does not catch on the knot and cause the cast to fall short).

- Use a braided shock leader instead of a monofilament. Monos tend to rattle through the rod rings.
- Use a large-spooled reel which is correctly filled with line (filled to the lip).
- Use an aerodynamically shaped lead (*see* section on rigs).
- Coat your line with a lubricant so that it flows easily from the spool. For this job we favour Kryston's Grease Lightning.

# FEATURE-FINDING WITH A ROD AND LINE

Feature-finding is a significant contributor to success in carp fishing. Knowledge of the formation of the lake bed gives the carp angler an all-important insight into the possible location of feeding areas, patrol routes or underwater snags. Feature-finding requires a little bit of effort, however, and because of this many anglers ignore it. Feature-finding is not difficult and can be carried out with a boat and echo-sounder or with a rod and line. It takes very little ability to operate an echo-sounder, but feature-finding with a rod and line is an art that needs skill and a lot of perseverance. It is also a skill that can be very beneficial to the carp angler when boats and echo-sounders are not allowed. Here's a simple look at how to do it.

## The Tools Required

Besides the usual rod and reel you will need a marker float, a bead, a lead and a pair of scissors for this job. Which marker float and lead you use is entirely up to you, but do remember that the larger the float, the heavier the lead needs to be, otherwise there is a risk that the float will lift the lead off the floor and give a false reading. As a guide, you should be fine with a lead in the region of 2½oz (70g) as this will cope with most sizes of float. As for the rod, you are better off using one with a medium test curve or tip action as they will recognize the lake bed a lot more easily than a sloppy or stiff rod.

## Setting Up the Rod

The setting up of the rod is straightforward. Simply thread the chosen lead onto the line, followed by the bead. Now attach the float to the end

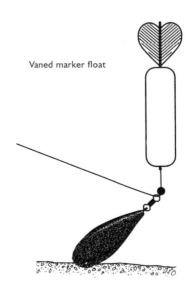

Vaned marker float

of the line with a good strong knot and cut off the excess line. We use a Grinner knot as it withstands the constant casting and abuse. Many anglers prefer to use two different set-ups for their feature-finding. They use the set-up shown for recording depths, and a further rod which has just the lead attached to the line for checking the composition of the bottom. The choice is yours.

### Checking the Depth

Once you have rigged up your rod with the chosen equipment, cast it out to the area which you want to check. Try to work your way around the swim in a methodical way. Start off on the left and work your way around to the right (or vice versa).

To check the depth accurately, tighten up to the lead (making sure that it does not move) and let the line off the spool, counting the depth it requires for the float to appear on the surface. A good tip here is to mark your rod 1ft (30cm) up from the spool to ensure that the depths recorded are as accurate as possible.

To help you make an accurate account of the depths, record all the information in a book. The best way we know to record the information is with a fan chart. Simply draw a fan of lines in the direction of each cast to be made and plot all the discovered depths. Each line shows the direction of the cast, with a dot showing the point where the depth was recorded.

### Know the Lake Bed

Dragging the lead to determine the make-up of the bottom is probably the hardest part of feature-finding with a rod and line. There are many different techniques used to drag the lead, but our favourite is to hold the rod at a 45-degree angle and pull the lead along the bottom slowly. Use the rod tip as a lever and pull the lead towards you using a sideways movement. Do not do this too quickly or the lead may jump about and give false readings. Keep your eyes on the tip at all times and feel for any vibrations which may be sent up the line. The make-up of the bottom is determined by the responses you recognise in these areas. It takes a lot of practice to be proficient at recognizing what texture the lake bed is and only trial and error will help you here. As a guide we have listed below what some of the features feel like when you drag a lead over or through them.

**Gravel** Gravel will cause your rod tip to bounce as you pull the lead over the top of it and you will feel a knocking vibration through the line. Once retrieved you will often discover that the lead has been scarred by the sharp stones.

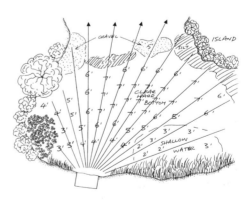

*Getting to know the lake bed will help you pin-point the feeding areas.*

**Silt** Pulling the lead through silt feels like you are dragging it across cotton wool. The rod tip will not bounce like it does with gravel, but it will bend every time you start to move the lead. The heavier the silt, the more your rod tip will bend when you pull.

**Weed** When pulling through weed, the rod tip will bend as you pull into it and then suddenly spring back as you pull out of it. The heavier the weed is, the harder it will be to pull through and, in most cases, you will drag in a ton of weed.

**Sand** The lead will move nice and smoothly across sandy areas with no resistance on the tip end of the rod.

**Clay** Clay can be discovered on the cast. The lead will normally sink into the clay once it hits the bottom and will usually only come free after a good pull.

One point worth noting here is that examining the lead after each cast will sometimes reveal strands of weed, gravel scars or fragments of clay or silt, which are all good clues.

As with depths, keep a record of the different textures of the lake bed that you discover. Record your information on the same map on which you recorded the depths as this will help you to draw up a more accurate final chart. To produce this, simply join up the dots of each group of different features you uncover. Depending on what you find, you should come up with a map similar in design to the one shown.

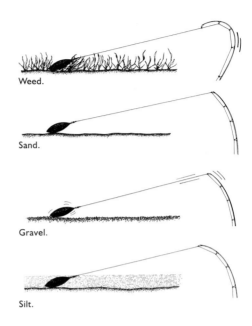

Weed.

Sand.

Gravel.

Silt.

## PLAYING FISH

There is nothing more disheartening than waiting ages for a pick-up only to have the fish drop off before it is in the net. The loss of a certain number of fish per season is both inevitable and excusable, and it happens to us all. Sometimes the fish will not have picked up the bait confidently enough, or taken the hook far enough into its mouth to ensure a secure hold is obtained. At other times the fish's mouth is so soft that the hook can be pulled out if the angler does not take care. However, many more fish are lost as a result of angler error and, with a little bit of thought, more takes could be converted into fish on the bank. In this basic guide we will consider the main reasons for fish losses after the buzzer has screamed in its excited tone to signify that a carp has picked up the bait.

**The Strike**

How many times have you heard anglers say that they picked up the rod, felt a couple of kicks – and then the line went slack? Some of the time this may be a result of the feeding style and confidence of the fish, but a fair amount of time it will be caused by the way in which the angler struck the run. Many anglers feel that they should really bang the hook home even if the buzzer is screaming a single tone, but a lot of the time the fish will have hooked itself and a strong strike will only serve, at worst, to pull out the hook or, at best, to enlarge the hole to increase the risk of a hook-pull later on. Gauge the strike according to the speed of the run, the distance you are casting, the action of the rod, and also whether you need to apply a 'hook-and-hold' strategy to keep the fish away from any nearby obstructions. Be especially careful in margin-fishing situations and apply only the minimum amount of pressure to ensure the hook will find its way home. The very fact that you are fishing in the margins means that there will be very little line between you and the fish to absorb the shock of any lunges it might make.

On the other hand there is the scenario where the angler did not strike the run hard enough, and this is particularly common with drop-backs. Something else frequently heard on the banks is that the run was missed, 'but it was a drop-back', as if this was a reasonable excuse for the loss. At the end of the day a drop-back is as good as a screamer in that the fish has picked up the bait and is running off with it – albeit towards the angler. All you have to do is adjust your strike to

*Here it comes!*

deal with the different situation and there should be no cause for concern. There is always the temptation to pick up and strike whilst the rod is in the rest and the buzzer is singing, but doing this will give only a minimal effect at the business end, as most of the force of the strike will have been lost in the bow of line in the water. Pick the rod out of the rest and reel in the slack line until you feel the fish. Give the rod a firm strike at this point and you should be attached to a fish.

As mentioned above, another major cause of fish loss is the fact that a lot of carp have soft mouths, out of which hooks can pull quite easily. This is often the case where fish are silt feeders and so do not have the tough, leathery mouths that they would need if they were feeding on snails and crayfish. If the fish in your lake are of this type then you will know that special care has to be taken when playing them. Our finding on a number of venues is that your choice of hook is vitally important. Fishabil is a prime example of this. Frequently you will lose batches of fish one after the other at this venue. A fine-wire hook is more likely to tear the skin of the mouth, so consider a change of hook pattern if you are encountering this problem. Or try altering the hooklink or hair (more on this in Chapter 5). Failing that, you will have to rely on your fish-playing capabilities and give the carp as little stick as possible.

## Setting the Reel

When it comes to playing fish, the clutch on your reel is one of your best allies. It should always be set at a slipping point just below the breaking strain of your line, so that if you get yourself into a danger situation with the fish tearing off and you unable to keep up with it, the clutch will save the day. Be careful when fishing near to snags, though, as it may be the case that you do not want to give the fish line under any circumstances. You can also use the clutch to play out your fish, and this method is much smoother than playing off the back-wind, although it does cause the line to twist a lot more, thus reducing its life. The clutch will also help you if you fish with stiff rods, where an angry carp on a short line in the margin will not stay on for very long if you are not careful. There is a clutch on every reel so make proper use of it.

## Snagged Fish

You've managed to get the fish to pick up the bait, the hook has been set properly and the battle has commenced. Five minutes into the fight with a good fish and it makes it to the sanctuary of a sunken tree about 30yd out to your right. What do you do? You tried everything to stop it getting in there, but it made it and now the fish is snagged. By all means give it a bit of pressure to see if it will pull out, but don't stand there tugging for ages or point the rod at the snag and walk backwards pulling for a break. This will almost certainly end up in a lost fish, and one which is probably tethered. At the very least the fish will suffer some damage as a result of the stress of the pull. If possible, seek assistance or use a boat. Wade out, but only if it is safe to do so. Alternatively put the rod back into the rest and open the bale arm or loosen the clutch. This will often encourage the fish swimming out of its own accord, leaving you to carry on the battle with neither your tackle nor the fish any worse for the experience.

## Battling under the Rod Tip

Whilst we all like a good scrap, the object of the game is to get the fish into the net as soon as possible. To delay matters gives the fish more of a chance to escape – the hook-hold will loosen as the fish twists and turns – and will only result in exhaustion of the carp, not to mention your nerves. As the fish gets nearer to the bank it is advisable, if at all possible, to keep low to the ground. The fish obviously knows that it is hooked, but the sight of the angler often has the effect of spooking the carp even more, causing it to make a quick dash for freedom. Dress in sombre-coloured clothing – bright apparel will stand out more than a dull green or brown. Have your landing net close to hand so that you don't need to shuffle around trying to find it, and try to keep any bankside disturbance to a minimum. Normally when an angler has a fish on, a crowd of onlookers gathers. Ask them to keep quiet, and pay no attention to any remarks they might make. Concentrate only on the job at hand, and worry about the well- wishers when the fish is in the net.

Most of us fish with a mate who can assist with landing a fish, but even if you do – and obviously if you fish on your own – it is worthwhile becoming competent at landing your own fish. There may come a time, especially at night, when you will be on your own and if you always rely on someone else you might find yourself in trouble. In our case we almost always land our own fish even if we are doubled up in a swim, and would certainly not trust anyone else to land a fish for us. We have heard no end of stories of anglers who have lost fish through the overzealous attempts of others to net their fish for them. If you lose it, you only have yourself to blame. Finally on this point, it goes without saying that you should always have everything to hand, and know exactly where your net and other essential items are, so that you do not have to shuffle around trying to find things and risk losing your fish.

Before you are in a position to land a fish, you should consider exactly where you are going to carry out the operation. Make sure that the water is sufficiently deep to enable you to bring the fish into the margins to net it. If it isn't, consider wading out if it is safe enough to do so. Many fish are lost by dragging them

through shallow water, and the sight of a fish grounded in the margins just out of reach of the landing net is not a pretty one. If you do decide to wade out, be very careful that the bottom of the lake is not too silty. The last thing you want to do is to get yourself stuck in the mud. Be aware of any marginal snags or obstructions in the water that might impede the landing of the fish, and try to keep it from getting into these in the first place to save you having to wading out to free it.

## Netting the Fish

One of the main danger times is when the carp is being drawn towards the net and sees it for the first time. The fish might not initially realize that it is so close, but once it sees the net it will often make a sharp dash for freedom. On a short line this can be fatal as the stretch in the line will be minimal, and if you are using a stiff rod and do not control the carp properly, it is likely the hook will pull free. This is where the clutch comes in. If it has been set properly you should

*Crowy with a long range thirty from France. This particular fish he targeted for two years, and he successfully caught it the following night that Rob caught his target fish from the water.*

have no problems. Do not try to bully the carp into the net at this stage as one false move could mean all is lost. You will know when the fish is ready as it will give itself up.

The final netting process is as important as any of the points we have considered. Do not try to chase the fish around with the net as you will, at the very least, scare it or, worse still, knock it off the hook. Sink the mesh until only the spreader block is above the water, and draw the fish over the cord until its nose is almost touching the spreader block before lifting the net. It is a good idea to tuck the mesh into the gap between the spreader block and the main part of the mesh itself. This holds the bottom of the mesh tight to the net and helps prevent snagging on the bottom of the lake as well as reducing the drag on the mesh, making it easier to move through the water. If you do net a fish for someone else, get them to bring the fish to you as opposed to you chasing around after it. If it does come off you can guarantee that you will, at least in part, be blamed for the loss.

Even when the fish has been safely landed there is still room for disaster. On a number of occasions we have seen fish lost prior to being photographed, even though they were safely banked and unhooked. On one occasion an angler we know had blanked all week. He eventually landed a fish only to have another angler unhook it and drop it back in prior to photos being taken. On another occasion, Simon caught a 20lb-plus grassy, unhooked it and left it in the net whilst he set up his camera equipment. The grassy jumped clean out of the net and escaped to freedom. It pays, therefore, to have everything organized and ready for the capture of a fish. If you do need to leave a fish in the water whilst you attend to other things, make sure someone is with it to ensure that it does not come to harm or, indeed, escape.

# 5 RIGS AND END TACKLE

Many articles have been written by many anglers on the subject of rigs, and all anglers have their own opinion on what is quite a complicated issue. One of the most important things as far as the beginner carper is concerned is that you should try to understand what you are trying to achieve and why, at the same time trying not to get caught up in the minefield that rigs can be. An awful lot of young carpers make the mistake of reading about the latest wonder rig and immediately try to tie one up, often getting it sadly wrong before taking it along on their next session without success. We should know, as we have both been in this position during our early years of carping. The main thing you should remember with the majority of rigs shown in the magazines is that they are designed with a certain situation in mind, so unless you are fishing under the same circumstances the rig may not be as effective as was intended – and it may even cost you fish.

We have been asked by beginners on a number of occasions if we will show them our rigs, and they are almost always amazed at how simple they really are. Don't make the mistake of over-complicating what needs only be a straight- forward subject. Consider what you want your rig to do or avoid, and then construct one to suit that situation. That is the basic principle behind rig design.

Because such a topic can be a very complicated issue, we will begin this chapter by looking at the fundamentals of what a simple rig comprises, then progressing to some of the rigs that we actually use for our fishing.

## BASIC RIG COMPONENTS

For the benefit of the beginners reading this book, the components of a rig are:

- Hook.
- Lead or weight attachment.
- Hooklink.
- Swivel.
- General items to enhance the use of the rig such as beads, tubing, and rings.

All rigs differ. Some comprise beads and buffers and in-line leads, whilst others are totally different, for example a free-lined hookbait, which has no lead attachment. It is therefore important to examine some of the major rig bits you will come across in magazines and tackle shops. When choosing which rig you are going to use for your carp fishing, the selection of hook, lead, bead, swivel and hooklink is vitally important. If you walk into any tackle shop you will see an array of many different types and models. All are designed for different situations and all have their own advantages. As you gain experience you will be able to decide which type to use in which situation, and you will be able to recognize when a change is needed. However, when you are starting out you can't be expected to get all the decisions right, so below are brief descriptions of what hooks, leads, beads, swivels and hooklinks are, which will hopefully set you off on the right track.

## Hooks

Hooks are probably the most complex of the five topics. Most tackle shops sell anything between one and 100 different types of size and pattern (design). To help simplify things, carp hooks can be classed into two different types: general carp and specific-purpose hooks.

Both types are available in different sizes, and with or without barbs. They also come in different designs, for example, with in-turned or out-turned points, different shank lengths, different gape widths or different eye positions. This is where the confusion tends to set in really for the beginner carper, as looking at all of the different patterns tends to leave an angler thinking, 'which one should I use today?' Obviously experience is the all important key here, as once you have used a number of the hooks you are sure to settle on a select few for use.

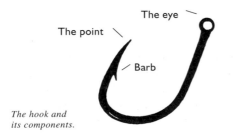

The eye
The point
Barb

*The hook and
its components.*

### General Carp Hooks
You will normally find that general-purpose carp hooks are very middle of the road in their design, simply because they have to be suitable for a wide number of different situations rather than a select few. They are made from a moderate gauge of wire and usually all have a similar design. Some of the most widely used general carp hooks are those available from Drennan, such as the Boilie hooks, Starpoint and Super Specialist. All these are designed on a similar line of pattern for all-round fishing and have been around for ages. In recent years, however, the general carp hooks have tended to be based on two particular modern patterns, namely the Pattern 1 and the Pattern 2 types sold by companies such as Fox International and Kevin Nash Tackle. They are basically seen as the two patterns that best accommodate the standard hair rig set-up as well as the now popular line aligner (*see* below). They are also chemically sharpened to provide a needle-sharp point, which assists with hooking.

### Specific-Purpose Carp Hooks
There are hooks these days that are specifically designed for either weed, snag, open water, boilie fishing, and so on. It is our advice that if you are a beginner, general carp hooks are more suited to your fishing. If, however, you are looking to approach a certain situation on a long-term basis, you may be better off with a hook that has added strength or a finer wire for the situation you are confronted with. As an example, if you are fishing a very snaggy water, you may opt for a heavy-wired hook such as an

Ashima Super Strong. Alternatively, if you are fishing for shy feeding fish, you may choose one of the 'en vogue' longer-shanked hooks like Carp 'R' Us' Long Shank Nailers, which tend to turn better in the mouths of finicky feeders.

*Our Choice*
We generally prefer hooks with an in-turned eye as they give a better hook hold when using the line-aligner set up (*see* below). We also tend to favour a size 6 hook for all-round fishing, as this tends to suit a wide number of different situations. The only time we will go above this size is when we are fishing amongst heavy snags, such as those we experienced at Romania's Lake Raduta, when we opted for a size 1. You tend to find that smaller hooks are more suited to shy feeding fish which have been put under a lot of angling pressure, but make sure that, if you opt for these, you are not risking losing fish: smaller hooks will pull out of the carp's mouth more easily.

As far as bait size is concerned, we generally follow the principle of a small hookbait for a small hook and a larger one for a large hook. This is to try to enhance hooking capabilities.

Another important point worth mentioning here is that fine-wire hooks will open up more easily compared with those made of a heavy wire. A large proportion of general-purpose carp hooks are made from an intermediate wire thickness.

*Barbless Hooks*
Barbless hooks are an item of tackle which seem to be overlooked by carp anglers. This probably has something to do with the fact that the majority of anglers are scared to use them because, in theory, they offer the fish a better chance of slipping the hook. These days we only ever hear about barbless hooks being used on waters that have specific rules in operation, and whilst barbed hooks do offer a better chance of landing fish, they too can actually be the cause for hook pulls on occasions. Hook barbs can restrict hooking efficiency by preventing the point from penetrating to a sufficient depth. In such instances the hook point will only be resting in the mouth tissue and thus be easier to eject by the carp, resulting in missed fish. In theory, this problem can be overcome by using a heavier lead, but as we all know, the carp can also defeat this advantage after a period of time.

Besides overcoming shy fish on occasions, barbless hooks are also a lot easier to unhook from the mouth of the fish, and thus minimize the risk of hook damage occurring. They are excellent in a number of other ways too. They can be

*Don't write-off barbless hooks! Rob with a 44lb mirror.*

released from clothing or material very easily if they happen to hook up accidentally, and they can be used to ensure that your rig is a completely safe one. Fish can shed barbless hooks very easily and we have even witnessed fish knowing how to roll off such hooks on waters where the barbless-only rule has been in operation for a long time.

We would never use the barbless variety in weedy areas, where you need to hook and hold fish in order to gain respect, but in open water they are completely fine as there is no need to bully the fish as much. Barbless hooks can be purchased from suppliers ready prepared, or you can save yourself a bit of money by purchasing a pack of barbed hooks and squashing the barb down yourself. If you do this you have the option of both types of hook, so this would always be our preference if we were short of money. Using a pair of forceps, simply squeeze the barb down flat, but be careful that you do not blunt the hook while doing so. Make sure the barb is completely flat by gently running your finger across it – once you are happy that it is not active the hook is ready to use – dead simple and sometimes extremely effective.

*Hook Tips*

One sight we see very often is anglers casting out without bothering to check the condition of the hook beforehand. Overlooking this simple task can quite easily be the reason for lost fish and missed pick ups. Try to get yourself into the habit of checking your hooks on a regular basis and making sure that they are capable of performing the task ahead.

So how does hook damage occur? There are a number of ways in which hooks may become damaged, but the most obvious way is whilst playing and hooking into fish. There is a great amount of pressure on the hook during this time and so it is vitally important that you give the hook a thorough check after unhooking. Look closely at the point of the hook. Is it still sharp? Is it still the correct shape? Compare the hooks to unused ones by placing them side by side and looking for a difference. Has the one you are using opened out or become disfigured in any way? If so, change it straight away and never think that a damaged hook will be fine, because the chances are it will let you down. You should also check new hooks in a similar way, as it is possible for faulty ones to appear in a brand new pack.

Playing and hooking into fish is not the only way that hooks may become damaged. Every time you reel in or pull the lead across the lake bed, the hook may rub on such surfaces as gravel, mussel shells or stones. Hooks can also be

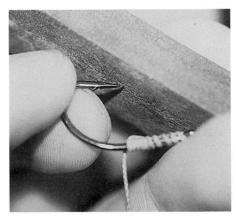

*Keep an eye on the sharpness of hooks.*

damaged in transport. Many anglers leave their rigs attached to their main line when they break their rods down, and despite the high quality of some of the rod bags on the market today, it is still possible for hooks to be damaged when packing your gear away in this way.

Finally, a point about hook sharpeners. Some anglers use these extensively, and we acknowledge that in the right hands they can be a valuable item of tackle. However, nowadays, where chemically sharpened hooks are the norm, hook sharpeners are not recommended. Any alteration to the needle-sharp points of modern hooks tends to weaken them, and for this reason we advise you to dispose of all damaged hooks regardless of how slight the   damage may appear. If you don't, you will only end up wishing you had done!

## Leads

Leads come in a range of different weights and shapes, and the carp angler should be quite sure what his requirements are before selecting, so he can choose the type that best suits the situation. We will look at some of the most common ones below.

### Arlesey Bomb

The Arlesey bomb is extremely popular amongst carp anglers and was designed by the late Dick Walker many years ago when he was fishing the   famous Arlesey Lake. The rounded shape of the lead makes it unsuitable for sloped bars or similar inclined features, but its streamlined shape and swivel attachment (which helps minimize twist) make it

*A selection of carp leads from Korda.*

ideal for long-range fishing. In recent times several new designs of Arlesey bomb have come on the market, with the most popular being the Distance Lead by Korda Rig Developments. This is a fantastic lead, designed with long-range casting in mind, but is suitable for a wide range of uses. It always has a swivel type attachment, but some anglers prefer to take the swivel off and simply attach it via the loop head.

### Ball Lead

Similar to the Arlesey bomb, the ball lead is unsuitable for sloped features as its rounded shape means it can roll. However, the rounded shape is ideal for bolt rigs as the full weight of the lead is

*The Arlesey bomb.*

central and therefore more likely to drive the hook home when the fish straightens the hooklink. When used in heavy sizes (for example 3oz), and combined with a short link, they are excellent for use on waters where the fish have been subjected to long links and light lead set ups. They are available in both in-line and swivel attachments.

### In-Line Leads

In-line leads do not have a swivel attachment but instead have a passage running through the centre where the line should be threaded. Once attached, the lead will be in the same plane as the line and terminal tackle, which makes it ideal for use amongst pads, weed, or snags, as it is less prone to snagging than one hanging free from the line.

### Flat Leads

Leads with flat sides are ideal for use on sloping bars or features as they hold themselves to the bottom better than those that are cylindrical or rounded. Some varieties (for example the pendant lead by Essential Products) also provide greater barb penetration, which is   another thing to take into account before making your final selection. Our favourite flat leads are those offered by Korda Rig Developments, which are pear-shaped and available in both in-line and swivel attachments.

*The in-line lead.*

### Riser Leads

As the name suggests, these leads rise up towards the surface when pulled through the water. There are many different varieties on the market, but they are all excellent for use when there are snags between yourself and the hotspot you are casting to. The flat pear leads by Korda are a good example, and come in both in-line and swivel attachments.

### Backleads

Backleads are generally small leads of less than ½oz. They are usually swivel type with an attachment connected to them and are used for a completely different purpose than the leads attached to the rig end. Backleads are used to sink the main line in the water, especially close to the rig end so that it keeps it discreet and away from the fish – thus avoiding spooking any line-shy fish. Backleads can either be purchased ready-made from tackle shops or made to suit the circumstances you need. Simply clip them onto your main line and flick them, with the assistance of the rod tip, into the required position. Make sure that you try to limit the size of the angle in your line, however, or you may cause problems with the sensitivity of your set-up (*see* Chapter 14).

### Which Size Lead?

All sizes of lead have a purpose. When deciding which size of lead to use you must consider:
• The distance you wish to cast out. If you wish to cast long distance, the lead must suit your tackle and technique. If you wish to avoid spooking fish, the lead must be light on

entry.

• The contribution of the lead to hooking. If you want the lead to perform a bolt effect then it must be heavy enough to drive the hook home.

We could write a book about lead size choice, but to avoid confusing you we will try to be as simple as we can. For backleading we always opt for a small lead of approximately ¼oz. For the actual rig end itself, we have used leads of all different sizes, ranging from ¼oz all the way up to 6oz. Obviously the 6oz leads are used for extreme-range fishing when we need to keep the line as tight as possible to enhance the sensitivity of the set-up, but we may also opt for a large lead when fishing short range but hoping to hook the carp well. A heavy lead will help drive the hook home, especially when you are using a short link. This is called the bolt or shock effect and is an excellent method to use when the majority of the fish in your chosen water have been caught on long, confidence-type rigs. For the majority of our fishing, though, which is on small English waters of less than 100 acres (40ha), we prefer to use a lead of 2–3oz. This intermediate size is suitable for all manner of different situations. For short-range fishing on small waters we do sometimes opt for a lead of 1–2oz.

There seems to be a feeling amongst carp anglers these days that you must use a large lead for your fishing. This is nonsense and anyone who follows this line of reasoning will make many mistakes. Angling pressure can change the reactions of the fish in a massive way, which is why we always recommend that

anglers analyse the situation first before making any choice. However, the following gives a brief summary of what size lead we opt for in certain conditions.

**¼–1oz** For backleading, small waters, stalking, confidence rigs and feeding fish that are at close range (up to 20yd).
**1–2oz** For fishing at up to 60yd range.
**2–3oz** For fishing at up to 100yd range.
**3–6oz** For fishing with braided mainline, bolt rigs, and at ranges over 100 yards.

*Lead Colour*
Leads not only come in a whole host of different shapes and sizes, but also in different colours. On some waters you will catch more fish with camouflaged leads, whilst on others you will do better with brightly coloured leads. It is a matter

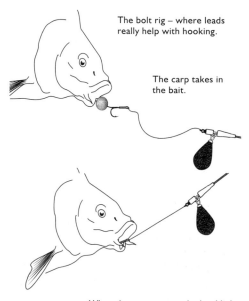

The bolt rig – where leads really help with hooking.

The carp takes in the bait.

When the carp moves, the hooklink straightens, driving the hook home.

of getting to know your water and using the method which responds best. If, like us, you regularly fish new waters, then your confidence in a particular method should be the deciding factor. On such occasions we choose a camouflaged lead, as our objective is always to keep the rig as discreet as possible. Blending into the environment is the best way, so if you fish a lake with a silty bottom a dark-coloured lead is best, whilst a light-coloured brown would be good when fishing over sand. We generally use Korda Rig Developments leads for our fishing, which are ready-made in different colours, but if you wish to colour your own leads you can buy a special kit from most tackle shops. In our minds, lead colour is an important issue regardless of what other anglers say.

*The Lead Link*
This particular item of tackle has been designed specifically with fish welfare in mind. The end of the 1980s saw a number of important changes occur in the world of carp fishing concerning the safety of rigs. Before this time, anglers overlooked the dangers of using permanently fixed lead set-ups, and a fish picking up a hookbait and the line parting above the lead was generally regarded as an unfortunate consequence of fishing.

Things have changed a great deal since then, and it is now a known fact that leads are normally the main cause of a fish becoming snagged. Once a cut-off has occurred, it is possible for the lead to end up either locked up in weed or wrapped around underwater branches if it cannot be freed from the line – leaving the fish tied up and stuck to the rig. The wide use

of modern anti-abrasive lines makes the latter even more likely if the line becomes completely engulfed in the snag, which is a common occurrence once the fish starts to panic and tries to free itself from the hook. A rig, therefore, that cannot ditch the lead has the distinct possibility of causing untold amounts of damage to a fish, with the likelihood being that it will remain permanently snagged and left to die – as has happened at some venues.

Initially, fish safety rigs incorporated a weak link between the lead and the main line. This method was not the most practical for casting long range, though, as the weak link, for obvious reasons, resulted in frequent crack-offs as well as heated arguments with anglers close to where they landed! This is where the manufactured lead links (as most are known) came in – and how welcome they are.

We've been using several models for some time now, and, to be honest, we wouldn't be without them now we've been using them regularly. Not only from the fish safety aspect are they beneficial to fishing, but they have assisted from the practical side of things also. As an example, if you regularly use swivel-type leads and like attaching them to the main line by simply threading the line through the swivel, after a period of lengthy casting you will more than likely find

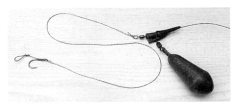

*The lead clip by Rod Hutchinson.*

*Kords's brilliant Lead Clips.*

your main line damaged close to where the swivel has been put under tension. Using a lead link here will protect your main line so that frequent casting can be carried out without you having to worry about the line parting after half a dozen full-blooded casts.

There are several models of lead link on the market, with the most widely used being those sold by Kevin Nash Tackle and Korda; we've been using Korda for a long time now. Each link comprises a main body and a 1in (2.5cm) silicon sleeve. Most of the others on the market are similar in design. They work by sliding your chosen lead over the point of the lower splice and onto the main body. This is held in place by the silicon sleeve which must be pushed over both of the spliced ends. The whole lot is then slipped onto the line, silicon sleeve first, and pushed up against the hooklink swivel, or if you prefer, you can slip each piece individually onto the line, fitting them together once they're all in place.

We've seen it written by some authors that lead links can be used in a running form of set-up. Whilst they can be used in such a way, it is our opinion that the bore of the main body is too small to allow the line to be passed through without causing some sort of tension on the hooklink end. We therefore normally opt for another set-up if we wish to present a running-type rig for shy feeding fish. We prefer to use a lead link for a semi-fixed kind of lead set-up. To do this, we simply push the hooklink swivel inside the plastic body of the lead link.

We have found lead links suitable for all manner of different situations (even weed), and will continue to use them ahead of all other forms of lead attachment.

## Hooklinks

There are hundreds of different hooklinks on the market, all acting in different ways to one another and all designed to overcome a certain problem. Here's a look at some of the more common types you will find.

### Buoyant Hooklinks

Buoyant hooklinks are possibly the most widely used link for carp today, and are designed for situations where the angler requires the hooklink to be suspended off the lake bed. An example could be when debris is present which may interfere with the action of the link (for example when fishing over very light silt). Although most lines float, buoyant hooklinks are usually braided materials such as Kryston's Silkworm and Super-Silk types, which are made from high-performance polyethylene (HPPE) which is naturally opaque and very supple.

### Neutral Links

For obvious reasons these links neither sink or float, but instead lie suspended

*The buoyant hooklink.*

in a neutral position – an example being Kryston's Merlin. Like most buoyant links, Merlin is also made from polyethylene, but it is balanced with polyester wraps (the material that gives it its camouflaged colour) and so acts in a completely different way.

Neutral hooklinks are excellent for use amongst weedy areas, as they look more natural in appearance than those suspended above the weed.

### Sinking Links

Sinking links offer a natural presentation by lying flat on the lake bed. However, they should only be used when there is little debris on the lake bed, or the link may easily become inefficient. Sinking hooklinks are usually a lot thicker in diameter than buoyant or neutral braids, so always consider whether or not this will effect your fishing before selecting

*The neutral hooklink.*

them for use. Kryston's Super-Nova is our choice of sinking link as it is both very soft and very supple.

### Invisible Links

When the fishing is becoming slightly difficult and the fish are wising up to the methods you are using, then changing to an invisible link may be the solution. Invisible links come in many varieties, with the most popular being Kryston's Multi-Strand. This is a buoyant link made up of many fine strands of HPPE, which separate when dispersed in water. Invisible links are also excellent for use when the surrounding lake bed is very clear and other types of hooklink stand out. In more recent years, several products made from fluorocarbon have hit the market and become popular. These are totally different to Multi-Strand and are monofilament lines. An example is Suffix's Invisiline.

### Stiff Links

Although supple links offer more of a natural presentation, the carp may easily eject them if they have become accustomed to their use. In this case, stiff links made from monofilament or Amnesia may be the answer, as the stiffness of the link causes ejection problems for the carp. The best way to attach a stiff link is to form a loop at the swivel end. This will give the link more mobility. Monofilament and Amnesia are also very durable, so they are also a good choice for tackling snaggy areas.

### Durable Links

Besides monofilament and Amnesia, there are a number of other durable materials that are suitable for use when fishing in snaggy areas. Although designed as a leader, Kryston's Quicksilver is probably the most widely used. It is very abrasion-resistant and has the added advantage of being supple. It is excellent for use amongst pads and reeds because it can cut through such plants without too much trouble.

*Combi-Links*

Combi-links comprise two or more different types of hooklink made into one and have become popular in recent years. Joining two different links together allows the angler to have the best of both worlds. An example could be a sinking/invisible combination, whereby the first half of the link will sink and the other half will be buoyant and invisible. Such combinations may be the answer to a problem (such as finicky takes), or they may just offer something new to a situation. Up until fairly recently combi-links were quite tricky to tie, so were not widely used. Then Dave Chilton at Kryston came up with the answer to the problem in the form of the first commercially available combi-link, known as Snake-skin. This material, which is absolutely superb for combi-links, is made up of Multi-Strand with a

plastic coating making it into a stiff link. All you need to do is to peel back a couple of inches of the plastic coating and you have a combi-link without the burden of a knot. A combi-link of this sort is ideal for pop-ups as it presents a bait with an almost undetectable hooklink. At the same time, the anti-ejection properties of a stiff link are retained, making the rig quite difficult to detect but very hard to eject. If this method has not yet been tried on your water then it is certainly worth a go.

*Hooklink Length*

The question of what length of hooklink to use is often asked. In our minds, there are three main areas to consider here:

• The distance to be cast.
• The size of fish in the target lake.
• The conditioned behaviour of the fish.
• The baiting situation.

Obviously the conditioned behaviour of the fish is a pretty straightforward thing

*Kryston's Snake-skin Combi-link.*

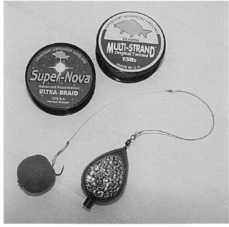

*Another form of combination link.*

to address, because if the fish have been subject to long links for a long period, it will almost certainly be beneficial to try short links (and vice versa). As for the size of the fish, many have different body shapes. Some waters are stocked with fish of the same race and strain, which will mean that for most of the year (apart from spawning time) they will have similar characteristics as far as body form is concerned. All fish feed by up-ending on the bottom and then levelling out. The deeper in body section a fish, the greater the angle at which it will have to up-end compared to one with a flat and straight belly. Obviously fish with a deep body section will be more likely to fall for a longer link as it will leave a greater margin for error. If the fish in your water are all similar then this should be the most significant consideration when designing your rigs. It is difficult to do this when fishing a water with mixed stock, and in these situations we generally opt for a link of 15in (38cm) as this seems to be an intermediate distance suitable for both fat and thin fish. Nevertheless, always

consider the conditioned behaviour of the fish alongside this rule of thumb.

Likewise, always consider the baiting situation. Tight clumps of bait mean that the fish doesn't need to move far to consume food items, so a shorter link is best. For a broader scattering of bait, a longer link is likely to be better. This topic is discussed in greater detail in Chapter 9.

On the distance-casting side of things, a shorter rig will create less resistance on the cast and thus enable you to cast further. Long links tend to spin in flight and limit the distance. All in all, the length of a rig is a vitally important topic to address. Talk to as many anglers as possible before tying your rigs, and then make sure that you have a reason for doing something specific. A good hooklink tip is to measure exactly how long the rig you are using is. We both carry tape measures with us for all of our fishing, and we know exactly how long our rigs are. We never settle for second best in this department and would rather abandon a rig than use it without good reason.

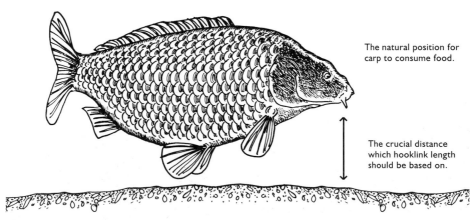

The natural position for carp to consume food.

The crucial distance which hooklink length should be based on.

*Do the carp in your water pick up baits in a level or up-ended position?*

*Hooklink Tools*

There are several hooklink tools on the market that allow the angler to alter the style of a hooklink. The two most popular ones are Drop Em! and Hauser made by Kryston. If you prefer to use a thinner hooklink, such as the buoyant types, but would like the link to lie flat, it is possible to present it on the bottom by adding weight. This can be done in a number of different ways, but by far the best is to apply Drop Em! to the material. Drop Em! is basically a block of tungsten putty. When you rub the hooklink through it, the braid will pick up minute pieces of the putty, which will make it sink in the water. Hauser is a stiffener which is applied to the hooklink, then left to dry. It will make certain parts of the hooklink stiff, such as the last two inches, so that the link will work in a particular way.

## Swivels

Swivels are used by the carp angler for any of the following reasons:

- To prevent twist in the terminal rig.
- To create a neat finish when joining two lines together.
- To act as a junction stop for the lead.

Like hooks, swivels come in a number of different sizes, strengths and designs. Many anglers have their own personal favourites, with the most popular being the oval eye-shaped type. In recent years, the long eye swivels of Rod Hutchinson are also becoming popular.

We generally opt for a size 10 swivel ahead of all others. These fit snugly into the main body of most lead links.

Although larger swivels tend to have extra strength, they are sometimes too bulky for the rigs we use. The choice is yours. Just make sure that the swivels are over 40lb in strength if you are fishing amongst snags, and ensure that you don't choose the type that are brass with twisted coils at the top. These can cause rigs to tangle or even separate if they are put under tension when wrapped around. The modern tungsten type that are available from most companies these days are the best as these are specifically designed for big carp.

## General Items

Besides the rig components mentioned above, there are a few other important items which need mentioning in this chapter. The most important are:

**Beads** These assist with presentation by giving rigs a neat and tidy finish. They are used to protect knots and to prevent the eye of the lead slipping over swivel heads and stop knots. They are available

*Correct hooklink selection did the trick on this occasion for Martin Davidson.*

in heavy-duty plastic as well as rubber. The rubber ones are usually favoured for protecting the knots as most are drilled with a bore in which the knot will lie protected. They also act as a shock absorber on the knot, especially when using a helicopter set up (*see* below). The harder versions are mainly used for their anti-tangle properties as well as keeping things neat and tidy.

**Tubing** We have mixed feelings about tubing. It is used mainly for its anti-tangle properties, but we're not convinced that it does this job – in fact, we generally feel that tubing tends to cause tangles more than avoid them. The only advantage of great lengths of tubing on the main line is that it protects the flanks of the fish by preventing the line from getting underneath the scales and causing damage. We favour tubing only in the 0.5mm size, and only use it for making the line aligner set-up described later.

**Rings** A number of modern tackle manufacturers are marketing small rig rings. These are mainly designed for joining lines together, but they can also be attached to the hook to design the D-rig set-up (*see* below), as well as acting as a pivot for a hook. We never use them because we tend to keep our rigs as simple as possible, but we do know plenty of anglers who do. The choice is yours. You will catch without them and you will catch with them.

**Tungsten putty** This is used for counter-balancing pop-ups, a topic discussed in great depth in Chapter 8.

# BASIC RIGS

## Side-Hooked Rigs
'Side-hooked' here refers to baits that have been hooked through the side (in the diagram you can see this with the boilie). Side-hooking is the oldest of the many carp fishing methods and is now somewhat overshadowed by more modern techniques. However, some anglers are now reverting to side-hooking in a bid to be different on some of the more pressurized waters.

### When to Use Side-Hooking
Although there are many techniques that are much more effective, side-hooking is very basic and offers great room for development. Unless you have good reason for doing so you should never enter a given situation with the best that you can offer. Always start simple and have something in reserve to advance to. For this reason, side-hooking should always be the foundation of your carp fishing, especially if you are fishing for virgin carp.

## The Hair Rig
The hair rig was designed as an advancement on side-hooking. Anglers became aware of the fact that fish were wising up, and that there was a need for a rig that didn't give the poor hookholds from which you sometimes suffered from with side-hooking. A hair rig basically uses a 'hair' (a length of line attached to the hook) to mount the hookbait on.

### A Simple Hair Rig
Making a simple hair rig is very easy. You

*A camouflaged lead and rig was its downfall.*

can use a number of different materials to make the hair. Some anglers use line, whilst others prefer braided material. Like everything, each has its own advantages and you will find out which you prefer through experience. For now, though, we suggest you use the knotless set-up, which combines the hooklink material into the hair. This is one of the most widely used methods of attaching your hooklink to the hook because it is simple to do and uses the same knot for both the link and the hair. To make it, all you need are your favourite hooklink material and hook pattern and some scissors. Here's how you tie it up:

*A side-hooked bait.*

1. After measuring your chosen hooklink and cutting it to size, take one end and thread it through the eye of the hook. Rest the hooklink along one side of the hook leaving a tail of about 2in (5cm) from the eye down past the bend, so that you can tie your hair.

2. Holding the tail in place, wrap the longer length of hooklink around the lower part of the eye of the hook (uppermost part of shank) ensuring that it is kept tight. If your link comes through the side of the eye, simply turn the hook over so that the gap is facing away from the tension.

3. Now wrap the link around the shank in the same way as in Step 2, working your way down the shank. Our experience tells us that the link needs to be wrapped around the hook at least ten times for it to hold firm. Ten wraps normally ends up finishing opposite the point of the hook (our favourite position for the hinge of the hair), but you can adjust this to suit your needs.

4. Keeping the wrap in position, loop the long hooklink end through the back of the eye of the hook and pull through.

5. Do not pull through too tight or the webbing around the shank will start to move up the hook – changing the position of where you want the hair to hinge. Just pull through so that the excess is taken out of the loop and tighten gently. If you do move the hinge position, simply pull the webbing down so that it is back where you want it.

6. The knotless knot has now been tied. To ensure that it stays in place and has suitable strength, you may wish to add a dab of superglue. Make sure this doesn't touch the tail left over for the hair

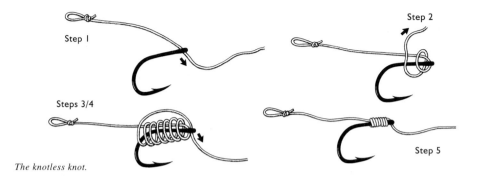

*The knotless knot.*

or it will become stiff in this area. Lastly, tie a loop in the end of the hair at least an inch (2.5cm) away from the hinge, on which you can now attach your hookbait.

### The Length of the Hair

The length of the hair is very important. If it is too long you may hook fish on the outside of the mouth or the fish may pick up only the bait. If it is too short you could find yourself hooking fish deep in the throat, which will lead to awkward unhooking and discomfort for the fish. Only trial and error will help you here as waters all respond differently to each method. As a guide, we usually make the hair long enough so that the top of the bait just touches the bottom of the hook bend.

### Ready-Made rigs

If you are still confused about how to make a simple rig or if you simply prefer not to make them, you can purchase them ready-made from most tackle shops. The rigs can be bought in many different designs, with different hooks or braids, at varying lengths. If you need it, you can guarantee that someone will have one on the shelf waiting for your custom.

## A FEW GOOD RIGS

Several points need to be taken into consideration before you can make your final rig selection:

- The nature of the lake bed.
- Angling pressure.
- The size of the fish you are fishing for.
- Surrounding snags.
- The distance you need to cast.

There are many products on the market, which, if applied properly in certain circumstances, will give you a bit of an edge over both the fish and the other anglers on your water. Carp learn by association, so after they have been exposed to any one method for a reasonable period of time, especially if everyone on the lake is using the same method, they will recognize the danger and will avoid capture. A change in tactics, even a small one, could be enough to give you that edge. Examples of this might be such things as the use of a stiff link if the others are using supple, or a double-balanced bait instead of a single. Even a change in the length of your

*We prefer the hookbait to just touch the bend of the hook.*

hooklink material can make a dramatic difference to your catch rates, and while we have given you an insight into some of our favourite rig components, these should by no means be adopted slavishly on every single occasion. Think not only about what you are doing, but also about what the others on the lake are doing. A lot of the time it pays to go along with the going method on a lake if you know that it is working, but other times it certainly pays to be very different. The hard part is knowing when to use which method, and that choice can only be made by you.

One thing that is vital for every rig is that it will hook fish. There is not a lot of point having a rig that the fish take every time if you then find that either the rig will not hook the fish or that the hook always seems to pull. In the mid/late 1980s many anglers started using a set-up known as the bent-hook rig. This rig incorporated a bent hook, and the idea behind it was that when a fish backed away with the hook in its mouth, the hook would always turn around because of the bend, and the fish would be hooked in the bottom lip. This proved to be the case, but one of the problems with the bent hook rig was that it caused damage to

the mouths of the fish hooked. Many waters banned the use of this rig as a result, but it was so effective that anglers thought their way around the problem of mouth damage, and eventually the line aligner was born. This set-up gives the bent-hook rig effect without any of the dangers of having a bent hook. It is one of the most widely used methods among carp anglers these days, and is certainly very effective – scientific tests have shown it to be 15 per cent more successful at hooking than other set-ups. Almost all rigs can, and indeed should, have a line aligner set-up incorporated into them, and we show how to set one up below.

### The Line Aligner
The line aligner can be used with almost all rigs, so the only extra piece of kit you need is some 0.5mm silicon tubing, or some shrink tube and a needle. We prefer to use silicon tubing but other anglers prefer stiffer shrink tubing. Either way the effect is still the same in that the tubing causes the hook to turn and prick the mouth of the fish. To make an effective line aligner, you need to have a pair of scissors, a needle, some 0.5mm tubing, and a ready-tied rig.

1. Thread the open end of your hooklink through the eye of the needle (you may need a needle threader to help you).
2. Cut a small length of 0.5mm tubing (this will be pushed over the eye of the hook so must be of the soft or shrink type). Our preferred length is one that just fits over the eye of the hook

(approximately ¼in or 0.7cm).

3. With the hooklink still attached, thread the needle through the tubing. Push the point of the needle through the wall of the tubing about three-quarters of the way up the sleeve.

4. Thread the tubing onto the hooklink so that it touches the eye of the hook.

5. Now push the tubing over the eye. Be careful not to split the side of the tubing when doing this or you may have to start again. A good tip is to work the tubing through your fingers for a minute or two to make it warm and more manageable.

6. Ensure that the face of the tubing where the hooklink comes through is in line and facing the point of the hook. If you haven't done so already, attach your hookbaits in the usual way.

We use the line aligner in the form outlined above for all our fishing, including pop-ups, bottom baits, criticals, double baits, particles, D-rigs and everything else. It is not enough simply to attach the hook to the hooklink with a strong knot. It has to be capable of hooking when inside the mouth of the fish as much as possible. Scientific tests have shown that the line aligner will hook eighteen times out of twenty, compared to sixteen out of twenty with the knotless knot set-up only. It is without doubt the most advanced hooking set-up of the modern years, and we will always advise anglers to use it.

**The Uni-Rig**

This rig is as simple as you can get. It is the rig which we use for over 50 per cent

of our fishing and is the actual rig we used to success in the World Carp Cup in 1996. It incorporates an intermediate 15in (38cm) hooklink which is suitable for all sizes of fish. The hook has an in-turned eye, which assists with the line aligner set-up, and is attached via a knotless knot. There is a lead clip and a standard hair, which can be adjusted to accommodate whichever size of bait you prefer. The rig can be cast average distances of over 100 yards, and is suitable for all manner of different situations, hence its name.

The only times we will modify this rig is if the type of lake bed demands it. We

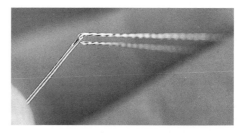

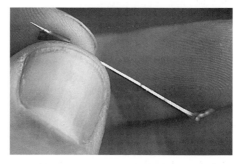

*Three photos displaying some of the steps involved in making the line-aligner.*

will change the type of hooklink as required, either opting for a Super-Nova hooklink over a clear bottom or a Silkworm link when fishing pop-ups or over debris. This is a great rig to use with both bottom baits and pop-ups.

## Standard Stiff Rig and Stiff Rig Pop-Up

In more recent years this has become one of our favourite alternative rigs. We use this a lot for wily fish that have become wise to supple hooklinks. All we do is take some stiff line and attach it to the chosen hook with a no-knot set-up, creating a stiff hooklink. The only downside to this rig is that it doesn't always give good hook holds because it can hook on the outside of the mouth. Usually this occurs with wily fish, so we prefer to fish the harder waters with the stiff rig pop-up set-up. This is basically the same as a standard stiff rig, but with a swivel attachment placed at the point where we want the bait to pop up (normally about 2in (5cm) from the hook). This creates a hinge at this point,

which helps somewhat with getting the hook into the carp's mouth.

## The D-rig

Although for a lot of our pop-up fishing we opt for the uni-rig, we do on occasions choose the D-rig. This rig can these days be purchased ready-made from companies like Carp 'R' Us. It is a little technical to tie up yourself, but is a great rig to use when tackling wily fish. It basically increases the chances of the hook catching inside the mouth of the fish by transferring the weight of the hookbait. The popped-up bait is attached to a small ring, which moves up and down the shank of the hook. This is inhibited by a float stop, which is slipped over the hook, usually opposite the point. The hookbait will sit in this position when on the lake bed and when initially sucked up by the fish. As the fish examines the bait inside its mouth and possibly realizes the danger, it will try to blow it out. As it does so, the ring will move down the shank, leaving the hook still inside the mouth. As the hookbait

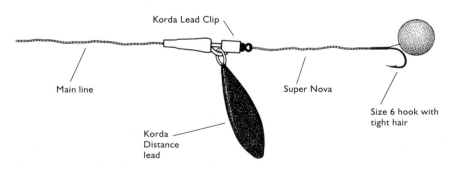

Main line

Korda Lead Clip

Korda Distance lead

Super Nova

Size 6 hook with tight hair

*The Uni-rig.*

*Stiff Rig Pop-Up Rig.*

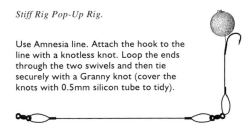

Use Amnesia line. Attach the hook to the line with a knotless knot. Loop the ends through the two swivels and then tie securely with a Granny knot (cover the knots with 0.5mm silicon tube to tidy).

*The D-Rig.*

Hooklink

*The Helicopter Rig.*

hits the eye of the hook, the force will hopefully pull the hook lightly into the skin of the mouth and then you're away.

## Short-Range Running Rig

This set-up allows the lead to be free-running so that the fish cannot sense any resistance from the lead. We only use a running set-up for short-range fishing of less than 30yd because over this distance it is a sure thing that there will be some sort of resistance created, rendering the rig useless for its purpose. As you can see from the diagram, the set-up incorporates a buffer bead near to the hooklink swivel followed by a hard bead and then the swivel. This must be a large-eye swivel such as one available from Hutchy, which is attached to the lead by a short link – this improves the free running as the swivel is more moveable than if it was simply the lead swivel. Usually we make the link at least 3in (7.5cm), but we may increase this depending on the nature of the lake bed (for example over weed or light silt).

## Long-Range Set-Up – the Helicopter Rig

As you can see from most of what we have said above, for most of our fishing we tend to opt for a lead attachment via a lead clip on the main line. We will, however, change this attachment when looking for a few extra yards in the cast. For this type of fishing we choose what is known as a helicopter set-up, which has the lead on the end of

*The Running Rig.*

the line. This is an easy set-up to make, but it is   important that it is not used alongside a leader knot, because if the line parts above the knot the fish will be dragging the whole rig around (unless you have a CV safety attachment which is now marketed by Carp 'R' Us). Because the lead is on the end of the line, there is less friction on the rig, so in principle it will go a few yards' extra on the cast than the uni-rig. There is also less chance of the rig tangling because the hooklink rotates around the main line when in flight. We recommend that for extra distance the hooklink should be kept as short as is possible for the situation you are confronting. A smaller hookbait will also help here.

### Snake-Skin Rigs

We've already briefed you about Snake-Skin by Kryston and its advantages for the carp angler, but what we didn't expand on is the number of rig variations you can design with it. Each has its own advantages in a given situation. Here are some of our favourites:

**Combi-link with stiff hair** Peel off half of the coating on the link. The peeled section should be at the swivel end. Tie the Snake-Skin to the hook with the knotless knot attachment but leave the plastic coating on the hair. The hook will move exactly where the bait is blown by the fish – excellent for wily fish.

**Broken-back rig** Peel back and break off a couple of millimetres of coating near to the hook. One centimetre from here, moving back towards the swivel, break the coating again, but this time don't peel anything off. This will allow the link to move freely at two points.

**Stiff link** Attach the Snake-Skin to the hook with a knotless knot. At the swivel end form a loop attachment by threading the link through the swivel once and tying a granny knot an inch (2.5cm) from the swivel. Don't peel any of the coating off and you have a straight-forward stiff link.

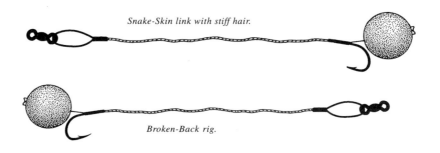

*Snake-Skin link with stiff hair.*

*Broken-Back rig.*

**Hinged/stiff link** Peel back a centimetre of skin at each end of the rig and you have a hinged stiff link. The idea behind this rig is to combine the anti-eject properties of a stiff link with the presentation properties of a supple link.

*Simon with a winter 27¾lb Birch Grove mirror caught on the Uni-rig.*

# 6  KNOTS

Although there are absolutely dozens of different knots you can use for attaching carp rigs and tackle items to your lines and braids, we ourselves use only five. Two of these we have already seen in the previous chapter (the knotless knot for hooks and the loop attachment for stiff rigs). This chapter looks at the other knots we choose.

Many of you may ask why we only use five knots for our carp fishing. The answer to this is that we have confidence in these knots, which we have settled on after many years of trying all manner of different variations. The one thing which we always advise is never try to confuse yourself with all of the different methods of tying knots and rigs. Stick to only a few and follow them through. Messing about with new forms on a regular basis will only lead to confusion and possible lost fish.

## TYING KNOTS

We have, in a previous chapter, mentioned that you should always check your knot strength before casting out, but it is worth mentioning again and again that there is no excuse for a fish lost because of a weak knot. We always check the strength with a knot tester, which can be purchased from most tackle shops. John Roberts makes a good one, but you can also test a knot by pulling the line firmly in the hand whilst the swivel or hook is attached to a stabilizer like a pair of scissors or a baiting needle. Make a habit of never casting out before testing a knot. When we say test a knot here, we do mean test it well and make sure that you have applied a lot of strength to it, not just a slight tug – carp are strong and powerful fish.

Besides knot testing, one of the main reasons for a line breaking is incorrect choice of knot. We use either the Grinner or the Tucked Blood for all of our swivel knots, and the Double Grinner for the leader knots. We have become proficient at tying these simply due to practice (practise knotting until you can do it in your sleep if you wish to be good at it. It also helps when tying knots in the dark). Also some knots are not suitable for some lines; for example, braids tied to swivels with a Blood knot cause slipping to occur, which is disastrous if you are playing a record fish. With mono knots, strangulation is also unavoidable if you do not wet the line first. Always remember to lubricate the knot well, either with spittle or Knot Lube before pulling it tight, as friction can damage the line, causing a weak spot.

## THE GRINNER KNOT

### For Braided Hooklinks and Lines
This is the knot we always use for tying braided lines (hooklinks or shock leaders) to swivels. It is a knot that, if

*The Grinner Knot.*

tied correctly, tightens itself up as pressure is applied to the line. Here's a step-by-step description of to tie it.

1. Thread the end of your braid through the eye of the swivel. Leave at least 2in (5cm) between the eye and the end of the braid.

2. Thread the braid through the eye of the swivel again, so that the attachment is doubled. Ensure that there are at least 2in (5cm) overhanging from the end of the braid.

3. Form a loop in the short length of braid by bringing the end back towards the eye of the swivel. Pass the end slightly over the top of the main length of braid.

4. Pass the end of the braid around the main length and weave it through the loop made in step 3. Repeat this four more times so that you have five turns on the knot.

5. Wet the braid with some saliva. Now gently pull the end piece of the braid so that the loop starts to close up and form a tightly grouped knot.

6. Slide the knot towards the eye of the swivel gently. When the knot is in place close to the eye, tighten it firmly by pulling both ends of the braid simultaneously, and then the main length so that it packs up tight to the swivel. The knot is now tied.

# THE TUCKED BLOOD KNOT

### For Monofilaments

For all of our mono swivel attachments, we always opt for the five-turned Tucked Blood knot. It is an easy knot to tie and one that has been used by thousands of anglers all over the world for many years.

1. Firstly, lubricate the line well with some saliva. Now thread the mono through the eye of the swivel just once and bring the line back towards itself so that it is parallel to the other side.

2. Keeping the swivel in a fixed position, cover a small gap between the two lines near the swivel with your thumb. Now wrap the short end of the line around the main line five times, ensuring that you still have a small gap between the swivel and the line.

3. Pass the end of the short length of line back across the twists and thread it through the small gap between swivel and the line. Don't pull the line tight at this stage, and leave a loop in its pathway.

4. Take the end of line that you've just threaded through the gap and double it back on itself by threading it through the pathway loop. At this stage, it will look like you have just tied a figure of eight with the main body of line.

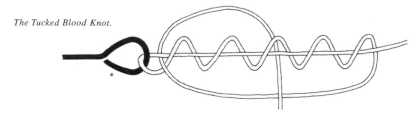

*The Tucked Blood Knot.*

5. Now begin to pull the line to a close by pulling the short end ever so gently. At the same time, push the knot together, still keeping it lubricated. When it is altogether, pull the short end tightly, and then apply pressure on the main line section. It is important to close this knot very carefully or you will strangle it. Once all appears done, trim off the loose end and test its strength.

## THE DOUBLE GRINNER KNOT

### For Joining Two Lines Together

The last of our favoured knots is the Double Grinner. This is very similar to the Grinner knot and also simple to tie, but instead of tying only one knot, you tie two knots back to back so that they pull against one another. We only use this knot for joining two lines together, such as a shock leader or a combination link. It can be used for both monos and braids, or combinations of both.

1. Lay both ends of the joining lines alongside one another, with one end pointing to the left and the other pointing to the right. Overlap the two by approximately 10in (25cm).

2. With one end, simply form a Grinner knot (*see* above) in combination with the other line (that is, at the looping stage incorporate the other line into the formation of the loops). When finished, pull this knot tight as you would a single Grinner, but make sure that you don't pull the other line free from the knot.

3. Turn the lines around so that the one which was to the left is now to the right, and vice versa. Now form another Grinner knot at the other side in the same way.

4. When the two knots have been tied, there will be a gap between the two knots. To finish the knot, you need to pull these together so that they are pulling against one another. To do this make sure that the two main lines are well lubricated and then simply pull gently on them.

5. Test the strength of the knot well and then trim the two knots to tidy it up.

*The Double Grinner.*

*One of South Africa's biggest carp. Simon with a 55½lb Klaserie Dam mirror.*

*A 32lb mirror known as Little Pecs from Hull & Districts Tilery Lake.*

*Tilery Lake's big mirror for Simon caught in June 2001.*

*An immaculate bar of gold from world-record breaking Lake Raduta in Romania.*

*(Left) A hefty mirror from France which took the liking to a single hookbait fished at 140-yards' range.*

*(Right) One of the most stunning fish we have ever seen. Steve Briggs with a fabulous mirror of 33¾lb from South Africa's Snagmere.*

*(Left) The Video Fish from Birch Grove, one of three mid-thirties caught by Simon in a three-day stint in March/April 2002.*

*One of four in a day from the tricky Motorway Pond in East Yorkshire – all on the day ticket! This one went 29¾lb.*

*A mint common and a super shot of Rob in action at an undisclosed venue. We do keep some things under our hats!*

*An ocean of blue and a featureless landscape surround Rob and this fine common at Romania's Lake Raduta. This shot was taken in May 2000, two years after our first visit.*

*(Left) Rob putting the net under the Birch Grove common as the lake freezes over around him. A truly incredible event.*

*(Right) The one from under the ice. Just when we thought it was time to go home, this 35¼lb common decided it wanted to feed in freezing cold conditions.*

*(Left) A day of all four seasons in one. In the snow at Lac de St Cassien, France, in February 2001. About an hour after this photo was taken, all of the snow had cleared and it was T-shirt weather!*

(Above) A super shot of our mate Derek Fell with an upper-forty common from Lake Raduta in October 2001.

(Above right) Happiness is a big, powerful carp on a sunny day! It took Rob thirty minutes to land this hard-fighting thirty-plus mirror.

(Below) A very, very memorable day. Catching big carp is a buzz, but standing on the podium after victory in the prestigious World Carp Cup is better. Take it from us! June 1996.

(Below) So close, you can almost touch em'!

*(Above) Carp legend Tim Paisley with a colossal Lake Raduta common of 73lb 13oz.*

*(Below) Another of the three mid-thirties from Birch in March/April 2002. This one is known as the Lovely Common and is the same fish that Rob caught from under the ice in 1999.*

*(Below) When it was –2 degrees back in England, we were lapping up the sunshine in South Africa in January 2000. A very memorable trip with some good friends and some lovely carp.*

(Left) Elvis Presley look-alike Rob and a glorious mid-winter common of 30lb-plus. It fell for a single bright hookbait and was one of four fish he took from the tricky Birch Grove in the space of two days.

(Right) A mint common of 28¼lb for Rob, taken in March 2001. Simple tactics were its downfall.

(Below) Returning a margin caught forty to its huge home of Lac de Madine in eastern France. It was one of five forties caught on camera for the Dream at Madine tapes shot in July 1999.

*(Above) Briggsy returning a forty-plus common to the daunting Snagmere. We had been tipped off that there may be a potential world record carp lurking in its depths.*

*(Below) Somewhere out there is a British record carp. A shot of Wraysbury when Mary was the fish that everyone wanted.*

# 7 CARP BAITS

It has become common for many modern-day carp anglers to believe that bait means boilies. The in-depth research and experiments that have been carried out on the boilie have provided us with a bait that perfectly fits the needs of the carp angler. Boilies can be resistant towards nuisance fish, used at excess range, designed for individuality, are easily digestible and so on. Basically the boilie is the ultimate in modern carp fishing baits and its popularity and success are evidence of this. However, its excessive use appears to have led many anglers into believing they are the only bait to use when in search of carp. There have been many occasions when particle baits in the form of peanuts, tiger nuts and chick peas have been the fashion, but rarely do we see the modern carp angler using any of the baits that have been so successful for us in the past.

There are many waters in Britain that impose boilie bans, thus forcing the angler to resort to using old favourites, but anglers who do not fish these types of water appear to be ignorant about alternative baits. There is no reason why the past success of maggots, worms or bread cannot be relived today and, indeed, one could well be surprised at how successful they could be when used on some of the boilie-orientated waters. Therefore, before taking an in-depth look at the boilie, we will begin this chapter by having a closer look at a selection of the forgotten favourites and

one or two other alternatives that may give us an edge on some waters.

## STANDARD CARP BAITS

Standard carp baits are the oldest of the many tried-and-tested baits and are classed as such because they are considered to be the standard to which other baits conform. They are found attractive by other species besides carp, but their effectiveness as carp baits should never be overlooked. All those listed below have been widely used with success all over Britain, and have accounted for many big carp. 'Standards' can be used effectively on their own or in conjunction with one another as part of a cocktail.

### Naturals
*Freshwater Snails*
Although found in nearly all our waters, freshwater snails seem hardly to be used as bait. The most commonly found snails in Europe are the great pond snail (*Limnaea stagnalis*) and the wandering snail, both being found easily during the summer months near to the surface of the water or clinging onto the sides of submerged branches. Most good aquatic shops will also supply them if you are unsuccessful in finding any at the lake.

You can guarantee that the water snail will almost certainly be a part of a carp's daily diet and that their use will rarely have been tried. They are a wonderfully instant bait and are definitely one of the finest natural baits for carp. We have found the best way to use them is to hook them through the shell, but be careful when doing this as the shells are very brittle. They can be successfully used on the lake bed or popped up via foam inserts and are best fished close to features where they are most likely to be found.

### Mussels

Like snails, freshwater mussels are widely spread throughout the waters of the world. The most commonly found are zebra mussels (*Dreissena polymorpha*) and swan mussels (*Anadonta cygnea*). They have been used for many years as carp baits and have a habit of producing well whenever used. Most anglers will be aware of the existence of mussels in their water, especially those who fish gravel pits. Mussels have a tendency to lock themselves onto rocks and sunken branches and can be one of the main causes of line fray and cut-offs where prominent.

They can obviously be obtained straight from the water, in which case the shell needs to be prised open to get to them, or in the case of saltwater mussels, they can be purchased pre-packed for human consumption. Pre-packed ones tend to be cooked and soaked in vinegar, which we find unsatisfactory, so try to purchase mussels from a fishmonger or dealer where you can get them untreated. They are an instant bait and are excellent for use when stalking fish with float tackle. The protein content is approximately 25 per cent and the fat approximately 3 per cent.

### Worms

Worms have, in recent years, become a much neglected carp bait, although they can easily outshine many other baits when fished on rich waters or when used for intercepting cruising fish. They come in many different varieties, but the most favoured are lobworms, brandlings and bloodworms. Although bloodworms are considered too small for use on the hook, their use in groundbaits is exceptional.

Worms can be very effective when used as static bottom baits, but they appear to be more successful when injected with air and made to float above the lake bed. They can be used effectively when fished over the top of other baits or when used as single hookbaits. They also have a tendency to wriggle off the hook, and therefore you may need to use a maggot or a piece of sweetcorn as a cocktail to hold it in place.

### Maggots

Maggots are a fantastic alternative to the boilie when presented in groundbaits. They can also be used effectively on the hook, especially when you are trying to intercept fish that feed heavily on natural baits. Very rarely do you see carp anglers fishing with maggots these days, as most tend to be put off by their tendency to attract small fish. The benefit of maggots, though, is that carp love them, especially when they are applied to a water in large amounts. Our favourites are white maggots, but we

*The Medusa Rig – superglue maggots to a ball.*

also like most other colours.

Although not maggots as such, small versions known as pinkies and squats can be purchased from most tackle shops. In our experience these are best used as feed or in groundbaits rather than on the hook. Their small size makes them fidgety and difficult to mount on the hair unless they are pierced with a needle and then threaded onto a very fine hair.

Finally, we should mention here that maggots in the caster form are also an excellent alternative. We tend to favour maggots and casters when boilies have been hammered on a water, or when it is known that the venue we are targeting does not contain many nuisance species.

## Human Food Baits

### Sweetcorn

Although sweetcorn is very attractive to many other species, one cannot overlook its attractiveness to carp. It has accounted for many, many big fish over the years and was the bait on which Chris Yates caught the former British record of 51½lb. Sweetcorn has a very strong and distinct smell and taste, and is excellent for use all year round. It contains small amounts of the amino acid lysine, and its success is often attributed to this.

Sweetcorn is widely available in tins or in frozen form. The tinned variety is often preferable as the juices in the tin give it more smell and attraction. We would go further and particularly favour sweetcorn in water and sugar over sweetcorn soaked in salt. It can be successful when used on the hook or on a hair rig and can be baited up at good distance with the use of a bait rocket or by freezing with water and stones into small cubes to give it more weight when using a catapult. As far as nutritional content is concerned, sweetcorn is approximately 3 per cent protein, 1 per cent fat and a fairly high 15 per cent starch.

### Maize

The use of maize as a carp bait has enjoyed a bit of a revival over the last

*Ready-prepared sweetcorn for carp.*

*Simon with an upper-thirty which fell to maize.*

few years. With the large number of anglers now travelling abroad to target carp, there has been an increase in demand for cheap and easy-to-prepare bait – and maize fits the bill perfectly. It has a distinct yellow appearance and looks very similar to large grains of sweetcorn, but with a firmer outer skin. It has excellent flavour-carrying properties and its crunchy texture and attractive appearance make it easy to understand why the carp love it.

Maize can be used in both small and large quantities, either on its own or as a base for additional baits. The best way to use it is with the hair rig, as when mounted straight onto the hook it has a habit of masking the point. It has a low fat content of just under 1 per cent, a protein level of 3 per cent and a high starch level of 16 per cent.

### Luncheon Meat

Luncheon meat is an instant bait and can be effective all year round. We have heard many stories lately of anglers who use this bait having more success than anglers pre-baiting with good-quality boilies on the same water. There are many different brands on the market,

mostly differing in texture and taste. Pork luncheon meat has been widely used to great success and has a good rubbery surface, which helps when mounting on the hook or hair.

Luncheon meat is best used in small cubes straight from the tin, or fried in oils to give it more attraction. It has a high fat content of approximately 25 per cent and a protein level of around 15–20 per cent.

### Bread

Although bread is susceptible to interference from nuisance fish, its effectiveness for catching carp cannot be ignored. As we all know, it comes in many different shapes and sizes, with both the brown and white type being productive. However, steer clear of granary varieties, which contain seeds and nuts, as the raw state of the grains may cause unnecessary distress to the fish when consumed (they swell inside the intestine of the fish).

Bread can be used as a carp bait in many different forms. It can be used on its own as a slow-sinking flake, as a paste bait, as a surface bait, or combined with other baits such as cheese to enhance its attraction. It can be said that bread is one of the best stalking baits around, and because of its practicality it will continue to be very effective in many situations. We recently caught a number of fish whilst stalking with flake, and although this may not sound like much of a feat, the fact that the fish totally ignored a couple of boilies we had thrown in furthered our belief that there is life beyond the boilie.

Never leave home without it!

# SEEDS, BEANS AND NUTS

Although we haven't the space in this book, the use of seeds, beans and nuts (otherwise known as particle baits) as carp baits deserves a special chapter of its own. The most important thing to note about these baits is that all seeds, beans and nuts need to be soaked in water for a day or so and then boiled in water before they can be used. If they are used raw, unnecessary distress or even death of fish may result (when immersed in water, raw beans, seeds and nuts swell as they soak). It is difficult to generalize as to how long a particle bait needs to be soaked and then boiled for. What we advise is always to have two parts of water to one part of seeds when soaking, and always leave them to soak for at least 36 hours. Some will need longer than this, so keep your eye on them. Basically they will be ready for boiling once they have swelled to their maximum and will swell no more. As for boiling, never overfill a pan, and always time the boiling from the

*Make sure you prepare all particles before use.*

moment the water hits the boil with the seeds immersed. We always boil the seeds for at least 30 minutes and always keep the particles moving whilst in the pan. You will know when they are done because the particles will have changed colour and some will have started to split. Check they are ready by taking one out and testing the texture. The softer they are the better, but the difficulty is in knowing when to bring them out. If you boil a particle for too long it will become mushy and a waste of time. There are some things that really can't be written about and can only be learned through experience. One of these is the preparation of particles. If in doubt about a bait, always ask a more experienced carper before you use it, just to be safe.

Not all seeds, beans and nuts are effective carp catchers, but those listed below have a proven track record.

### Hemp Seed

This seed has to be one of the most famous and effective carp catchers of all time. It has accounted for thousands of carp over the years, and is best used as a loose feed with sweetcorn, a tiger nut or black-eyed bean fished over the top. It is very difficult to present hemp seed on the hook, but products similar to Kryston's Bogey can be effective. This is basically a sticky product which can be rolled into a small ball and then into the hemp itself. The small grains of hemp will stick to the Bogey and blend in well with the feed. It will basically look like a hemp seed boilie and is very useful for fishing over the top of hemp. Another

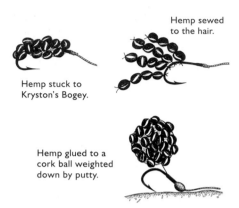

Hemp stuck to
Kryston's Bogey.

Hemp sewed
to the hair.

Hemp glued to a
cork ball weighted
down by putty.

*A few ideas for presenting hemp.*

method, which is very fiddly, is to thread the small grains onto a very fine hair using a small sewing needle. This is an effective method of using hemp, but many anglers prefer to opt for the Bogey because of the difficulty of threading the hemp onto the line. For this method you are better off using a 2–4lb line so that the grains do not split open.

Although it is effective, there is one problem with hemp seed. We have both found it to be very good at causing preoccupation – the fish will not pick up anything other than hemp once they really do get their heads down on it. We both tend to use it in small doses on a 'little-and-often' basis.

A larger grain, known as tares, are another favourite. Both tares and hemp are available from most tackle or pet food shops.

**Tiger Nuts**
Probably the next most popular particle bait is the tiger nut. Carp absolutely adore this bait, probably due to its

natural-looking appearance and its crunchy texture. We are both firm believers in the theory that carp love to feed on items that are crunchy and very similar to their favourite natural food items such as mussels and snails.

Tiger nuts are best used popped up off the bottom; our favourite form of presentation is two tigers on the hair separated by a small piece of cork. This would be fished in the middle or on the edge of a baited area laced with tigers, hemp and chopped boilie. However, tigers can also be used very effectively on their own. They don't require pre-baiting before use as they are an instant bait.

**Black-Eyed Beans**
Black-eyed beans are easily identifiable by the black scar on their sides. They are otherwise cream-coloured with a firm texture and a peanut-type flavour. At one time they were considered to be a killer bait on some waters, especially when prepared with tomato soup. Both of us know of many anglers who have scored exceptionally well using this combination. The beans can be purchased both ready-prepared or in the raw form, but usually the ready-prepared type have been soaked in salt water. It is therefore better to purchase them raw, so that you can add whatever flavours and attractors you desire. They are best used when mounted on the hair rig and, when combined with a number of free offerings, they will often achieve the point of preoccupation. They are 9 per cent protein and 20 per cent starch.

*Borlotti Beans – a superb bait that is hardly used.*

## Borlotti Beans

Borlotti beans are another overlooked bait. They very much resemble a peanut and are oval-shaped with a chocolate-coloured skin and a sweet taste. We first started using them over ten years ago, when one of our local waters, which was going crazy for peanuts, put a ban on their use. They can be purchased in the raw form, and therefore need to be boiled and soaked in the usual way before use, or they can be purchased in tins ready-prepared. Flavours and additives can certainly be added when you are preparing them yourself, but the sweet flavour of the natural bean appears to be a good enough attractor. They are by their nature an instant bait and it is always useful to have a tin at the bottom of your rucksack as an alternative when the action slows up.

## Particle Mixes

Over the last few years, blends of particle seeds have become very popular. Hinders sell a mix known as Partiblend whilst Haiths sell one called Red Band amongst others, which have accounted for loads of big carp. They combine crushed maize with hemp, niger seed, millet and other seeds and crushed

pulses. In 1999 Dave Poxon and Mark Redding won the World Carp Classic at Lac de Madine in France using a bait known as the Madine Mix which also contains a variety of tiny seeds. This is a fabulous mix to use and has been very successful for us. Simon used it with Tim Paisley to win the 1999 Orchid Lake British Carp Angling Championships eliminator. More recently we both used the Madine Mix in January 2000 at African Gold's Bushcamp venue on the Klaserie Dam in South Africa. On that occasion we held the fish in our swim for eight days. This is the advantage to using tiny seeds and baits like this – they really can hold the fish. The beauty about these crushed blends of seeds is that they don't need to be soaked for days on end. They just need to be scalded with boiling hot water and left to soak for an hour or so.

## OTHER BAITS

### Chum Mixers

Whilst on the subject of alternatives to the boilie as a carp bait, we must not forget the humble Chum Mixer-type dog biscuit. This product is very popular amongst stalking and surface anglers as it can be flavoured and prepared in a number of ways by the angler. For further information about Chum Mixers, refer to the section on stalking and surface fishing in Chapter 10.

We have so far taken a brief look at a broad choice of different types of carp bait. However, all of those mentioned above are generally considered as alternatives to those which we will now turn our attentions to – namely the boilie and the increasingly popular pellet.

## MODERN CARP BAITS – BOILIES AND PELLETS

The creation of the boilie came about when carp anglers searched for a bait that would overcome the annoyance of nuisance fish. Standard baits are attractive to several species, and because of this the long-stay carp angler found himself being constantly plagued by such fish when using such baits.

So what is a boilie? Basically a boilie is a collection of dry ingredients and liquid additives which are mixed together with eggs to form a dough. This dough is cut into usable shapes and sizes, and then boiled to give it a tough

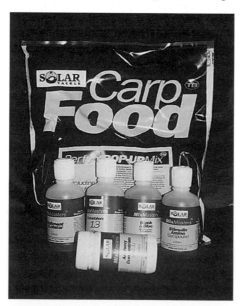

*Solar – Yes please!*

outer skin. Precise instructions on how to make a boilie are given later in this section. The preparation is always in three basic stages:

**1. The Mix Stage** Where powdered ingredients are mixed together to form a powder.
**2. The Additive Stage** Where liquid additives and sometimes powdered additives are added to eggs, to which the mix formed in stage 1 is added. This stage is sometimes known as the attraction stage, as the additives are usually the main source of attraction for the bait. The mix is added to the additives and formed into a dough, which is then cut into pieces.
**3. The Boiling Stage** Where the cut pieces are boiled for a specified length of time.

As far as boilies for the beginner carp angler are concerned, we advise you to buy the ready-made type or, if you fancy having a go at making them, one of the commercially available mixes. This is basically because designing your own mix can lead to many problems if you are unsure of what you are doing.

Commercially available mixes have a proven track record for catching fish and have been specifically designed to make preparation as easy as possible. We have nevertheless listed a few   details about boilie mix ingredients below just as an insight.

### Boilie Mix Ingredients
In general there are two classifications of boilie mix that can be used by the

carp angler. These are known as Low Nutritional Value (LNV) and High Nutritional Value (HNV). The former basically relies on the additives to attract the fish in a short space of time (a one-off visit to a water), whereas HNV mixes rely on the nutritional content of the bait to attract the fish on a long-term basis. Believe it or not, scientific studies and field experiments have proved that carp can learn what is doing them good or harm when a food source is applied on a long-term basis. Understanding how deep this learning goes, however, is something that is difficult for even the seasoned carper to attain, so we will leave that for another time to avoid confusing you. Just remember that if you wish to catch carp from your local venue on a regular basis, you will need an HNV mix and you will need to pre-bait the venue on a regular basis so that the fish get a good taste for your bait. When pre-baiting we also recommend that you keep the liquid additives to a minimum so that the nutritional content of the mix does the job rather than the chemical flavours. On the other hand, if you wish to attract carp instantly on a water you are likely to fish only once or twice, forget using quality and expensive ingredients, and instead concentrate on the chemical attractors to send out the food message. Both approaches have their advantages in different situations.

The ingredients used to make boilies vary from manufacturer to manufacturer, but as a guideline you will come across the following types: cereal, fishmeal, birdseed, milk, meat and bonemeal, or a mixture of two or more of these. There are a whole host of suitable ingredients and each will have its own characteristics and uses when added to the mix. Some act as binding agents to hold a mix together, whilst others combine to increase the nutritional value. The list of uses and varieties is endless, so we have listed below a rundown of some of the tried-and-tested types to help you on your way.

Before we examine these, however, it is important to mention that products used for boilie mixes should be of the highest possible quality: not only are high-quality ingredients far superior in performance, but they are also of more benefit to the fish as far as nutrition is concerned. Always ask for top-grade quality and only purchase products from reputable manufacturers.

*Milk Proteins*
There are several proteins derived from milk, both insoluble and soluble. Many are used in the food and confectionery

*A cold-water thirty which fell to a simple fishmeal mix.*

industry and are very expensive additions to a base mix. Beware of low-quality milk proteins, as some are used to make glue. Top-quality milks can be purchased from selected companies and advertisers, and although they are used in a wide range of mixes, these are usually HNV (High Nutritional Value) mixes.

Recommended milk proteins are:

**Casein** The main protein derived from milk. It is insoluble and available in different mesh sizes from 30 to 100, with 30 being coarser and 100 very fine.
**Lactalbumin** The secondary protein from milk, which is soluble.
**Calcium (or sodium) caseinate** Soluble casein.
**Whey protein concentrate** The powdered substance left behind when the liquid is removed from whey.

*Fishmeals*
As the name implies, fishmeals are composed of fish parts. They are formed by drying out fish products and then grinding them down to fine powder. They are very nutritious to the carp as they provide a high level of fat and protein, and they are an excellent additive to a bait because of their high attraction properties. The only drawback is their incredibly strong smell. There are a large variety of fishmeals available to the carp angler with the following four being some of the more popular:

**White fishmeal** North Atlantic cod and other white fish.
**Capelin meal** North Atlantic smelt fish.
**Anchovy meal** A strong-smelling fish

from the herring family.
**Ground trout pellets** Ground pellets used for rearing trout.

*Birdseed*
These products are used primarily for the rearing of birds, but when fishmeals and milk powders became popular amongst carp anglers in the 1980s, they were soon incorporated into boilie mixes as another alternative. They are very nutritional in that most provide a range of vitamins and minerals, as well as a balanced blend of fats and energy products. Recommended birdseeds are:

**Robin Red/Roger Red** Bird food containing ground peppers.
**Red Factor** Dried egg yolk, niger seeds and carophyll red.
**Nectablend/Honey Blend** Dried egg yolk, mixed seeds and honey.
**CLO/BLO** A mixture of seeds and binding ingredients.

*Meat Derivatives*
Meat meals are an excellent additive to a mix and have become quite popular in recent years. They come in all sorts of varieties and, like fishmeals, you should always seek permission before bringing them into the house as they have an overpowering smell. The most popular are:

**Meat and bonemeal** Dried and ground animal flesh and bones (government anti-BSE precautions have placed severe restrictions on the use of mammalian meat and bonemeal, which may restrict future supplies).
**Liver powder** The dried and ground liver of various animals.

**Blood haemoglobin** The dried red blood cells of vertebrates.

*Cereals and Flours*
These are the cheapest ingredients available and possibly the most widely used. Although there are absolutely hundreds of different types available, cereals and flours used in carp fishing normally refer to those listed below:

**Semolina** The hard grains left behind after milling wheat.
**Soya flour** Ground soya beans.
**Wheat gluten** The ground protein of wheat grain.

*Other Mix Ingredients*
The following additives are also extremely popular amongst bait buffs and are certainly worth a mention here:

**Kelp powder** Dried seaweed.
**Egg albumin** Dried egg whites.
**Dairy Lac** Milk powder used for rearing calves.
**Multivitamin supplement.**

**Boilie Additives**
Now you have seen what forms the basis of a boilie mix, we will briefly examine some of the additives added to the egg at the second stage of boilie-making. These additives primarily serve as the main source of attraction for the boilie. Certain powdered additives, such as appetite stimulants and vitamin supplements, are also incorporated in small doses at this stage. Most additives are flavours, oils or sense appeals. These each have a specific use and we will take a look at some of our favourites below.

*Rob with a South African mirror which fell to a cereal-based boilie mix. The successful bait was Rod Hutchinson's Scopex ready-mades. Scopex is one of the most famous flavours in the world, developed by Rod Hutchinson himself.*

## Flavours

As we saw in the first chapter, carp rely on chemoreception to locate food items, so adding certain chemicals to the bait helps them to find it. Flavours are probably the longest established and most popular chemical additive and are available from a wide range of suppliers. They are formed from either natural or artificial chemical bases, with our favourites being ethyl elcohol (EA) or propylene glycol (PG). The most important thing to remember with flavours is not to be fooled by their smell, but to be aware of its chemical signal when it is immersed in water. Carp don't smell the strawberry or blackberry, they only sense its signal. Also, always stick to recommended flavour dosages as too much flavour can be detrimental not only to the fish but also to the aquatic environment.

## Amino Stimulants

Amino acids are known to be one of the best attractors of carp. They can be used in a boilie mix by themselves or in combination with others. Most are available in a blend, such as the Sense Appeal range or the Multimino and Ambio types. It is our opinion that they are best used as a soak for a bait rather than an additive before the boiling stage, because most of their benefits are lost in boiling. They can be used in large doses and, in our opinion, the more you use the better they are.

## Sweeteners

It has been proven that carp are attracted to sweet items as well as those which don't contain sugar. We both like using baits that are bitter to the taste, but have caught carp on plenty of occasions with the assistance of a sweetener. Most sweeteners are based on saccharin and are of the liquid type, but you will come across powdered ones based on either lactose (milk) or fructose (fruit) sugars. They are recommended if no one else on your water is using them, but don't go overboard with sweeteners, as too much will turn a bait hot to the taste. Sweeteners are one of those additives that you don't necessarily need, but that can be beneficial on occasions.

## Essential Oils

These additives are extremely strong and obtained by distillation from organic substances. They can be used by themselves or in combination with flavours and are very effective both ways. They are very popular on hard waters where anglers strive to keep the bait as natural as possible. They are also very effective in HNV baits that are intended as a long-term food source. Two of our favourites are ylang ylang and cinnamon.

## Bulk Oils

A bulk oil in a bait is not only nutritious but also very attractive to the carp. Bulk oils can be found in various forms, with the fish and food varieties being the most popular. Some anglers like to glug their baits in these oils as well as use them at levels of 10–15ml in a kilogram mix. Some of the most popular bulk oils are fish feed oil, mackerel oil, herring oil, vegetable oil and sunflower oil. Our preference is to use these oils in large quantity during the summer and warmer months, but to use them sparingly during the winter. It has been proven that fish find oils and fats difficult to digest in cold water. Use them in quantities of up to 15ml maximum per kilo of dry mix.

**Powdered Additives**
**Colours** Do colours matter? To our minds, yes, they do. Some waters are clear whilst others are coloured up. In the latter, a bright bait usually outperforms dark-coloured baits because the fish can locate the food source easily. There's no use in having an attractive bait if the fish cannot find it. There are a wide range of colours available on the market, with both liquid and powdered forms on offer. We don't bother too

*The Rod Hutchinson label has been around for many, many years and their products are certainly amongst some of the finest available.*

much with colours other than to examine the colour of the water and make sure that the bait is visible to the fish. On occasions we will opt for a bait that is subtle in colour when angling pressure is high, such as during the World Carp Cup of 1996. During these times it is important to make your bait as discrete and natural-looking as possible. Colours do matter, but make sure you have a good reason for using one.

**Vitamin supplements** These are added to a bait to enhance its nutritional quality. If you are after a long-term bait then you may need one, but most of the time they are not required – unless you wish to do your bit for the fish, that is.

**Appetite stimulators** Basically these aim to induce the fish into taking 'one more' by stimulating its taste receptors. We're not convinced that most of those on the market work. Many companies seem to base their stimulators on those used in the confectionery industry rather than the fish food industry. We have found that the best are those which are nucleotide-based, such as those in the Rod Hutchinson range.

It is possible to use all of the above additives in the same boilie, but please remember that the more additives you apply to your mix, the lower the dosages should be.

Now that we have given you a brief introduction to what a boilie is and what they are made from, we will now go one step further and take a look at the formation of a mix and some of the functions the ingredients perform.

*Get the attraction properties right and you'll soon see this over your baited area.*

### Designing the Boilie Mix

Boilie mixes generally contain a blend of ingredients, with each mix broken down into 16oz (450g) totals for reference purposes (for example 8oz of ingredient 1 + 8oz of ingredient 2 = 16oz). We looked at the ingredients used for boilies earlier so there is no need to tread old ground here. However, what we will say is that there is no point in mixing any old ingredients together and hoping a bait will turn out right. A great deal of thought is required at the production stage as a mix needs to fulfil different requirements if it is to work correctly.

Firstly a mix needs to be attractive to the fish, both in terms of smell and taste. Secondly it needs to meet the necessities of the angler (that is, it needs to roll well, be capable of withstanding use in a throwing stick, carry flavours, be highly nutritional, coloured if necessary and so on).

As far as attraction and taste are concerned, only trial and error and experience in the field will help you come up with a suitable mix by yourself, but always remember that it will almost certainly be altered at the final stage if you aim to include liquid additives when making your bait. The needs of the angler, on the other hand, can be met through choosing the correct ingredients for your mix.

When designed, a mix will normally be categorized and referred to by the majority ingredients included in it (for example, one containing mostly fish products will be termed a fish mix). As is usual in carp fishing, however, things are not quite this simple, as in order to obtain the very best from a boilie mix, it is sometimes necessary to use a variety of products in the same amounts. This obviously makes it difficult to categorize boilies, but as you will gradually find out through experience, it is also the objective of the mix which can determine its classification. At this stage we will avoid this issue and focus on the basics.

## Function

Once you have decided on the requirements of the mix you wish to design, it is a matter of selecting the individual ingredients. All ingredients are capable of performing specific tasks; some are extremely attractive to carp but useless at binding, whereas others are quite the opposite. It is therefore necessary to understand how the different ingredients perform and how much to use. To assist you here we have drawn up a table as a guide (see next page). All of the listed ingredients have a proven track record in carp baits, so there is no need to worry about any not being attractive – just make sure you stick to the recommended levels!

## Suggested Recipes

Forming or examining the following mixes will help you to design your own as you will be able to recognize the different functions of the individual ingredients. As we have seen above, designing and making your own boilie mix is not as difficult as it appears. It is a part of carp fishing we should all go through because it gives us more knowledge and understanding of how carp baits operate. Furthermore, you will feel a sense of achievement when you catch your first carp on a mix that you have made for yourself.

### Fishmeal Mix

This instant mix has accounted for some very wily carp over the years. It is one of our favourite mixes for short session fishing but is best used in the summer.

4oz (115g) white fishmeal
2oz (57g) capelin meal
5oz (140g) CLO/BLO birdseed
2oz (57g) 90 mesh casein
2oz (57g) semolina
1oz (28g) liver powder

Use with Rod Hutchinson's Monster Crab and Shellfish Sense Appeal.

### Carrier Mix

A low-budget mix that is useful for carrying flavours and testing at which levels additives work best. An excellent mix to use on rivers.

6oz (170g) semolina
6oz (170g) soya flour
2oz (57g) Dairy Lac
1oz (28g) whey protein concentrate
1oz (28g) multivitamin supplement

Use with Rod Hutchinson's Chocolate Malt or Scopex.

### HNV Milk Mix

This mix is a very good bait to use on a long-term basis, for example for pre-baiting a water. Our experience is that the more you apply before fishing, the better it will be in the long run (as a guide, bait regularly for at least six months before use). This mix has often been responsible for the capture of

| | ATTRACTION (SMELL) | ATTRACTION (TASTE) | BINDING | NUTRITION | MAX PER 16oz MIX |
|---|---|---|---|---|---|
| CASEIN 90m | XX | | X | X | 6 |
| CASEIN 30m | | | | X | 6 |
| LACTALBUMIN | | | | X | 2 |
| C. CASEINATE | XX | XX | X | X | 4 |
| WHEY P.conc. | | | XXX | | 1 |
| WHITE FISH M | XX | XX | | X | 4 |
| CAPELIN M | XX | XX | | X | 4 |
| ANCHOVY | XX | XX | | X | 2 |
| Gr. TROUT P | XX | XX | | XX | 4 |
| ROBIN RED | XXX | XXX | | XX | 2 |
| NECTABLEND | X | X | | XX | 4 |
| CLO | | | XX | XX | 6 |
| MEAT & BONE | X | X | | X | 4 |
| LIVER P | XXX | XXX | | X | 2 |
| BLOOD Hmgn | | | XXX | X | 1 |
| SEMOLINA | carries flavour well | | X | | 6 |
| SOYA FLOUR | carries flavour well | | X | | 6 |
| WHEAT GLUTEN | | | X | | 2 |
| KELP POWDER | XX | XX | | | 2 |
| EGG ALBUMIN | | | XXX | X | 2 |
| DAIRY LAC | X | XX | X | XX | 2 |
| MULTI VIT | | | | XXX | 1 |

*This table identifies the properties of certain ingredients. X = Not bad. XX = Average. XXX = Excellent. The more Xs overall does not mean the better the ingredient.*

almost 50 per cent of the fish in a lake.

6oz (170g) 90 mesh rennet casein
3oz (85g) Lactalbumin
2oz (57g) calcium caseinate
2oz (57g) egg albumin
2oz (57g) soya flour
1oz (28g) multivitamin supplement

Use with Rod Hutchinson's Maple Cream in a low dosage.

*Birdseed Mix*
An instant mix that is suitable all year round. It is especially effective when fishmeals have been used extensively on a water.

4oz (115g) Robin Red
2oz (57g) Red Factor
2oz (57g) CLO/BLO
7oz (200g) semolina
1oz (28g) whey protein concentrate

Use with Rod Hutchinson's Fruit Frenzy.

# A GUIDE TO BOILIE-MAKING

Most of you will be using boilies from the excellent ready-made ranges such as those produced by Rod Hutchinson, Nashbait, Nutrabaits, Richworth and so on. These will be perfect for most of your fishing needs, but most of you will want to know how to make your own boilies, and basically try something different from the usual shop-bought ready-mades.

It is quite a big step moving from shop-bought boilies to ones you have made yourself, but once you have mastered the technique of actually getting the things the right shape and consistency, it is very satisfying catching a carp on bait you have made yourself.

Another advantage to making your own bait is that it is a lot kinder on the pocket: a 1kg bag of mix will make nearly five times as many boilies as a small bag of ready-mades at the same cost. For your first attempt it may well be worth you and your mates clubbing together to buy a bag of base mix between you so you can all have a practice, and share the cost in the process.

As far as the choice of mix and flavour is concerned, any mix from any of the top companies will catch you carp. The end choice is down to you, so it will be worth speaking to your tackle dealer for some advice, or alternatively keep your eyes on the catch reports in the papers to see which are the 'going' baits. We would suggest buying the cheapest 50/50 or carrier-type mix available until you become proficient at rolling. You will make mistakes, we guarantee it! It is better to waste a small amount messing up a carrier mix than a large amount getting an HNV mix wrong.

One of the most important things to

*Welcome to the whole new world of boilies!*

*The sort of gear you will need.*

remember when you start to make your own bait is that you must follow the instructions on the label exactly. The bait companies have put them there for a reason, and if you try to go your own way, the bait may not work as well, or even at all. Another advantage is that if it then doesn't roll, at least you know that it's you that has done something

*Flavour levels need to be exact.*

wrong and not the mix!

Having decided on your base mix you should now get all the things    together that you will need to make your bait. These are as follows:

Base mix rolling table.
Flavour.
Bait gun.
Oil/sweetener.
Amino (if required).
Saucepan and sieve.
Mixing bowl.
Cloth for drying bait.
Fork.
Colourings (if necessary).
Syringe.
Measuring implement.
Eggs.

**Mixing the Bait**

1. Break the required number of eggs into a bowl. Most base mixes have a direction as to how many eggs to use per pound or kilogram of dry mix.

2. Add your flavours, additives and so on to the eggs or the mix. As a general rule of thumb, add liquids to the eggs and powders to the dry mix.

3. Mix all the additives in well, either by shaking the base mix and powders around in a bag or mixing the eggs well with a fork. Do not be tempted to whisk the eggs as this will trap air and may make the baits float.

4. Now add the dry powder slowly to the eggs, mixing it in as you go. This is where the hard bit starts because if you put too much in, the mix will be too dry and will not bind

together or roll. Too little and you will have a bowlful of a gooey substance resembling baby sick. It is much better to add the mix slowly. You can always put more in, but you can't take it out.

5. When the eggs have sufficient dry mix in, take the bait out of the bowl and knead it with your hands until it reaches the consistency of dough.

6. Using your bait gun or rolling table, roll out a number of sausages the same diameter as your rolling table. Make sure the diameter is correct because if it isn't, it will not roll. If it is too large the baits will go egg-shaped; too small and they will go barrel-shaped.

7. Cut the sausages to the same length as your rolling table and place one on your table and roll. Only use one sausage at a time; if you use more than one they may roll together. You can try more than one when you get more proficient.

8. When you have rolled all your sausages, place the baits in a pan of boiling water and boil for up to 3 minutes, depending on the hardness of bait required. The longer you boil the baits the firmer they will be. Always time from the moment the baits and water come to the boil. Always be accurate with your timing and never overfill the pan with bait or it will take too long for the water to begin boiling.

9. Take the baits out of the boiling water and place them on a cloth, preferably a tea towel or old bed sheet, to dry for an hour or so. Baits left longer to dry will generally have a firmer skin.

*(above) Three stages of the boilie-making process.*

10. The bait is now ready to freeze or use.

### Common Problems when Making Bait

**Problem** Bait floats

**Remedy** Too much air either whisked into the eggs or kneaded into the mix or too many light ingredients may have been used to make the mix. Use baits as pop-up hookbaits or throw the mix away.

**Problem** Bait sticks to table

**Remedy** The mix is too wet to roll so add more powder to dry and firm it up a little; or the rolling table is dirty so clean it off and give it a light covering of polyunsaturated oil to assist rolling.

**Problem** Bait cuts into squares and not rolling
**Remedy** The table is too slippery so wipe it with a damp or dry cloth.

**Problem** Bait rolls into 'eggs'
**Remedy** The sausages are too thick in diameter. Try using a larger roller or smaller nozzle on the bait gun.

**Problem** Bait rolls into 'barrels'
**Remedy** The sausages are too thin in diameter. Try using a smaller roller or larger nozzle on the bait gun.

**Problem** Bait is breaking up on the table
**Remedy** The mix is too dry and brittle to roll. Throw the bait away and start again or use it as paste/crumb groundbait next time you fish in the margins.

### Preserving Baits

It is not always possible to make bait just before you go fishing and it is more convenient to have a supply made up at home. There are a number of ways of preserving baits – using chemicals, covering in oil, freezing or air drying – but by far the best methods are freezing or air drying.

Freezing, as its name implies, involves placing the baits in the freezer. This effectively halts the denaturing process and can keep baits fresh for a long time. They will, however, start to go off once they have been thawed out or kept in the freezer for too long (you can tell if the latter has happened by the white patch that forms on the bait where all of the moisture has been taken out).

An alternative to freezing is air drying. In order for a bait to go off, it requires air and moisture. If you take the moisture away, then the baits will stay preserved. The way to air dry baits is either to put them in the airing cupboard on a towel or purpose-made/bought drying tray for a few days (three to four usually does the trick) or, for quicker results, place them in a pillowcase and put them into the tumble drier for anything between 20 minutes and one hour. Both methods will dry out the baits sufficiently to preserve them for over a week. They should then be placed into a pillowcase or hessian sack (so they don't sweat) and stored in a warm, dry room. Make sure the room is dry as any moisture will cause the baits to go mouldy in time. Another method is to vacuum seal them in bags using a domestic kitchen vacuum sealer, which can be purchased from most cooking/department stores.

Although both of the above methods work well, certainly the most convenient way to preserve a bait is to bake it in the sun. This will take all of the moisture out of the bait and turn the bait rock-hard – perfect for those venues where nuisance species are a big problem. Simply place the baits on a tray or towel, ensuring that they are not touching one another. Leave them in the sun for a full day, or more if desired, turning them regularly. Make sure that you do turn the baits, or you will end up with soft patches in places.

### Don't Write off Ready-Mades

Ready-made baits are fast becoming a favourite amongst bait manufacturers and anglers alike. They are available from all of the major bait manufacturers and rollers and can be bought in all manner of different sizes and mixes. Some experienced anglers, however, appear to be very critical of them because they don't have the advantages of home-made baits or those made by a rolling company (for example, individuality). It is our experience that ignorance about a ready-made bait may be the difference between catching and blanking so our advice is to not write them off.

As two anglers who fish short sessions at lots of different venues, if we had to put our faith in one bait ahead of the other for this type of fishing, it would always be ready-mades. We have caught a lot of good carp over the years using ready-mades, with some of our favourites being Hutchy's Fruit Frenzy, Mainline's Fruitella and Nashy's Scopex Squid Liver. These have been successful on both easy and very difficult waters, and most of all, we know they have been through rigorous tests around the globe before making their way to the shop shelf. Ignore the rumours you'll hear on the grapevine about ready-mades being for beginner carp anglers. Pick and choose them wisely and they will put a lot of carp on the bank for you. They will also save you a lot of time rolling and field-testing.

## PELLETS

### The Ball Pellet

When compared with other carp baits, the Ball Pellet is a relatively new concept but one that has already been used with great success in numerous countries world-wide. In the UK it has accounted for some of the hardest and largest carp in the country since its release in 1996. Indeed many of you may already be aware of its existence, but no doubt some of you would like a closer look at this ingenious design.

The brain behind the Ball Pellet is experienced carp man Clive Deidrich, who is well known to the carp world for his connections with Richworth and the production of the first commercially available ready-made boilies. Following on from numerous other innovative ideas, the Ball Pellet is Clive's latest little gem, and it has taken him eight years to perfect its design and make-up. To take advantage of the now huge carp fishing market, Clive has teamed up with numerous British tackle and bait manufacturers such as Kevin Nash and Nutrabaits for the promotion of the Ball Pellet, and since its release in

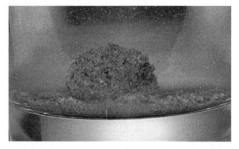

*The Ball Pellet – one of the best modern-day bait inventions.*

September 1995 people have already started to brand it as one of the best modern-day angling inventions.

The Ball Pellet is very similar in make-up to the boilie, but instead of being boiled at the final stage, it is dried and compressed to free it from moisture and form its shape. However, its use is remarkably different to any other form of bait as it is effectively designed as a method of introducing the 'food message' into a swim without any possibility of over-baiting. What happens is that after a period of time, when submerged in water, the Ball Pellet breaks down and leaves a crumb-like effect on the lake bed. The time it takes the pellet to dissolve can be modified to suit you (ranging from as little as five minutes to two days if required), and once broken down the crumb may be eaten by all sizes of fish. Although carp may consume broken-down Ball Pellet, the crumb does not easily satisfy large appetites and the reasons for this are twofold:

- Mouthfuls of crumb are washed out of the gills during the feeding process
- It requires a great deal of effort and time to feed upon it

Given that the small pieces of crumb may easily become dispersed into your swim, you can see that Ball Pellet has a number of advantages for the carp angler, most obviously that you can introduce it into a swim as a form of attractor without worrying about over-baiting. In the colder winter months such an advantage can have an absolutely startling effect on catch results: in the winter of 1995 alone, the Ball Pellet accounted for some incredible carp captures on some of the country's hardest carp waters.

**Other Forms of Pellet**

Besides Ball Pellets there are other forms of pellet available to the carp angling market, although only the Ball

*Simon with the biggest fish of the World Carp Cup 1996. Boilie fished over a bed of Ball Pellet did the trick.*

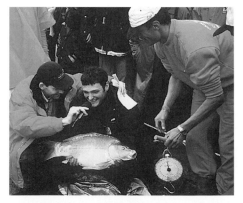

*Another fish from the World Carp Cup 1996 when Ball Pellets proved their worth.*

Pellet comes in an oval shape. Some of the other pellets are the Hemp Pellet from Nutrabaits, Formula Majic by Rod Hutchinson, The Pellet by Solar, The Halibut pellet marketed by several companies, Betaine pellets and of course the infamous trout pellet, which can be purchased almost everywhere. All of these different pellets can be used in various different ways, both on the hook and as feed, similar to the way in which the Ball Pellet is used.

On the matter of small waters, one of our favourite methods of fishing with these pellets is with a PVA bag. These are basically small bags that can be filled with bait and a rig and dissolve upon contact with water. When combined with any one of the many pellets on the market, the method leaves a small pile of bait in a tight concentrated area. It is a deadly method, and one which has accounted for many a wily carp, especially with trout pellets.

**Groundbaiting for Carp**
A tactic that has accounted for plenty of carp on some of the heavily pressured waters around Europe has been groundbaiting. Obviously groundbait can simply be applied as instructed on the bag (just add water, mix to consistency and then roll it into balls and apply to the water), but it can also be used by moulding it around the lead of the rig, a practice known as the Method (*see* section on bait application through the rig).

Whilst groundbaiting for carp has caught us plenty of fish, in our experience it is an excellent method for catching lots of fish but not necessarily the bigger ones. Also, look out for lead twitches with this method, as bream and roach will also favour the presentation. You can purchase groundbait either in its ready-made form or you can have a go at making up your own mix. The procedure for this is similar to making boilies, as not only will such a bait require attractors but it will also need binding ingredients. We prefer to use coarse ingredients in our groundbait, but we do know plenty of anglers who like fine powdered ones also. Some of the birdseeds such as PTX and Prosecto (available from Haiths birdseed manufacturers) are our favourites, as well as the fishmeals, but we have been known to use chopped boilies, nuts and other particles, as well as hemp, maggots and bloodworm. It's all down to trial and error really. Our advice is to start off on the ready-made groundbaits and then progress to making your own.

# 8 HOOKBAITS

Most of the baits listed in the previous chapter can be used on the hook in their natural form, with only the pellets being unsuitable for this type of presentation, for obvious reasons. However, even pellets can be used on the hook if they are prepared in the correct way, as we will see later on. In this chapter, we will give you a brief introduction to some of our favourite methods of presenting hookbaits. To catch carp successfully these days, it is necessary to be able to present hookbaits on the bottom, popped up off the bottom or even critically balanced. Here's a look at how we offer them in these ways and under which circumstances we would use each method.

## BOTTOM BAITS

Most baits can be used on the hook directly from the bag without any further preparation. In these cases, they should be applied to the hair in the way outlined in the rig section, or simply side-hooked. We would use bottom baits in the following situations:

- When the lake bed is firm enough to make the hookbait apparent to the carp.
- When the fish have been pre-conditioned that popped-up hookbaits are dangerous (that is, when a natural form of presentation would be the best line of attack).

Bottom baits can be used on their own as singles or in multiple numbers. It's worth noting that the more baits which you use on a hair or hook, the less efficient at hooking the rig may become; especially when using multiples of large boilies such as 18 or 22mm sizes. Nevertheless, piling more baits onto a rig can increase your chance of catching bigger fish (refer to big water carping for more details on this) so it is important not to neglect this method on occasions.

For most hookbait hair presentations, it is possible to attach the baits with the use of a standard carp fishing needle or by side-hooking, but for some of the smaller baits, like hemp seed and maggots, you will need to sew them onto a hair with a dressmaker's needle. This is easy enough to do, but a bit fiddly if you are having to keep up with constant fish action. The best approach is to sew a bunch onto a separate piece of cotton/ fine line and then, instead of tying a loop in the end for a hair stop, simply attach one end to the shank or bend of the hook,

*Bottom baits, the most natural form of presentation.*

and the other to the hair of the rig so that it forms a loop between the hair and the hook.

Bottom baits probably cover approximately 90 per cent of our fishing, simply because we prefer our hookbaits and rigs to look as natural as possible. Generally, we present the bottom baits on a tight hair, and this method has accounted for a massive number of our carp over the years.

Most of our bottom bait-caught carp have been taken on poly-pop inserted hookbaits. This includes fish we've caught from tough venues like Motorway Pond, Orchid, Withy, Birch Grove and Cassien, as well as the numerous easy and middle-of-the-range venues we've fished. We tend to think that there are very few anglers in circulation these days who go to the lengths of counter-balancing the hook with a couple of poly-pops or a slither of cork or foam. Most either use baits straight from the bag or criticals of less than an inch. For us, there's more to bottom baits than just these two presentations, and we think the carp have been getting away with it on more occasions than many of us would like to think.

One of the main reasons why poly-pop inserted bottom baits aren't used as much today is because you can't buy them ready-made. The angler has to go to some lengths to make them for himself, unlike pop-ups or baits from the bag. All we do is take our chosen hook, generally a Hutchy Vice size 6, slide a poly-pop onto the shank, and then immerse it in a cup of water. We'll bob the hook up and down in the glass checking its buoyancy because even a small poly-pop can make

a very heavy hook float if it isn't sunk beneath the surface. The water surface acts in a rather strange way with light objects in that it helps to keep some things afloat when they actually shouldn't be. If you sink them below this barrier, you'll see a different reaction so we'll keep doing this until we have found the equilibrium. You usually find that the same sized poly-pops will keep the same pattern and size of hook balanced. The aim is for the poly-pops to just keep the hook afloat. We will then wrap them in boilie paste and then boil for three minutes to give them a good protective coating.

## POP-UPS

A hookbait and its hook can be popped up off the bottom in a number of ways, but before we look at methods of how to do this, let us first consider why a bait should be popped up in the first place. Some reasons for this could be:

- The presence of debris on the lake bed.
- The desire to fish over smelly black silt.
- To make the hookbait stand out from the free offerings.
- To present the bait in front of mid-water cruising fish.

The easiest method of popping up baits has to be through the inclusion of a piece of foam or cork on the hook or hair. These items can be as big or as small as you wish, and should be shaped with a sharp knife to the size required. When using

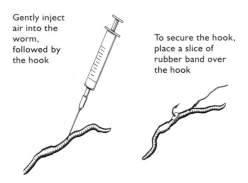

Gently inject air into the worm, followed by the hook

To secure the hook, place a slice of rubber band over the hook

*Worms can be made to float by injecting them with air. This is an excellent presentation for mid-water cruisers.*

boilies, however, there are much better methods available. Besides, a further piece of foam can sometimes make the hookbait act differently or even obstruct the hook point.

Most particle and natural bait pop-up fishing is done with foam or cork, although it is possible to make worms pop-up by injecting them with air. This is a simple process to carry out, and can be devastating for intercepting cruising fish. Maggots can also be made to float by leaving them to soak in a very thin layer of water. To do this, take a handful

*Making hookbaits is now a science to some anglers.*

of maggots and leave them to crawl about in the water for approximately an hour, until they froth. They can then be attached to the hook, but remember that they will need to be used in combination with a piece of foam or cork to hold up a heavy-wired hook.

To use cork or foam to pop-up your baits, simply take a largish piece and attach it to the hair or the hook itself in the same way you would a bait. We have found that cork is best suited to seed and nut baits like tigers and peanuts, whilst foam is better for sweetcorn and other bright or dark-coloured baits. This is because cork is very similar in texture to nuts, whilst foam can be purchased in different colours to suit the type or colour of the bait. The object here is to keep the cork or foam as discreet as you can so that it makes the hookbait appear as natural as possible.

Although it's not necessary, for confidence reasons you may wish to trim the foam or cork to so that it looks as similar to the bait as possible. To do this, attach the buoyant material in place and then trim it with a sharp knife or a pair of scissors. We have found that a piece of cork is much more buoyant than most foams, and may in fact pop-up three tiger or peanuts of the same size together with the hook. Therefore, if you only wish to keep the hook and a single bait popped up using cork, you will need to use a very small piece. Foam, on the other hand, may need to be much larger than the bait, so a tip here is to camouflage it even further with a drop of flavour or similar additive.

*Our favourites are the commercial hookbaits.*

## Popping Up Boilies

To pop-up boilies a different form of presentation and preparation is necessary. We prefer to use boilies that have either been microwaved or that have a foam or cork insert in them. In both cases, it is possible to purchase hookbaits ready prepared from tackle shops, but we prefer to make them ourselves as we can then make them as buoyant as we wish to suit the situation. Some ready-made pop-ups may be buoyant for only a short period, or may in fact be too buoyant.

To make a boilie pop-up using a microwave oven, simply take a non-boiled paste bait and insert it into the

*This fine common fell to a simple pop-up presentation.*

microwave on high power for a minute or two. Keep watching the bait as it is cooking. Do not overcook it or it will burn. At the most, you will need to cook it for three or four minutes, but make sure you test a few first before you use them, as you are sure to burn some.

The other way we make our pop-ups is to take a piece of boilie paste (the stage before boiling), mould a piece of cork or paste into the centre, and then boil it in the normal way (for two minutes or so). You will need to test the pop-up prior to boiling to see if it is as buoyant as you wish. Make sure that when you make the pop-ups in this way, you always cover the insert completely or during the boiling stage the bait will open up even further where the crack is. Like all pop-ups, you can use one, two, three, or even more boiled baits to pop the hook off the bottom.

There are now even specialist pop-up mixes available which make the process of making boilie pop-ups much easier. Some of the most popular are those available from Nutrabaits and Solar, so if you are having difficulty making them yourself, we suggest you get hold of one of these and follow the instructions on the back of the packet. If this still doesn't work, revert to ready-made pop-ups, of which there are numerous brands available.

### Shotting and Weighting the Pop-Up

For obvious reasons, all pop-ups will need to be anchored to the lake bed in some form or another, unless you wish to fish on the surface. As we point out in Chapter 10, it is possible to intercept cruising fish in mid-water by fishing a

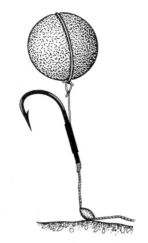

*To regulate the speed at which the hookbait sinks, pinch pieces off the putty until you achieve the desired presentation.*

strong). Instead, we normally attach a small amount of shot and then apply some tungsten putty around it. This should be rolled in the hand first to warm it and make it malleable, and it should be moulded all around the shot. Tungsten putty can be applied direct to the line instead of over a shot, but we have found that it normally slips on the cast if the anchor shot is not first attached. If you don't wish to use the shot, you can add a float stop to the hooklink to mould the putty around. This will hold the putty in just the same way as the shot.

## CRITICALS

Critically balanced baits are a fantastic method to use for fishing over very light silt or to try and trick the fish into sucking the hookbait further down into the throat. They are basically made by making a popped-up bait sink very slowly. To do this, you will need to use tungsten putty to sink the pop-up so that the weight can be balanced to make it sink slowly. It can be done by selecting the exact weight of shot to

*When using Tungsten putty always place a shot on the hooklink first. The putty will not slip on the cast now that it has something holding it in place.*

pop-up directly off the lead. Whilst this can be a very effective method, on most occasions pop-ups are used to fish only a few inches off the bottom. To anchor the pop-up in these instances we normally opt for a simple shot, which can be purchased from most outlets.

We prefer to opt for the size that sinks the pop-up with as few shots as possible, and we very rarely choose to overweight it (make it sink faster than the freebies). The only time we may overshot the pop-up is during windy conditions in shallow water, when the bait could fly all over the place (or rivers when the flow is

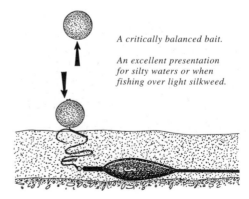

*A critically balanced bait.*

*An excellent presentation for silty waters or when fishing over light silkweed.*

use, but the easiest method is to mould putty to the line and pinch off bits to make it sink. The speed at which the bait will sink can be modified to suit the situation you are fishing, but do bear in mind that the hookbait will soak up more water the longer it is submerged.

The critically balanced approach can be applied to baits popped up several inches off the bottom, or only a few inches, or even to make them sit on the bottom itself. This depends on where the putty or weight is applied. When you want the hookbait to sit directly on the bottom, the putty can be moulded around the eye of the hook. This can trick the fish into thinking that the hookbait is similar to the freebies, but the light weight of it will make it fly back far into the carp's mouth (it would be lighter than the freebies so it would catch the fish off guard) and hopefully cause it to panic and register a very confident take.

## HOOKBAIT PROTECTION

Before we take a look at presenting pellets as hookbaits, we will briefly mention a couple of ways to protect our hookbaits from dreaded little creatures like poisson chat, crayfish or fresh-water crabs. The first is by making our hookbaits out of Rod Hutchinson's Clawbuster product. This is a base mix which contains an added food polymer which reacts with the sugars in the bait, causing it to set hard. The effect will last longer than 72 hours if prepared in the correct way and is also excellent for waters where the hookbaits need to be immersed in water for long periods. It can be flavoured and styled in the same way as boilies, and is also suitable for inclusion in baits which are intended to pop up. For extra hardness, place the baits in direct sunlight for a few hours, making them bake rock hard.

For even further protection, enclose the hookbait in a wrap of nylon stockings or tights. This prevents the fish from

*A cracking mid-twenty for Rob.*

*The result of nuisance species.*

taking any bits off the bait, and therefore keeps it at the original, intended size. On some occasions, where nuisance species are very common, you may find that they cut through a single wrap of nylon, so it may be necessary to double it around for extra protection. Here's a look at how we prepare netted baits:

1. Take the chosen hookbait and wrap it in the tights. We generally use ones that are thick and very finely meshed.

2. Pull the tights as tight as possible around the whole of the hookbait. Make sure that the bait is totally covered or the fish will break through easily.

3. Twist the top of the tights so that the bait is secure within.

4. Now tie a secure knot around the neck of the tights with a piece of braid. We normally use the Grinner knot (*see* Chapter 6).

5. When the knot is tied, simply trim off the loose ends of both the knot and the tights. When doing this, make sure that you do not cut the tights too close to

*A crayfish with its weapons fully loaded!*

the neck or they will open up again.

6. To finish off, apply a dab of superglue to the knot of the braid. To give the bait some added attraction, we sometimes soak it in flavour. This also serves to mask any smell on the tights that may repel the fish.

As always seems to be the case these days, you can now purchase ready-made hookbaits which will withstand constant attacks from nuisance species. Rock-hard baits or ones wrapped in stocking can be purchased from selected tackle shops. To go one further, you can even buy hookbaits in an armour casing. This ingenious idea is the brainchild of Dave Poxon and the lads on a water in Essex known as the Arena. The casing, which is shaped like a boilie and has holes all around, can be opened up and filled with boilie paste. The whole lot is then boiled in the same way as normal boilies. As the paste takes on board water, it swells,

*Wrap ladies' stocking all around the hookbait and secure with a good knot.*

filling the casing and giving the bait a natural, but protected, appearance.

## PRESENTING PELLETS

Believe it or not, besides using pellets as feed, it is also possible to present them on the hook. This may sound like an impossibility, but it can be done in an effective way. You will need to wrap a pellet tightly in a fine piece of ladies' stocking (*see* above). This will prevent most of the particle from dispersing into the water and keep the pellet as whole-shaped as possible. The pellet will swell in the water and become soft, releasing attraction ever so slowly, depending on which flavours have been added to the bait. Some of the particles will even make it through the mesh of the stocking

*Simon with Orchid Lake's big mirror known as Diana.*

during the whole time it is in the water, and this is just one reason why this form of presentation can be an excellent carp catcher when used first on a water.

*Rob with a super mirror taken on a pellet hookbait.*

# 9 BAIT APPLICATION THROUGH THE RIG

Whilst the main object of the rig is to present a bait to a feeding carp, it can also be used as a means of bait application. There are numerous methods of putting bait into the swim using the rig, and because they affect the way your rig works, we will discuss our favourites within this chapter.

## PVA

### PVA String
Available in many different forms, PVA is a soluble substance that can be added to the rig so that bait can be applied around and close to the hookbait. The most common form it comes in is string. Stringers, as they are known, are basically a string of baits threaded onto a length of PVA string and tied to either the hook itself or the lead. When cast out the stringer dissolves, leaving a tight cluster of bait around your hook. They are very popular and also very effective, although at some of the harder waters the fish have got used to them and their presence can cause the fish to be wary. We prefer PVA string from Kryston, known as Meltdown, but many other companies supply similar products. It must be noted that some do not dissolve in low water temperatures so bear this in mind before you select a brand for use in winter. Meltdown is specially designed for use by the carp angler all year round.

PVA can be used with as few as one bait up to as many as you can effectively cast out. Like rigs, great wads of PVA and bait applied to your rig will inhibit the distance you can cast. For long range therefore you would probably opt for a two- or three-bait stringer, whereas for short range you can try anything. It is worth noting, however, that two or three freebies around the hookbait is a popular form of using PVA so the fish may have wised up to this strategy at your chosen venue.

Here's how to prepare a simple stringer:

1. To prepare a stringer, you will need a ready-tied rig, a stringer needle plus some PVA string. Our preference is for Kryston's Meltdown, but there are plenty of excellent types on the market from which to choose.

2. Depending on how many free offerings you wish to present near to the hookbait, cut a strip of PVA string to the

*Two of the many PVA products now on the market.*

128

size you require. On this occasion we are going to present three 16mm freebies on a 6in (15cm) length of string.

3. Take the stringer needle and carefully thread on the three baits. Try to pierce them as close to their centre as possible or the baits may crack.

4. Knot one end of the PVA string with at least a couple of granny knots. Once

*(above) Three photos displaying how to tie a simple PVA string.*

the baits are threaded onto the string, the knots will prevent them from coming free on the cast.

5. Take the opposite end to the knots of the string, and form a 1½in (4cm) loop. Hold firmly and attached the hook end of the needle to the loop. Now thread all but one of the baits onto the string. The final bait should be threaded on top of the loop and left there. This will leave a small gap between the end bait and the end of the loop (approximately ½in or 12mm).

6. Thread the point of the hook of your chosen rig through the strands of the small loop of PVA. Do not close the gap between the top bait of the string and the bend of the hook as this will make the PVA near the hook take longer to dissolve. You are now ready to cast out.

**PVA Bags**

Another popular form of PVA is bags, in which you place your bait. This method is very good for accurate baiting with small baits such as trout pellets, or chopped boilies. Press reports indicate that this method is particularly effective if it has not yet been used on your water. PVA bags are not a new concept, but despite all that has been written about them, there are still remarkably few people using them. Certainly on some of the more commercial venues they are a common sight, but many anglers on other waters give them a go for a short time and then bin the idea as not really being that much more effective than other methods.

One of the main advantages with the bag method is that it presents the

*PVA bags are excellent for those small weedy lakes.*

hookbait and a small number of freebies in a way that few carp have seen before. A tight, intense presentation of small-diameter baits is quite similar to how the carp's natural foodstuffs appear, so the carp are not that suspicious.

To use a PVA bag, simply open it up and pop your hookbait inside. Next apply a small amount of bait so that it covers the hookbait. Do not add the lead until you have done this, or you will more than likely cause a tangle. Once the hookbait is covered, add the lead and then apply some more bait. Now seal the opening. The easiest way to do this is to tie a knot at the top. However, this will cause a wad of PVA to settle in this area which will not dissolve as quickly as the rest of the bag. Instead of tying the knot, lick the edge of the bag and stick it down. Then pull the corners of the bag down and lick

these into place. Don't lick the bag too much or you will make it open – practice makes perfect. Pulling the corners down gives the bag extra strength as well as making it more aerodynamic. The main line should leave the bag through the centre of the opening, and the PVA should be strengthened as much as possible here. It may need to be doubled over a few times, but don't cast until it is strong or you will risk wasting your time.

The reason we apply the hookbait first is that if no holes are inserted into the bag, any air trapped inside will probably be towards the hookbait end. This will cause the bag to role over so that the lead is at the bottom and the hookbait at the top. The main residue of the bag will be near the opening by the lead, leaving the hookbait clear. Ideally what will also happen is that the hookbait will be thrown up into the water as the air from the bag is released, leaving it in an untangled position.

Here's a look at a couple of alternatives to the standard PVA bag presentation.

**Floating Bags**

On more than one occasion the call of 'your bag's floating mate' has echoed across the lake, but the reply is always silent. Whilst the angler opposite may think that we are complete beginners for filling the bag with air, we are happy to sit there with an open bale arm and the rod in the rests, waiting for the bag to burst. When it does, the lead will sink straight down, coming to rest on the lake bed directly below the bag, whereas the bait, especially if it is an irregular or

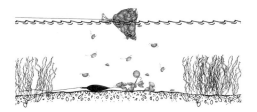

*The floating PVA bag. As the bag dissolves it spreads the freebies all around the hookbait. A different form of presentation to the normal PVA bag method.*

*The floating bag method in action.*

uneven shape, will descend at a much more sedate pace. If our plan has worked, it will spread out a little on the way down, thus baiting the immediate area of the hook, but not in the way of standard bag presentations. It goes without saying that for this method, the bale arm should always be left open to allow the lead to free fall. If the bale arm is closed, when the bag bursts the lead will probably kite on the line until it comes to rest away from the area in which the free baits have been deposited.

One of the shortcomings of the floating bag method is that it is difficult to control in the wind. For a start, the wind will often cause a bow in the line, but the lead and line should not be tightened for fear that the hookbait will

move away from the freebies. The other effect of the wind is on the accuracy. You may want to place the bait with pinpoint accuracy, for example into a small hole in a weed bed, but the wind will often blow the bag away from the drop zone during its floating stage, thus depositing the baits into the wrong place. Clearly this method is at its most effective on calm days.

As far as the rig set-up is concerned, we always use Nash PVA bags. Nashy's bags come in three different sizes (small, medium and large), and for the purposes of a floating bag set-up we have found that the medium-sized bait bags are the best choice. They are big enough to take the rig, lead and also a reasonable quantity of bait, but will still float if required. The best way to fill them (and indeed any bag) is the way described above. Although the lick and stick method may not look very strong to the newcomer, if done correctly, it certainly is. If you aren't convinced, you can staple the opening with a standard stapler as an alternative.

You must use baits of different shapes if you want to spread out the grouping of your free offerings. Round bait will not be affected by twist on the way to the bottom, and will thus end up in more or less the same position it would have done if a standard bottom bag method had been used. Chopped boilies are ideal for creating a good spread of bait as they can be broken into all manner of shapes that will each descend at different speeds and in different directions.

Don't forget that the fundamental principle of this rig is that the bag should float. Filled with air, the bait bag is normally buoyant enough to float a 2oz lead when air is kept inside if you do not pack it too tightly or squeeze out the trapped air. If you want to be really clever, you can critically balance the bag by making a number of punctures through the side, but this takes a lot of trial, error and wasted bags. If you are prepared to take the time to do it, make sure the type of lead and exact amount of bait is recorded most accurately, as even the slightest deviation will affect the bag. A balanced bag is useful over weed, but it is virtually useless for deep water as normally it will have dissolved by the time it reaches the bottom. This is another reason why we have found the Nash bags to be the best as they do tend to last a little longer in the water than some of the others.

## Popped-Up Bags

A pop-up bag is just a slight variation on the floating bag theme, and is our choice when it comes to fishing over weed. For this method we prefer to use the smaller bags, or if we want to put out a lot of bait (on the PVA bag scale) we will use the medium-sized ones with a bigger lead that is weighty enough to hold bottom whilst the bag pops up above. Only the hookbait is placed into the bag this time, and the bag is left filled with air but sealed so that it can pop up above the lead. As the lead is not secured in the bag, the hook is more prone to tearing out during the force of the cast, so it is imperative that the hook is pierced into the side of the bag, and that the cast is more of a gentle lob. Casting anything over about 40yd is a bit wasteful as the

*Another method of PVA bag presentation, this time the PVA pop-up bag. Simply fill the bag with air before you attach the seal. Remember, you don't need to site the lead in the bag for this method.*

bag splits in mid-air and peppers you with bait or dumps it unceremoniously into the margins at your feet.

Once you have cast the rig out to the required position, it pays to watch the water for a while, as after a short period you should see an air bubble breaking the surface of the water. When you see this you know that the rig has landed as you intended it, and that the hook should

*PVA bags can also be very effective on the big lakes. Here's Rob with a beautiful Madine mirror.*

by now be sitting in the middle of a nice little spread of bait. A tip in windy weather is to include a 20mm brightly coloured pop-up in the PVA bag with the freebaits. When the bag bursts and expels the freebait, the pop-up will be liberated and will rise to the surface thus indicating to you that the hook is also free of the bag. This can be taken one step further when fishing over weed with a critically balanced bottom bait, as the pop-up can be PVA'd to the hook stringer-fashion. The bag bursts, the freebies sink, but the hookbait is held above the weed by the pop-up. When the PVA holding the pop-up to the hook melts, the hookbait will sink slowly down to rest on top of the weed, and the pop-up will rise to the surface telling you that the hook is clear. Using this method, those nagging doubts about whether the hook is snagged in the weed should be a thing of the past.

## The Twin Airbag

This final PVA fine-tuning method basically incorporates the previous two. On one occasion we couldn't decide which of the two methods to use so decided that there was no reason why we should not adopt both methods. The twin airbag system was born! If cars can have them, why can't anglers?

The best bags for this method are the smaller ones. In one bag put the lead together with an amount of chosen bait. We both favour boilies or pellet for this bag. Use the lick and stick method to seal the top, although residue around the lead is less prejudicial than around the hooklink, so the twist and tie method can be used for the lead bag if you prefer. Then put the hookbait into another small bag before filling it with bait and some air. The bait in this bag needs to be irregular in shape and very light so that it will spread out a little on the way down

*(Right) The double air-bag presentation.*

*(Left) Simon with a super forty-plus mirror taken on the twin air-bag presentation.*

(the idea is that this bag will be floating above the first bag which contains the lead). Maggots or chopped baits are ideal for this. As far as the hook length is concerned for this rig, we normally use a long hooklink of 18in (45cm), with a couple of drops of Drop Em! on the link to pin it to the bed of the lake out of harm's way.

The set-up is quite difficult to cast and does not lend itself very well to distances over 40yd or so. A gentle lob is all that is required to prevent the hook pulling out of the bag, and it feels strange at first to be casting out two bags in one go. Once the bags hit the water, the lead will sink the first bag, but the air and the lack of weight in the other will cause it to pop-up above the lead. As each dissolves, the lead bag will leave a tight group of baits around the hook, whereas the other bag will pop in a nuclear explosion mushroom- style, spreading out the lighter baits around the outside of the tight group. If all goes according to plan, the hookbait will sink towards the middle of the tight group, and you will be left with another fabulous form of presentation.

We find this method mimics quite well the natural feeding areas that carp will be on the lookout for. It is unlikely that it will have been used widely on your water so if your local lake has been taken apart in the past on the standard PVA bag method, but catches are now a lot slower than they used to be, this may be the answer to your problem. Obviously all these methods are really designed for small waters, but the same principle can be applied to large waters if you are allowed to bait up from a boat.

# THE METHOD

One of the most widely used methods of baiting via the rig in recent years is the presentation of groundbait around the lead, known as the Method. Although not renowned for producing the big fish, it is a method which frequently proves effective for catching large numbers of fish in short bursts. It is a difficult tactic to master because of the many false indications you can get as the carp twitches the lead when feeding on the groundbait. Here's a look at how you use it.

1. Our favourite groundbait when using the Method is Rod's Method Mix groundbait. This is usually combined with some cooked hemp and chopped boilie. We will mix 1.1lb (500g) of groundbait with ¼lb (115g) of hemp and twenty chopped 20mm boilies.

2. Mix the ingredients for the groundbait to the right consistency (one that is easily formed into solid balls when compressed in the hand). To do this mix the dry ingredients first, and then slowly add water until a damp consistency is achieved.

3. You can use either a lead or feeder presentation for the groundbait. Take the lead/feeder of your rig and bury it in a large handful of the groundbait. You will need to cover the whole lead/feeder in the mix.

4. Compress the groundbait tightly around the lead within the hand. Make sure that there are no soft, broken gaps amongst the groundbait or it will fall from the lead during the cast.

5. Hold the lead off the floor to see if it is compressed correctly. If pieces fall

off, it will need compressing more. If it is too crumbly, you will need to add some more water to the groundbait.

*(Top) The Method Mix needs to be at the right consistency to make it bind to the lead.*

*(Left) Perfect!*

*(Bottom) Tiny little pieces dissolve into the water and attract the carp. A great method to try on difficult waters.*

The Method is a very effective way of fishing for carp and is an excellent alternative to the standard stringer boilie presentation. Upon contact with the water, the groundbait will begin to break away from the lead/feeder and disperse in the water column. It can be used alongside a number of different presentations, with our best results coming when combined with a short 6in (15cm) link and a critically balanced bottom bait.

## The Pellet Rig

Carp, being simple creatures, learn by association, and as a result have become conditioned into recognizing certain things as a danger source. If you think about most modern carp angler strategies, there tend to be two very common features found from angler to angler:

- The boilie.
- The baiting approach.

As a result we are all constantly on the lookout for something that is different in order to lower the defences of the carp and induce them to feed without too much caution. The success of pellets has been well documented throughout these pages and, indeed, almost every angling paper in Europe, but as more and more anglers recognize that they can be a deadly method if used in the right way, the more the fish will come to recognize it as a source of danger too.

Being round, Ball Pellets can be fired out with a Cobra, but this type of application is used by many anglers and gives a scattering of baits around the general vicinity of the hookbait. In situations where there are a number of carp competing for food, this method can be deadly as it makes the fish search for the food source. However, in waters with a lower stocking density or where you are fishing for patrolling carp, one of the methods that we have found to be effective is to fish a single bait over a stringer of pellets. This tends to be an exceptional 'ambush' method. When it comes to the stringer method of presentation, most anglers would choose PVA, but with most of the larger pellets, a number of new options are also available. Due to the fact that pellets dissolve, they can actually be threaded onto the hooklink, thus dispensing with the need for PVA. We have successfully used pellet rigs in this way on a number of occasions. One of the advantages of a pellet rig is that, in the same way as a PVA bag, it can present bait in the immediate vicinity of the hook thus creating a very attractive feeding area for a passing carp. In addition, being streamlined, the pellet rig has the advantage over the standard PVA bag set-up in that it can be cast out a lot further. In fact, in good conditions it is possible to fish a short pellet rig at distances of 100yd or more.

Our first concern with such a rig, and indeed one which has been expressed to us by a number of our friends to whom we have shown the rig, is that the pellets might not dissolve quickly enough, therefore giving aborted takes should a carp pick up a pellet on the hooklink that has not completely dissolved. In order to counter this, it is imperative that you know how long it will take for your

pellets to dissolve completely, and adjust this according to the feeding patterns of the carp you are after. Pellets often vary in dissolve time depending on their constitution and the temperature of the water they are immersed in. At the very least, test them at home before you use this method or, better still, immerse some in the lake water to get a more accurate result. You could even sink them for a few minutes before you cast out.

When we were putting the initial concept of the Ball Pellet through its paces (during the World Carp Cup of 1996), we had two different dissolve times to play with, these being three- and six-hour breakdowns. Realizing the advantage of a quicker breakdown time prompted us to ask Clive Diedrich (the maker) for some quick breakdown pellets of approximately half an hour. It was these that we used successfully in the World Cup, and which have now been altered slightly and are on general sale. At present most pellets dissolve in around an hour, but if you feel that this is too long for you, they can be 'doctored' by drilling extra holes in them to make them dissolve from the inside as well as externally. They can be made to dissolve in around fifteen minutes with some strategic drilling, but if you feel that even this is too long for you, let us know where you are fishing as we wouldn't mind a ticket!

The standard pellet rig that we use is a 12in (30cm) hooklink of either mono or our old favourite 15lb Kryston Super-Nova, with the pellets threaded onto the hooklink before the swivel is tied on. We put around twelve pellets onto each link before tying on the swivel, and leave a

*Another method of presenting Ball Pellets on the rig.*

hinge

*The method of presenting the Ball Pellet on the hooklink. A very effective method with quick-dissolve pellets.*

*The Pellets are drilled out and the hooklink is then doubled through the centres. The Pellets are then held in place by a hair stop.*

couple of inches of braid clear so that there is a tail between the lead and the first pellet. As the rig is cast out, the pellets will slide towards the hook, but this does not have a   detrimental effect on the presentation of the set-up. In fact, it often enhances it, as when the pellets sink to the lake bed, they straighten out the hooklink and hold it on the bottom. Quite often they will even bury it in a mound of dissolved pellet. The short tail that is left free allows some movement of the link should a fish pick up the bait and back off with it in its mouth. If it is preferable to use a confidence set-up with a longer hooklink this can still be accomplished. It is also a little less fiddly to set up, as instead of threading the pellets onto the link before the swivel is tied on, you simply double up your hooklink to make a loop, and thread the pellets onto the link using a stopper to prevent them falling off in flight. One point to note here is that the acceleration force exerted on the   pellets during the cast is very high, so a normal hair stop

often pulls through the end couple of pellets, thus reducing the effectiveness of the rig. Instead of a standard hair stop we prefer to use a piece of strong, smooth grass, which is less likely to pull through the pellet.

In addition to its effective properties in the fish-catching stakes, the pellet rig in both its formats is very good at preventing tangles. The string of pellets fly behind the lead and prevent the hooklink tangling around the lead and swivel. Problems though, can still   occur if the pellets are not drilled as near to the middle as possible. When the pellets are threaded onto the link you can tell whether they are straight enough, as a pellet which has not been drilled straight will cause the whole rig to curve. This will cut down on the   distance that you can cast, and will also increase the risk of a tangle. Dangle the line of pellets by the lead and see if the line is totally straight. If it starts to curve, remove the offending pellet.

# 10  THE FOUR SEASONS

Most of what we have looked at so far in this book should serve as the foundations for your carp fishing career. The information considered will be useful to you time and time again and will help you to be successful on a number of occasions. In this chapter we wish to move onto the next step, which is where carp fishing can start to become confusing to the beginner. Simply put, all waters are different and all carp are different. For this simple reason alone, your tactical considerations should never be stereotypical in their approach and must be logically thought out with reasons to back up your decisions.

This point can be understood all the more by examining fishing in the four seasons of the year. Winter, spring, summer and autumn are all different, not only to the human, but also to the carp and the water, in the biggest way possible. Being cold-blooded creatures, the carp's feeding is dictated by water temperature and daylight hours, which both differ immensely at different times of the year. The same can be said of the water, as at certain times of the year the lake undergoes a number of biological changes which in turn affect the way the fish feed. Ultimately the carp angler will have to alter his tactics to suit the situation and the way the fish are. Certainly you may find similarities between your tactics in one season and another (for example snag fishing can be successful all year round), but more often than not you will find that during a specific season you will follow

one approach more than at other times of the year.

We cannot stress enough the point that an angler will become a more successful and better equipped angler if he fishes all year round and experiences all manner of different situations. We have both fished all year round, all over the world, and have drawn together a number of important points that must be considered by the modern-day carp angler. We have broken this chapter up into the four different seasons, and have outlined some of the common tactical approaches that will be required for each of the different seasons. We will start with winter, which in our minds deserves the most attention of the four due to its unpredictability.

## WINTER
## TIME FOR HARD WORK

Winter is a time when catch rates drop considerably, and when only the hardy or crazy ones amongst us continue to pursue our goals and dreams. Winter fishing can be very unpredictable and certain things need to be considered if one is about to confront it for the first time. Remaining warm whilst on the bank is very important. Good-quality footwear, underclothes and oversuits are necessary if you are to remain enthusiastic and happy during the long dark and damp nights which you are almost certain to encounter. Confidence plays a great part in success during the

*Frozen over, but don't be put off.*

winter, and it is obvious that shivering to death in the wet and cold will not do much for your morale.

In temperate zones the climate has a habit of changing very quickly during the winter months, and it is vitally important you are prepared for such circumstances should they occur. Among the most recommended items of clothing are Wychwood Tackle's Four Seasons clothing range, Sundridge's Silcatex oversuit and boot range, and Rod Hutchinson's range. Suitable protection can also be purchased at reasonable cost from most camping shops. The best time of the year to buy your winter clothing is during the summer months, as you will often find things at reduced prices and on special offer. If you shop around and do not get drawn into buying the first item you see, you should be able to get yourself kitted out with a full set of winter warmers for less than £200. It is worth pointing out to you here that you should always take spare items with you as it is quite easy to slip on the muddy banks which are so common during the winter. Remember also that lots of thin layers are better than a couple of thick ones.

Lastly, to keep warm whilst asleep at night obviously requires a sleeping bag. There are a number of different types on offer to the carp angler, with the majority costing somewhere in the three-figure region. Do not take much notice of all the advertising hype surrounding these as you can obtain some excellent sleeping bags for half the price. Have a good look around the camping shops and don't be drawn into buying the most expensive. We know plenty of guys who use a couple of cheap bags, one inside the other, all through the winter.

**Find Those Fish**

Water temperature is another important factor when it comes to winter carping, and although many people have said it before, it is worth repeating a few points again here. In the olden days many of the top carp anglers believed that the carp went into hibernation for the winter when the water temperature dropped below a certain level. We now know that this is not the case, although temperature has a marked effect on fish in that their body temperature is governed by the water temperature around them. They will

*You'll normally find the best winter spots are the same year-after-year.*

normally try to seek out the warmest area of a lake, although this may not necessarily be the deepest. As water cools it sinks to the bottom of the lake, so this area is often the coldest. However, as soon as water gets colder than 4°C it starts to rise to the surface of the water. When the air temperature is -1°C it cools the surface layers of the water until they too reach 0°C and turn to ice. In very cold conditions the water at the bottom of the lake will still be around 4°C, and as long as the weather is fairly even, the temperature will be quite constant and the fish will feed happily at this depth. When choosing a swim, however, it is worthwhile fishing somewhere that has a variety of depths in the same area, as the carp will often move up and down in the water column depending on light and heat penetration. We have often found that even where there is a level area of, say, 8ft (2.5m) deep, the carp will prefer to lie up at this depth but are prepared to move up a bar or shelf into shallower water to feed in the daytime, especially if it is a warm day.

Nevertheless the carp can be increasingly harder to locate in our waters in the winter months. They become less active as the water temperature lowers and can often be found huddled together in only one area of the lake. If you are having difficulty locating the fish in your water, before abandoning winter carping as a bad idea, give the following areas of the lake a thorough try and investigation:

**Snags** Carp like to feel safe when dormant, and so the first areas we would always try are the snaggy areas of a lake.

Always consider submerged features alongside those which are visible, and don't forget to check that your tackle is up to the job when fishing close to them. Losing a winter carp due to bad preparation is one of the worst mistakes you can make (refer to the section on spring for ideas of how to tackle snag fishing).

**Reed beds** are another excellent area to try, especially if they offer sufficient depth and cover for the fish. Such areas will also offer natural food items and so you may have to cast quite tight to them if you wish to entice the fish out. Once again, don't forget to use good, strong tackle when fishing here.

**Islands** usually shelve or slope off and therefore offer a wider choice of depth than other areas of the lake. A specific depth of water will be more comfortable for the fish at a particular time, and thus carp will lie close to islands because they can adjust to the most comfortable depth without having to expend much energy. Islands can also provide overhanging bushes and safe areas, so they are always a favourite for the carp in winter.

*Water inlets are a great attractor of winter carp.*

**Warm water inlets** from a variety of sources are an obvious place to look during cold water temperatures. Probably the most common form of this type of inlet is from a power station. We know of several sections of canal in both France and Holland where warm water is fed in via cooling towers or similar energy supply stations. These are great areas to fish for carp in the winter, and if they weren't so few and far between, would almost certainly be our preference ahead of snags.

**Mid-water** During prolonged cold spells where water temperatures settle below 6°C, expect some carp to lie-up in mid-water or, at least, a couple of feet off the bottom. This applies particularly on waters where springs seep through the lake bed. Spring water is a constant temperature above 6°C and will rise up in the water as it disperses. The easiest way to locate springs is to wait for the lake surface to freeze over and then look for unfrozen patches which will probably have been caused by warmer water dispersal.

**Warm wind** On most waters, the presence of a strong warm wind will usually signify good carp feeding conditions. If such a wind is present on your lake, the end which is receiving it will always be worth investigating. The water here will be well oxygenated, at a constant temperature throughout, and possibly coloured and full of disturbed food items.

**Shallows** On a warm day the shallow areas of the lake which catch the sun's rays will warm up very quickly. The carp will be aware of this and may visit such areas of the lake to feed or, indeed, just lie up for the day. Scan the shallows regularly with a pair of binoculars, and keep an eye out for any black shapes which happen to be moving.

**Summer hotspots** Although bloodworm and other natural foods will be less abundant than during the warmer months, summer hotspots in open water may still be visited by the carp in the winter. A single hookbait fished in these areas can often be a winner.

**Dying lily beds** also offer natural food in winter, and the carp will recognize this and visit them.

**Water inlets** Providing the water depth is sufficient, a water inlet area offers a number of advantages to the carp in winter: the water temperature in such an area is usually more constant than elsewhere in the lake; the area will have an abundance of oxygen; and food deposits from upstream will gather here. Don't neglect them.

### Winter Tackle

You don't need special tackle to fish through the winter although the 'business end' of your line needs to be spot on if you want to make the most of your winter fishing. You may be able to get away with something not quite perfect during the summer months, but during winter your presentation needs to be absolutely correct. You get precious few chances in the colder weather as it is, without

*Snow on the ground and one of two English thirties to fall in two days.*

fluffing your chances because your hook was blunt or your knots didn't hold. There is no excuse for that sort of loss in the summer, let alone the winter, so don't let it be you who loses fish as a result of silly slip-ups.

One item of tackle which can be scaled down in the winter is the hook. We have used a size 8, or even a 10 or sometimes a 12. We do this because usually there are less obstructions such as weed around in the winter, so you may as well make the most of it by opting for a less obtrusive hook. Besides hooks, we may also scale down such items of tackle as line and hooklinks. Although we obviously cannot tell you what will work on your water, you may find that if in the summer you have to use a main line of 15lb in weed, you may be able to use 12lb line in the winter. The reduction in the diameter may entice the fish to feed in the vicinity of the hookbait instead of being spooked out of the swim because

of a visible line. The same can be said for hooklinks, and we will normally opt for a breaking strain as low as we can get away with.

### Bait for Cold Water

There is a bad saying in England that fishmeal baits don't work in winter. This has started all sorts of rumours that any bait which contains fishmeal will not work in cold water. If you have heard this sort of statement then our advice is to totally ignore it. Fishmeals work in winter, end of story. We have caught countless carp in the winter using these baits, including thirties in the snow on very hard-fished venues. The important thing to understand is that carp require fats and protein to survive in the winter; as they do in the summer. They require the same levels as they do in the summer as well, albeit they will not require food as often because they are not exerting as much energy.

For carp, some fats become very hard to digest in the European winter months

*More snow. This time small baits did the damage.*

because digesting enzymes present in the gut are less active because of the cooler temperature. Although no scientific research to our knowledge has ever been carried out on the effects of fishmeals on carp in the European winter, we can assume that if they overdo the amount they feed upon, they may become stressed (certain fishmeals are fairly high in fat). No self-respecting carper wishes to cause the carp any discomfort, especially if it may have an effect on their results, so it is no wonder that word has spread around that fishmeals are ineffective. Yet we both use fishmeals all the time in the winter. They are a superb bait and very nutritious to carp. The secret is to use only a small amount in the bait. No more than a quarter of the mix should be made up of fishmeal, and this will be of the pre-digested sort which will assist with assimilation. We don't use any of the fish oils we would normally add in the warmer months, and instead just add our favoured flavours/attractors.

We're very big fans of fruit flavours in the winter months. Before we started work for Rod Hutchinson, we used all sorts of different fruit flavours in the winter. Probably one of the most effective was Esterblend, which is marketed by Solar. We couldn't tell you why it is so good, but it may be something to do with the solubility of the esters in the compound. Esterblend is made up of twelve different fruit esters. Esters are, according to Rod Hutchinson, who, believe us, is the biggest authority on bait in the world, a fabulous attractor of carp. These days, we tend to use Rod's Fruit Frenzy for our winter carping. It is very similar in make-up to the Esterblend, but

based on Rod's own favourite esters rather than Martin Locke's. We've only been using it for three winters, but each winter it has produced some stunning carp. In addition to this, we haven't really fished much over the last few winters so to be able to rely on a flavour like that is just what we need. We also like tangy flavours such as tangerine or mandarin. We used Nashy's Squid Mix with Tangerine and Esterblend for two seasons and it caught exceptionally well.

The main point worth noting when it comes to flavours in winter regards the solubility aspect. If you carry out some tests with flavours in your tank at home, you will see that all compounds react differently in water. Take a few drops of your test flavours one at a time and drop them into cold water (that's been chilled in the fridge). Some will sink and lie on the bottom like bricks, whilst others will shoot up to the surface and spread out. Others will even sit mid-water. The important point about this is that you are best targeting your winter fishing with a flavour combination. Never just rely on one flavour in the winter. If you can find a compound which sinks and mix it with one which floats and another that tends to act neutrally, then you are on your way. This is possibly one of the reasons why the Esterblend or Fruit Frenzy combinations work so well.

### Winter Baiting Strategies

There are hundreds of different ways to approach your winter baiting and the correct choice is obviously related to the type of venue you are fishing and the conditions on the day. Nevertheless, here are a selection of methods which have been successful for us in the past. Pick and choose them wisely, and we're sure they'll be successful for you.

**Bait lightly** Over-baiting is often the biggest fault of many anglers in the winter. The fish do not burn up energy very quickly as they are less active and, for this reason, they will only feed sporadically. Single hookbaits in known feeding areas are a deadly method and have accounted for thousands of carp all over the country.

*With small baits, the carp needs to eat more to fulfil its needs. This prolongs the feeding spell.*

**Three or four-bait stringers** are an excellent method to try on a roving rod. Instead of sitting behind static baits for hour after hour, try to entice a carp into feeding by hunting it down. Loaded with a stringer, recast a rod every hour or so in an attempt to disturb a fish and tempt it into feeding.

**A natural livebait** such as a worm is also excellent for use on a roving rod. The release of natural attractors, coupled with the movement of the bait, seems to be far too appealing to be left alone.

**Reduce the size** Because the carp does not always feed for lengthy periods during the winter, try using tiny baits instead of the standard 14mm or 18mm ones. This way the fish will need more of the baits to fulfil its needs. The more it wants, the greater the chance of the fish finding the hookbait.

**Increase the range** If the small bait method has already been tried on your water to great effect, then try five or six larger baits spread over a wider area. This will keep the fish searching for food and they will therefore be more susceptible to sampling hookbaits.

**Chopping baits** will not only result in more samples of bait in your swim, but it will also increase the release of attractors. This can be a deadly method if used for the first time on a water and is certainly one of our winter favourites. We have had some excellent results with this on various day-ticket waters. Five to ten 18mm baits chopped into quarters is an ideal starting point.

**The Ball Pellet** has been the biggest advance in bait technology for many years. Its use allows the angler to regulate the amount of attraction in the swim without worrying about over-baiting. Our results show it is best used alongside a single hookbait and on a 'little-and-often' basis (ten to fifteen pellets after every fish, or shortly after the dissolve period of those previously fired out has elapsed).

**Bring enough bait** You may find that when the fish do feed on your water they will feed in large numbers. The environmental conditions will appear to stimulate almost all of the fish in the lake into a feeding frenzy. If this happens you can capitalize on it if you are armed with enough bait. There are countless times when we have caught more than one fish in a winter session simply by giving the fish what they want – food. 'Little-and-often' baiting strategies tend to work best on these occasions, and it is better to scatter bait broadly rather than in tight clumps.

## Hookbait Strategies

One of the biggest mistakes a winter carp angler can make is to look at winter as simply that – winter. To us, this season of the year is one of the most unpredictable, and for this reason we generally split it into three different sections, namely the beginning, middle and end.

### The Beginning of Winter

For a lot of our early winter carping we opt for a pop-up type presentation. During the first part of winter there is an incredible amount of fallen leaf matter at most fisheries and a certain percentage of this will inevitably make its way into the water. This will eventually come to rest on the bed of the lake, where it will begin to break down. Such leaves frequently move around on the bed of the lake and can come to lie over hookbaits as well as mask the hook. Obviously this may cause problems if you only have standard bottom baits, and it is for this reason that we prefer pop-ups in November and December. A lot of the time we favour double pop-ups, as during the winter it may be necessary to keep the hookbait in the water for a couple of days, or even more. Single pop-ups tend to soak up water after about 24 hours and then become critically balanced or light bottom baits. Double pop-ups, on the other hand, are an excellent way of overcoming this problem as the combination of the two keeps the hookbait afloat for longer periods. To anchor the pop-up we will use either shot or Kryston's Heavy Metal.

### Mid-Winter

Because carp generally feed quite gently (with slow movements) at the height of winter, snowman-type presentations are another favourite of ours in January and February. We will use these after the lake has finished its natural breakdown of leaf matter (when the bed is fairly clean) as the hook needs to rest on the lake bed with this set-up. We always use this type of rig in conjunction

*Pop-ups, especially very buoyant ones which don't have to be re-cast every hour or so to see if they are still popped-up, are a favouite at the beginning of winter when there is plenty of leaf matter on the lake bed.*

with a long hooklink of over 12in (30cm). This is because we are trying to get the hookbait to the back of the carp's throat as soon as it sucks it up. It really works on the same principle as critically balanced baits, but we prefer the snowman because it doesn't seem to be as widely used as single, critically balanced hookbaits. We normally use this method in the depths of winter when, if the fish are moving, they will be in a semi-dormant state and not particularly focused on examining hookbaits.

To make up a snowman simply thread a normal bottom bait onto the hair and then follow it with a pop-up. You can use the same type of bait for both or you can try two different ones. Our preference is for something different and we normally favour a single Scopex-flavoured boilie combined with a fruit-flavoured pop-up.

*The End of Winter*
Towards the end of winter, when the water temperature starts to rise slightly, we return to our favourite summer

*The Snowman presentation – brilliant in the middle of winter.*

strategy of bottom baits. At this time of the year the fish are beginning to wake up and are therefore increasingly more likely to notice a 'hooky' hookbait amongst a selection of free offerings. We use bottom baits straight out of the bag at the end of winter on most    occasions, but for heavily pressured  waters we make up a selection of bottom baits including a couple of poly-pops to help counteract the weight of the hook. We begin to use bottom baits towards the middle of March.

**Indication**
In winter you should pay special attention to indication. A single bleep which may have been ignored in the summer could mean a fish on the bank in   winter. Try and watch your line as much as possible where it enters the water, as any movement here may be a tell-tale sign of a fish which may not register on your alarm. Also try to keep the line as direct as possible from your alarm to the lead. The more angles there are here the longer it will take to register a bleep and, as we all know, fish don't move as much in the winter as they do in the summer. They can be tightly shoaled up and will not move around much, so screaming runs can be few and far between.

*Bottom baits for the end of winter.*

As far as alarms are concerned, you should try and make them as sensitive as possible. You will want them to pick up the slightest movement at the business end so, if you have alarms with sensitivity controls, turn the sensitivity up. If you use Optonics it is worthwhile changing the wheel inside to a twelve-vane or twitcher wheel.

## SPRING
## TIME FOR WEED

With spring just around the corner the fish start to move about in search of food, before getting ready for the ritual of spawning. March is another of our favourite months of the year, with the spring sunshine warming the water and the leaves starting to grow on the trees. All seems rosy above the water, but below the surface the carp are at a very delicate stage in their lives. Many of you will have heard about the disease called SVC. This stands for spring viraemia of carp, but exactly what is it?

This is a virus which is carried by some fish and can be fatal at this time of year, when the carp's defences are at their lowest. As the water temperature warms up the virus becomes active (hence the 'spring' viraemia). SVC is by no means the only disease which can affect or even kill carp at this time of year. It is, in fact, very rare but it is also very contagious, so if you see any fish you think are distressed, note down where they are and tell the nearest responsible person, or inform a club official when you can. All suspicious fish deaths should also be reported to the water authority, for if they are investigated early enough the lives of some of the fish in your lake may be saved.

As far as fishing is concerned, spring is the time of year when the fish start to get themselves back into their regular feeding patterns and behaviour. The carp is a cold-blooded creature and the extent of its activity is governed by such things as water temperature and, to a lesser extent, the penetration of sunlight into the water. The fish may have been laid up in the same place in a semi-dormant state for some time during the winter, so you may find that they are covered in leeches when you catch them in spring. This is quite a common sight with early season fish, and whilst it does not look nice to see the carp with a collection of leeches on its body (especially in its mouth), it is a natural occurrence that will rectify itself. The carp will get rid of their unwanted visitors either by leaping clean out of the water, by means of suction through the gills, or by the simple action of feeding. If you come across any fish which have leeches on them, do not remove them unless you are equipped with antiseptic solution (such as Klin-ik). This is because removing leeches leaves

*Carp just love weed, whether it's for shelter or the food that's found there.*

open wounds where they have been attached, through which secondary infection can attack the fish.

As the fish begin to wake up, so does the other life in the water. The most obvious sign of this has to be the growth of weed in certain waters. If the lake you are fishing falls into this category, then no doubt the weed will become more and more established as the spring months settle in, posing the carp angler plenty of problems. One of the biggest mistakes many anglers make when fishing next to weed beds is to consider weed as just weed, without giving further thought to the type it actually is. There are hundreds of different water plants which exist in and around water bodies and, as is usual with living things, each type of water plant has a particular classification, these being: emergent and marginal plants, floating-leafed plants, submerged plants and algae.

Before we look at the most common form of plant life within a water it is worth mentioning that not all water bodies are the same, so it is possible that you may not find specific types of plant life at your chosen venue. The characteristics (depth, size and so on) of individual lakes, rivers and ponds are all different, and this naturally has a bearing on what plant life will be found within and around a water. That said, certain types of plant life are very common around the lakes and waters we fish and we shall begin by taking a look at some of these.

## Types of Weed
There are a number of different types of totally submerged plants found in water bodies and most of these are perennials (last several years). Many of these have overcome the problem of how to survive through winter by sinking to the bottom and producing winter buds which stick into the lake bed. The winter buds contain food material which is used up during spring when tiny buds float to the surface to form new plants.

Submerged plants show the greatest adaptations and consist of limp and weak stems which are supported by water. The most common forms are:

**Canadian pondweed (*Elodea canadensis*)** The best known of the totally submerged plants. It was first introduced to Britain in 1840s and is now very common throughout the country. It displays a feature that is common in most water plants – that of multiplication by vegetative means rather than by sowing seeds. Such is Canadian pondweed's growth that most lakes containing it soon become infested. It is a rooted plant which has extremely long and slender stalks with minute lilac flowers attached (these are often overlooked). It is often found on sale in aquatic shops for inclusion in fish tanks.

**Hornwort (*Ceratophyllum demersum*)** This is noticeably different from Canadian Pondweed in that it is not a rooted plant, but a free-growing plant which can be found just below the water surface. On rare occasions the plant can become fixed to the lake bed by what are known as rhizomes (shoots), which sometimes develop in older forms of vegetation. It is an erect plant with green, forked (once or twice) leaves and a long, limp stem. Flowering and pollination takes place underwater and, because of this, it is said to be one of the most completely adapted plants to aquatic life. The male and female flowers appear in late summer.

**Water Milfoil (*Myriophyllum spicatum*)** This rooted plant is most noticeable during the flowering stage, when it extends its flowering shoots above the water. It has long stems which carry large quantities of dissected leaves of four or five whorls which end in a short, spiky, small pin flower head. As mentioned above, a number of submerged plants produce tightly packed buds which are filled with food material to assist with surviving the winter months. Water milfoil is a good example of this type of plant and often survives the hardest of winters. It is usually found in very shallow marginal areas.

**Stonewort (*Chara vulgaris*)** This is usually found in deeper parts of lakes and ponds and is a favourite food of the grass carp. It is a much larger plant than most and is included in the green algae classification. There are over thirty different species of stonewort in Britain and because of this it is a complex plant to identify individually. There are, however, one or two qualities found in all the different species, these being the brittle nature of the plant and the frequent presence of a limy coating on their surface.

Weed classifications fall into a number of different categories but those mentioned above are the most commonly found. If you are still having trouble recognizing the many forms of weed which can be found within lakes, get your hands on a good field guide to help you with identification. Although this can be a difficult and tedious process, it is certainly worth pursuing. Understanding how thick the weed actually is and how it may affect your presentation may be the difference between catching and blanking.

**Tackling Weedy Waters**
Once you have successfully identified the weed type you have in front of you, you then have to familiarize yourself with the area in which it lies. Although on many occasions you will be able to see what lies beneath the surface and where the actual weed beds lie, the use of a marker float as a means of locating specific areas is invaluable. With the correct set-up, and through practice, you will soon be able to discover the shape and size of clear areas and weed beds, as well as discovering any underwater pathways the fish may use. Pen and paper are useful here to record your findings for future reference.

*A lovely springtime shot of an English estate lake.*

There are dozens of different makes of marker float available to the carp angler. Our favourite is the Fox Weedy Marker model as it is extremely visible and capable of withstanding heavy use. It also has a dumpy but streamlined shape, which makes it very buoyant and enables it to be cast long distances. A good tip when using marker floats in weedy areas is to attach 12in (30cm) of stiff line to the lead attachment. This prevents the float from lodging in the bottom weed on the cast, and ensures that it has an easier passage to the surface. If you decide to use this set-up, don't forget to add the extra length of line to your depth readings.

### Where to Fish in the Weed?

Once you have mapped out your swim and discovered where the clear and weedy areas lie, you will then be in a position to ask yourself: 'Should I fish in the weed or in the clear areas?'

The weed itself will hold profuse

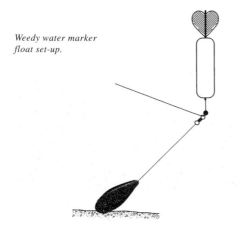

*Weedy water marker float set-up.*

amounts of natural food such as snails, shrimps and beetles, while the clear areas may well be clear due to the fish feeding on bloodworm in the lake bed. Certainly all waters are different but both clear and weedy areas offer the chance of producing carp captures. Your choice of which area to fish is therefore a difficult decision if you have no previous experience of the swim; if this is the case, you should consider the following factors:

**Past capture records** Is the weed a known producing area, or are the clear areas better? Who has been fishing the area before you, and what were their results? Try to find out as much information as you can about your swim through consultation with other anglers who are fishing or have knowledge of the water.

**Your chances of landing fish** Can you successfully hook and land fish from the area, or are you more than likely to lose them? Try to fish a swim which gives you a direct pull on a hooked fish. If the negatives outweigh the positives then you should look elsewhere.

**The behaviour of the fish** Are the fish visibly feeding in one specific area? Do they appear to be feeding in the weed, in the clear areas, mid-water, on the bottom, or in the upper layers?

If you are still unsure where to fish, try each rod in a different area and change if you have sufficient evidence to do so.

## Rod and Tackle Selection

Once you have selected your fishing area you still have to think about what tackle to use.

### Rod

As well as being affordable, your rod should also be able to cope with the hard and fast lunges of hooked carp.

If you are fishing at close range, a rod with a test curve of 1¾lb and a through action would be ideal, but if you are hoping to achieve distances above 65yd you will have to consider rods that give you more power. The development of technology in recent years has meant that far-off weed beds can now be reached by rods which also maintain incredible performance abilities, and the once stereotyped 'stiff broomstick' label for all rods with a 3lb TC has become a thing of the past. This does not mean that all rods of higher test curves are suitable for weed fishing – it merely tells us that some are more appropriate than others. If you are unsure, always ask before you buy.

Whatever rod you decide to use, you should always stay close to it once you have cast out and you should never go wandering off into the next swim if weed is close by. If a hooked fish does become embedded in weed, try to keep steady pressure on at all times and always allow the rod to have some action in reserve. By keeping the pressure steady rather than heaving and jerking the rod, you should eventually, depending on the density of the weed, coax the fish out and into a more manageable position.

### Line

You are certainly going to have to rely heavily on the quality of your line when fishing in weed, so your line has to be strong and durable enough to withstand

*You need good tackle and some good decisions to be successful in weed.*

*Expect to see this sort of activity in the spring at most lakes. This is a shot of the carp spawning at Hull & District's Motorway Pond in 1997. Most of the lake's population of carp were in this area just off the road bank close to the motorway.*

a great deal of wear and tear. There are many lines on the market that are suitable for carping in the weed, but some are definitely better than others. Our favourites include Rod Hutchinson's Sabreline and Hutchy's Monster Line, which is thicker. From our experience, we would not select any line less than 12lb for fishing in fine weeds (such as blanket weed) or 15lb for tough plants (such as the lily beds).

We may also opt to use a braided line, such as Sabrebraid, which is non-stretch. This line will cut through all manner of different weeds very easily and is fairly abrasion-resistant, but we only recommend it to advanced anglers as it can be very tricky to come to terms with. The lack of stretch often results in the hook coming free as the fish bounces around on the end. To play a fish on a short braided line requires skill with either the back-wind or the clutch to ensure there is sufficient give in the tackle.

Lastly, if you wish to increase the strength of your line without having to increase its diameter, Granite Juice by Kryston is your answer. This is a lubricant which is available from most tackle shops. Apply the juice to your line using a cloth and allow it to dry for a few minutes. This is an excellent product for use not only amongst weed but also trees and other snags.

*Terminal Tackle*
Rig safety is an extremely important part of carp fishing and it is essential that all of your rig developments are governed by the safety factor ahead of anything else. By this, we mean that if you lose

*Good strong line helped with this fine 25lb mirror.*

direct contact with a fish through your line parting, the rig you are using must be able to release the lead from the set-up, thus preventing the fish from towing a lead around with it and becoming tethered in the weed.

Following on from the safety aspect, it is necessary to focus on the durability of your rig to ensure that it will land fish rather than just receive 'pick-ups'. Not only is losing fish frustrating for you, but leaving hooks in the mouths of fish through carelessness is not the practice of the responsible carp angler. Make sure that your chosen hooks are strong enough to do battle in the weed whilst also keeping a firm grip on the fish, and that your hooklink will withstand any friction caused through   contact with the weed. Our suggested hooks for weed and snags would be the Hutchy Vice or Precision, Nash Pattern 1 or 2, the Drennan Continental Starpoint, or the Ashima

Super Strong. The bigger the hook the more chance you will have of exerting pressure in the weed without it popping out.

You must also ensure that the lead is positioned so that it is less likely to become snagged. In-line leads are OK for use in weed and have become widely recommended as they do not freely hang from the line, but even they can prove problematic in thick weed. A modified safety clip attachment is a much better way of connecting a lead for use in weed. Simply disregard the tubing and the neoprene sleeve which come with the set-up and use only the clip that houses the lead. Now trim off part of the clip and use. Should the lead become caught in weed, the clip will open out and release the lead very easily, leaving you in direct contact with the fish. This may cost you a fair bit of money for each lead lost, but will certainly catch you more fish. Other than this, a weak link attached to the lead is sufficient. Simply attach the lead to the line via a low breaking strength line such as a 2lb link (if you are fishing at a distance of about 20yd). Obviously this is a little tricky if you wish to fish at extreme range on the cast, and in these circumstances we will normally risk the in-line lead.

### Suggested Rigs for Weed

Let's take a look at some basic rig ideas for fishing in both the clear areas and the weed itself. We will begin with the clear areas.

*Fishing in the Clear Areas*
Without a doubt the clear areas of weed

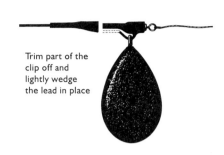

Trim part of the clip off and lightly wedge the lead in place

*Modified Safety Clip.*

beds offer excellent presentation possibilities for the static angler, and in these instances we would certainly try to keep the hookbait looking as natural as possible. Bottom baits would be our preference and, depending on whether or not the lake bed was clear, we would normally use a hooklink which offered the natural presentation of lying flat on the lake bed (such as Kryston Super-Nova). If the lake bed is not extremely clear (for example if there are leaves present which may interfere with the hooklink) we would use a buoyant hooklink such as Kryston Silkworm and a pop-up of a couple of inches (5cm) to keep the rig out of contact with the debris.

*Fishing in the Weed*
If the fish are visibly feeding in the weed, or the clear areas on your lake have been hammered by previous     captures, you may wish to try fishing in the actual weed. An excellent approach is to present your hookbait  actually on top of the weed, and this can be done by choosing a buoyant hooklink such as Kryston Silkworm, combined with a critically balanced bottom bait or pop-up. Rest the hookbait lightly on top of the weed rather than amongst it, by ensuring that your

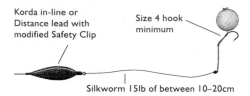

*Clear area set-up.*

hooklink is longer than the depth at which you wish to present your bait (for example, if the top of the weed is 1ft off the bottom use a hooklink longer than this). Other successful methods that have accounted for many carp include fishing a pop-up straight off the lead or using a very light lead and a short link (the lead will not sink through the weed).

## Weed and Snags – a Similar Approach

Before moving on, it is worth pointing out here that all of the tactics and considerations we have mentioned for weed fishing apply equally to fishing near snags – you need durable gear, you must sit close to your rods in the best swim that gives you a direct pull on the fish and you must be positive in your thinking. The main difference probably lies in the fact that with some snags you will need to upgrade your gear to super-heavy. For many overseas venues, where sunken trees line the margins, we use

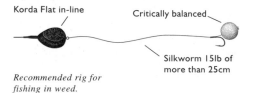

*Recommended rig for fishing in weed.*

35lb main line and hooklinks combined with size 2 Hutchy Precision hooks. For the dreadful conditions which anglers are faced with at Lake Raduta in Romania we would be prepared to go even heavier: we tend to use 50lb monofilament here. Mono is much tougher than braid when it comes to withstanding both cutting and abrasion on buildings and submerged trees, so bear this in mind.

## Springtime Bait

Bait is always a very difficult topic to address as people all have different opinions about which type of bait should be used at which times of the year. Traditionally high-protein baits (usually milk-based) are used throughout the winter with a change to high-energy baits, such as birdseeds, once the water starts to warm up. If you are at the stage in your angling career where you are making your own baits then consider this when deciding upon your mix. In our opinion birdseed-based baits definitely have an advantage over other bases in the spring as they have excellent flavour-leakage properties and also lend themselves well to colouring. Later on in the season we don't find bait colour matters that much, apart from on turbid waters. Throughout the winter and the early part of spring we especially find bright baits to be very effective. They are very easy for the fish to locate visually and our preference is usually to opt for those coloured yellow. Don't worry if you don't make your own bait as there are plenty of excellent ready-mades on the market, in a range of colours and bases. Hutchy's

Fruit Frenzy pop-ups have proved themselves to be very successful on a number of waters, as press reports will confirm, so it is certainly worthwhile trying them to see if they work on your water.

# SUMMER
# GO LOOKING FOR THEM

Whilst all manner of different tactics will work well during the summer months, in this section we will focus our attentions only on the matter of stalking. Summer is that time when the fish can be hunted down by the angler a great deal more easily than at other times of the year, as the warmer water makes the fish a lot more lethargic. Stalking can be one of the most exciting – and also most infuriating – aspects of our sport. By stalking, we mean attempting to catch a fish that you have either searched out, or alternatively know is there. You may have seen a ruffle on the surface of the lake, or some reeds moving as a fish swam through them, but in both cases you know it is there.

It is possible to stalk fish off the top, the bottom, and in mid-water, but the rig has to suit the style of fishing. Generally speaking, most stalking is done in the margins, or within a reasonable distance of the bank. It is difficult to see, let alone stalk, a fish out in the middle of the lake unless it is on the surface, so the methods we will consider only really apply to close-range fishing. Some of the methods, however, will adapt themselves to long-range stalking.

*Found them! Now you've got to catch them!*

## Surface Stalking

In our opinion surface fishing for carp is possibly one of the most underused tactics of angling. We have both regularly fished for carp on the surface for a number of years now, and it is surprising how few anglers we have seen doing likewise. Why this is so we have no idea. It could be down to sheer laziness, as more often than not anglers are required to search out the carp first and then try to tempt them to feed – both of which pursuits require more effort than sitting behind a set of buzzers and waiting for the moment to arrive.

Most surface stalking is done in the margins, or within a reasonable distance of the bank. In order not to spook such fish it is important that the angler is well hidden from view, so we always wear

*Rob with a lovely fish from a small estate lake in Somerset.*

camouflaged clothing when attempting to stalk fish. A good pair of Polaroids is also useful so that any fish can be clearly spotted and not spooked from distance. Our favourites are the Optic Cormorant version with the amber lenses, which are available from most tackle shops.

When fish are located in the summer, they often appear to be in a semi-dormant state and trying to lap up the warmth in the upper layers of the water. However, with the right technique it is possible to tempt them into feeding. Observe the fish for a short while and study their movements before you attempt to apply any floating bait. The wrong move here can result in the fish drifting away, never to return. The fish has to be convinced that the food item is safe and that there is no danger in the vicinity. Keep yourself well back from the water's edge and crouch down. If possible, hide yourself behind any bankside foliage. Never just throw the surface bait in, in a haphazard sort of way, or directly on top of the fish. All this will do is spook the fish and ruin your chances. If there is a ripple present on the water then use this to your advantage by throwing a handful of baits upwind and letting them drift over the head of the fish. This is the best way of applying bait on the surface as the fish is not spooked by any splashes overhead. If, however, there is no wind then apply your baits individually with a short one or two-minute delay between each one. Again, fire these out in the vicinity of the carp and not on top of their heads.

The quantity you fire out depends on the number of fish you have in your swim as well as the pressure they have been subject to. Only your experience on the

*They're about somewhere!*

water can help you here, but as a general guide we would recommend a little-and-often approach as opposed to piling them in. You can't get back any bait which has already been fired out, and so it is always better to work your way up instead of watching your chances fade away as the fish fill themselves up before even seeing the hookbait. Generally speaking, for one fish we would fire out about four or five baits. Our favourite surface bait is Chum Mixer dog biscuits (*see* below) as these can be customized very easily (attractors

*Rob with a fabulous mirror caught from the margins at his feet.*

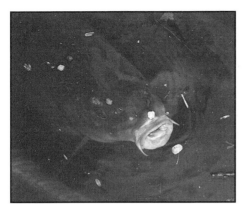

*There's nothing as exciting in carp fishing as seeing a fish take the hookbait.*

*A big mirror in Motorway Pond on the lookout for food.*

and colours can be added). When Chum has been hammered on a water, we will try alternatives like bread, trout pellets or even breakfast cereals.

## Timing the Cast

The next stage of surface fishing is possibly the hardest part, as presenting the hookbait needs to follow a strategic approach. Instead of just firing out the hookbait and sitting and waiting for the fish to find it as anglers may do when bottom bait fishing, we prefer to wait for the fish to be feeding heavily on the bait and then cast out. We try to wait for the moment when the fish are competing for the surface baits. Get the fish feeding confidently on your surface baits by applying them on a little and often basis. When they are feeding confidently and beginning to compete for any remaining few, fire out the hookbait. With this kind of approach you will have developed the fish to a stage where they have lowered their defences. If you had applied the hookbait earlier, the fish may not be at

what we call the 'trigger stage' and would be more likely to notice any danger/ unsafe aspects with the hookbait or rig, resulting in aborted takes. On some of the hard-fished waters in Britain we frequently observe carp taking all the freebies whilst leaving the hookbait completely untouched.

## Surface Presentations

There are a number of surface fishing presentations available. Dapping is possibly one of the most effective. This involves the angler fishing to carp lying beneath branches or snags overhanging the water with the line draped across a branch and the hookbait lowered onto the surface of the water from above. This method eliminates any problems with line-shy fish, but for obvious reasons it can only be used when the fish are in close range. For the hooking set-up with this presentation, simply attach the hook to the line with a simple blood knot. Now place the bait onto the hook, either by side-hooking or with a hair rig. We always favour side-hooking for surface fishing, but we do know of several anglers who prefer the hair.

You can also fish with the bait just resting on the surface, like dapping, in another form of presentation known as the beachcaster rig. This is a fairly technical rig to tie up, but is excellent for long-range fishing or where there are no bankside branches to assist with presentation. It can be difficult to cast out, and you will always need plenty of clearance behind the swim so that a long drop can be laid out behind you. The diagram below shows exactly how to set up the beachcaster rig.

The only other forms of surface presentation we use are what is known as the driftwood rig and the standard controller. As for the standard controller, this involves using a controller float (available from most tackle shops)

attached to a hooklink, much the same way as a standard bottom bait rig. The only difference is that on this set-up the lead is replaced with a float so that the whole lot can be fished on the surface. You can buy controllers in different weights depending on how far out you wish to fish. The hooklink we opt for is almost always a length of main line monofilament, usually longer than 24in (60cm) to ensure that the float is a fair distance from the bait.

### The Driftwood Rig

This is one of the most effective rigs for surface fishing. It is set up in the following way:

1. This rig gets its name from a product known as Driftwood, made by Kryston.

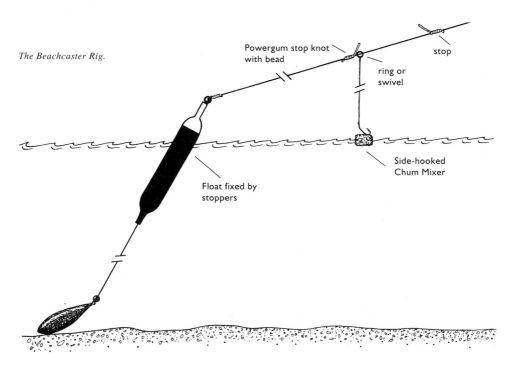

*The Beachcaster Rig.*

Powergum stop knot with bead

stop

ring or swivel

Side-hooked Chum Mixer

Float fixed by stoppers

This is a buoyant putty which can be moulded onto the main line. For most of our surface fishing we use 12lb main line straight through, but because the Driftwood sometimes slips when attached to line only, we advise you to attach a hooklink swivel approximately 24in (60cm) away from the hook.

2. To form the hooklink, simply cut a length of line to the desired length. For a link of 24in (60cm) you will need approximately 30in (75cm) of line. The swivel should be attached between the two lengths with a strong knot. We favour the five-turn tucked blood knot either side of the swivel for all of our mono knots.

3. Attach your chosen hook to the hooklink. Once again we favour the five-turn Tucked Blood knot for this.

4. Take a small piece of Driftwood putty and mould it around the hooklink swivel. You may have to warm the putty in your hands first to make it fit comfortably. Balance the amount of putty you use with the distance you wish to cast as well as with the weight of the swivel you are using.

5. For the hookbait of this rig, especially when using feed like Chum Mixer (*see* below), we favour a cork ball; Nash Tackle make a good model. Alternatively you could try the imitation Chum Mixer which is now marketed by some companies. We may add a drop of flavour to the ball to give it a form of camouflage. If you are using something else, you may wish to opt for another form of hookbait, but always consider the distance you wish to cast and the length of time the hookbait will be in the water. If you do use cork, we have found the best way to position it is nipped through

the side and close to the eye with the main section lying upwards. The Driftwood rig is now ready.

This rig is easy to make and very rarely tangles if set up correctly. It is an ideal rig to use when stalking fish in the margins of lily pads and weed, and because it looks very natural you may witness the fish themselves taking the Driftwood instead of your hookbait.

Depending on the weight of the Driftwood/controller used, this rig can be cast distances of up to 100yd. If you go this far you will need a pair of binoculars to see when the hookbait has been taken.

The length and material of the hooklink is one of the most important aspects of the surface fishing rig. This will always depend on the situation you are fishing (for example, when fishing tight against an overhanging tree – a difficult cast – a shorter link would be easier to use). Perhaps more importantly, the confidence of the fish is another deciding factor, as they may not want to go within 4ft (120cm) of a controller, so you will have to use a long link. Only you can make the decision based on the circumstances you are facing, but we recommend that you start off with a link at least 2ft (60cm) long and take it from there.

**Preparing Chum Mixers**
The most versatile and practical of successful surface baits is Chum Mixer dog biscuit. It has many advantages over other surface baits as it is very easy to use and is adaptable to a number of

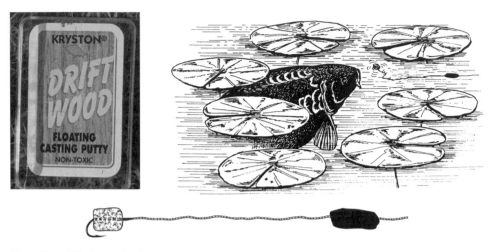

*The Driftwood Rig is excellent for use amongst pads or open water.*

different situations. It is possible to catch carp on Chum Mixer in its biscuit form, but one of the best ways of using it is to soften it and add attractors. The following is a step-by-step guide.

1. Get together plastic bags, a measuring jar, your chosen flavours/attractors and a set of weighing scales.

2. To help soften the Chum Mixers you will need to add water to the biscuit to moisten it. The ratio of biscuits to water is important – we work on the basis of 1lb (450g) of Mixers to 100ml of water. Using your weighing scales and measuring jar, measure out 1lb (450g) of Mixers and 100ml of water. When done, tip the Mixers into a plastic bag large enough to allow the mix to be shaken: for 1lb of Mixers, we use a bag measuring 13 by 9in (33 by 23cm). Do not add the liquid.

3. Add your desired flavours, colours and attractors to the water. Stick to the recommended quantities stated on the

bottles as you would when preparing boilies (say 5ml to 1lb (450g) base mix/dry mixers).

4. Shake or stir the solution to ensure that the attractors are evenly dispersed.

5. You can now add the liquid to the dry Chum Mixers. Make sure that there are no holes in the plastic bag.

6. Fill the plastic bag with air by blowing into it and forming a balloon shape. Seal the top tightly so no air can escape.

7. Shake the bag well so that the liquid is evenly distributed (this usually takes about five minutes). If you are using colours you will know when to stop, as the bag will change from coloured to completely clear. When the attractors are evenly spread, you can let the air out of the bag and fasten the top with a simple knot or elastic band.

8. To allow the Mixers to soften thoroughly, you must now store them overnight in a cool, dark place. When they are done, they will be completely

moist all the way through and will resemble small sponges. Change the bag as soon as they reach this stage and label them for reference purposes. If necessary the Mixers can now be stored in the freezer until you need them.

## Timing the Strike

Seeing the hookbait being taken by a surface-feeding carp is what surface fishing is all about. Watching the fish feeding really gets the adrenaline flowing, especially when the hookbait gets anywhere near the lips of the fish, and especially if the fish is big. Once taken by the fish, the strike of the rod has to be accurately timed. Strike too early and the hook will not be set; too late and the fish will have enough time to eject the bait. The strike has to be so precise that only experience can assist the angler here. If we had to generalize, we would say that as soon as the fish has taken the hookbait, count two seconds and then strike. This is a very good guideline but again it depends on the pressure which the fish have been subjected to. Carp which have been fished for heavily can be very wise and

*A bag of Mixers ready for use.*

uncertain of a surface rig, even if the water is coloured up.

If you are getting problems with fish shying away from your hookbait, try using a finer breaking strain line (within reason) or try Multi-Strand as a link. The latter also assists the hooking arrangement by being more supple than monofilament. You can also try doubling up the amount of baits you have on the hook. On many occasions a double bait fished amongst a group of single baits is sufficient to lower the carp's defences.

## Stalking Fish on the Bottom of the Lake

If you can locate a fish which is browsing around in the margins there is a good chance that you will be able to catch it if it's already on the lookout for food. A good place to start your search is near weed beds, especially pads. In the early part of the year the carp will be heading up to the shallower water and if there are any lily pads in these areas the carp won't be too far away.

Stalking is easier said than done, though, and sometimes you can only put the bait where you think the fish are, or alternatively where you think they will visit. Every now and again we are all in the position where we stumble across a carp feeding in the margins just screaming to be caught. Its tail is in the air as it smoke-screens and digs for food, and it all looks so simple. It's just a case of lobbing a bait out, and away it will go. Right?

Wrong! More often than not we will spook the fish as we stomp off to get our tackle, or alternatively it will bolt out of

*The Motorway Pond's Long Fish off the top at 29lb.*

they do not make any splash at all when they land on the surface of the water, and when they settle they create a carpet of food that the carp will find irresistible.

If you only have a few hours in the evening after work to go fishing, don't spend that time sitting behind a pair of rods hoping for action. Pack some bait and a small tackle box into your car, just take one rod and a landing net, and stalk around the margins of your pool, looking for signs of feeding fish. Dawn and dusk are the ideal times for this, and they are also the perfect times for you as you can fit in a bit of stalking either before or after work.

the area when it hears our lead landing in the margin in front of it. In this situation the best thing to do is to take off the lead completely, as the less splash the better. If that is impractical use as small a lead as you can get away with, or better still some Kryston Snag Safe putty. Putty is our preference as you can flatten this to reduce the splash. It will also pull off the line if you get into difficulties with snags. Always try to use a slack line in this sort of situation, so that if the fish touches it, it won't be as spooked.

If you do get to feed the fish, and it starts to take baits, flick them in one at a time. Broken boilies will make less of a splash on entry and will also sink more slowly and be less likely to scare the fish. One of the best baits to use in this situation is the humble worm. The fish might be feeding on naturals and a boilie might be ignored, but a free-lined worm sinking slowly through the     water is an excellent method for margin browsers. Maggots, too, are a pretty good bet as

## Visible Bottom Feeder Rig

For fishing on the bottom, although we do now and again use free-lining, most of the time we opt for a lift method presentation. This involves using a standard quill-type float which is shotted overweight either with shot or tungsten putty. It is also set overdepth. Once cast out, the line is pulled tight between the rod and the float, so that the latter sits in the upright position. The line is kept in a tight position, with a registration of a bite occurring when the float lifts upwards and comes to rest on the surface in a horizontal position. When using this rig we tend to opt for a small hooklink of approximately 4in (10cm) so that an indication of a bite is received sooner rather than later. What will happen is that the fish will lift the putty or shot very quickly as it upends and then levels out. This will cause the float to rise very quickly, giving very early indication. With this presentation, if done correctly, it is possible to hook carp before they realize what has happened.

## Mid-Water Stalking Rig

A lot of the time it may be difficult to tempt carp down to the bottom or up to the top to feed but, with a little bit of thought and application, there is no reason why you should not catch a fish or two from mid-water.

When they see cruising carp, many people tend to fire out some floaters in the hope that they will be tempted to feed on the surface. Whilst quite often they will, a bait that is presented in mid-water will frequently be more effective than either a surface or a bottom bait. There are a number of methods that can be used when fishing mid-water, including float fishing at a shallow depth, or using a rig known as the zig-rig.

If you choose to float fish for carp, one of the better methods that we have tried is to use a light float with a slow-sinking natural bait such as a large, juicy lobworm. This method of presentation will seem very natural to any carp that stumbles across it, as they are used to

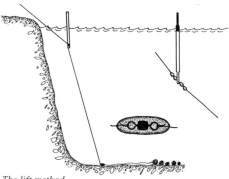

*The lift method.*

insects and other natural food items falling into the water from overhanging trees. It is especially effective as the worm is falling through the water 'on the drop'. The advantage of float fishing is that it is easy to reel in and cast back out to a different spot without making too much of a disturbance in the swim, and, if you can actually see carp in the area, it is an incredibly exciting method of fishing.

If you prefer a static approach and are sure that there are carp swimming around in mid-water, then the zig-rig may be just the thing. This tactic often gets a result when the going is tough and you are really scratching around for a bite. It is especially effective during very hot weather, when the carp are clearly cruising around. We have found that the lakes where it works best are slightly coloured, but not so much that the fish would not be able to see the bait at all. The diagram shows how a zig-rig should be set up. The first thing you should do is plumb the depth of the lake, and hazard a guess as to how deep the fish are cruising. Then set up the rig with a long tail between the lead and the bait, and use a pop-up with no balancing weight. Effectively what you are doing is fishing a pop-up off the lead, but with a hooklink that could be 3, 4 or 5ft (90–150cm) long, or more if necessary. The bait should be a nice, bright pop-up so that it will be easily seen by the carp. If you find that you have problems casting the rig out because the bait touches the floor, simply PVA the link into a concertina and then cast it out. Once the PVA melts it will pop-up to the required depth.

The zig-rig seems to be successful

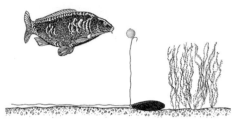

*The zig-rig in action. Go on, take it!*

because the carp stumble across the bait in an area where they are least expecting it to be and, more often than not, will take it out of curiosity rather than hunger. Carp have been known virtually to bump into the bait when they are swimming along at that level and, instead of going around it, they sample it.

Returning to the point of water colour and its effects on the rig, we have found that whilst the fish can see the bait a lot more easily in clear water, they often avoid it earlier. This method is most effective when the carp is more or less surprised by the bait, and just snaps at it instinctively.

The choice of material for the link is entirely up to you, but we have found Multi-Strand and monofilament are the best. Avoid thick and heavy braids like Merlin or Super-Nova, and stick with something that the carp will not see as easily.

## AUTUMN
## GET ON THE WIND

Autumn is renowned for its contradictory weather patterns and continuous leaf fall, which make life on the banks very uncomfortable for the angler.

Nevertheless, autumn is also the period of the year when some outstanding carp catches are made. Like most other fish, carp build up their energy supplies for the onset of winter in the autumn, usually beginning during the first sharp temperature drop. In Britain the first frosts always signify a huge feeding spell around the country, and you can almost guarantee that most of the     bigger fish will come out during a mad two-week spell.

Aside from the initial temperature increase in the spring, we would have to rate autumn as one of our most successful as well as favourite periods of the year. The big winds oxygenate the water following the warm summer months and they tend to stir up the bottom and turn the fish on to feed in a big way. Albeit at lower weights, the start of autumn usually sees the fish at the windward end of the lake, with warmer winds generally being the most productive. We have absolutely no idea why this is so, but we would guess that it has something to do with the     comfort of the fish. Cold winds usually decrease the water temperature, so the fish, being cold-blooded, are shocked into resting up. Warmer winds have the opposite effect and stimulate them into feeding.

Such is the force of many of the first autumn winds that fishing from the offside banks is often more suitable than setting up directly into them.   Besides assisting with casting distance it makes life more comfortable and pleasant for you. If the fish are not to be found at the windward end of the lake, then try looking for them off the wind. At this time of the year the windward end is where the fallen leaves collect and start their natural breaking-down process. As they are broken down into detritus, the oxygen in the water is utilized as carbon dioxide is released. Carp may avoid such areas if they do not provide the necessary water quality, and a significant factor that you will frequently notice is those summer hotspots that are affected by leaf matter in the autumn fade into completely fishless areas. Don't let yourself get caught out by this and always keep your eye on the weather and its effects.

As regards the back end of the autumn, if the fish are not on the wind itself, or off it, then try looking in the snaggy areas for them. Snags are a favourite haunt of the carp as they provide shelter and safety during times of rest. At the end of the autumn the fish will usually come to rest in such areas when their big feed comes to a close and the onset of winter comes ever closer.

## Autumn Bait

In autumn the weather conditions basically determine carping results, as water temperature is usually very unstable at this time of the year. Sharp frosts tend to kill off natural food productivity and the fish are turned towards anglers' baits in an attempt to build up their fat stores for the winter. Fishmeal baits are an excellent choice for the autumn period, and we would almost always opt for a fish oil to be included in our boilie mixes. Effective oils are capelin oil, salmon feed oil or blended fish oil, and we would use about 20ml of oil per pound (450g) of dry mix. We also add a drop of oil to the bag of baits just

before use and make sure this is distributed evenly among the freebies. This is a bit of a messy process, but is very effective as the oil quickly disperses into the water and is an excellent attractor. As another source of fat in the bait, we use ingredients such as white fishmeal, herring meal, capelin meal or salmon fry crumb in our boilies. All are excellent additives and have a proven track record as excellent carp catchers. An ideal mix for the autumn would be:

4oz (115g) white fishmeal
2oz (57g) capelin meal
5oz (142g) mixed bird food
1oz (28g) egg albumin (powdered egg white)
3oz (85g) 30 mesh casein
4oz (115g) semolina

Add the necessary consistency of mix to six eggs mixed with 20ml of blended fish oil and 5ml of Fruit Frenzy flavour. Boil for two minutes.

As at any other time of the year, bait quantity in the autumn is a very difficult subject to generalize on, but more often than not it is much better to start off with

*Damp and foggy – Autumn has arrived!*

smaller amounts and work your way up. If our results are anything to go by, we would use more bait at the beginning of autumn when the fish are confronted with the first frosts, and taper this down as the colder weather sets in.

## End Tackle Selection

The final, and probably most technical, decisions that have to be made by the autumn carper are those concerned with end tackle selection. Fallen leaf matter poses immense problems with presentation, and very often hookbaits become masked by debris and thus prove ineffective. Unless we are both absolutely sure that our rigs are going to be effective, we would never go for bottom baits in the autumn months.

For 90 per cent of our static carp fishing we will use boilies, and in such cases we will create popped-up baits with the use of foam inserts or by microwaving. These are suspended an inch (2.5cm) or so above the lake bed, depending on the density of the debris, and are attached to the bottom with lead shot or, preferably, tungsten putty. Autumn is usually a very windy time so you may be wise to pin your hookbaits down a bit by overshotting them somewhat. At least then you aren't going to have a hookbait that is dancing all over the place!

As a final piece of assurance, we will normally cover the hook with PVA tape to minimize the chances of it catching on the debris. We also never pull back the end tackle once it has been cast out at this time of the year.

# 11 FISHING THE RIVERS

The River Trent in England surprised everyone with a 45lb ghost carp in the summer of 2001, whilst both the River Thames and River Nene have continued to throw up the odd surprise. Whether the floods have been the cause of many of these surprises, or if they are previously unrecognized beauties, is anybody's guess, but for a long time now the rivers have been the talking point of many an angler in search of the unknown. In mainland Europe it has been the same, and many anglers over there are also turning their attentions away from the heavily pressured Cassiens, Orients and Madines of this world, looking for the dream fish which may be hiding somewhere in the miles and miles of river water that can be found in big countries like France. Some of them have been lucky with the odd monster turning up, whilst many have not. Fishing the rivers isn't easy, there is no doubt, so let us see if we can help any of you along the way by considering some of our experiences from over the years.

*Sunset over the River Mayenne in France.*

## TACKLE SELECTION

Playing fish in rivers can be tricky when a lump decides it wants to bolt off downstream. To our cost, we have found out that a lighter rod doesn't particularly help in any way. These days, we tend to use exactly the same sort of gear for river fishing that we use for lakes and all other forms of carp fishing. Our trusty, and they really are trusty, 13ft 3½lb TC Dream Makers are ideally suited for all types of situation, within reason. We've used them for rivers, canals, margin fishing, long-range casting as well as huge reservoir fishing and so on. To be honest with you, whether it is a Nash, Fox or Harrison rod that you use regularly, we'd bet any money that so long as it is one of today's 'en vogue' style rods, it will be suitable for rivers. Most high-profile carp rods these days tend to be all-rounders that are suitable for a variety of different types of water. Just make sure it is loaded with a decent-sized reel that can reach the distances you need to fish at.

On the line front, unless we are fishing at extreme range on the big rivers in France, we tend to only use lines of 15lb or above. We know there will be spots where you can get away with 12lb, or even 8lb lines before any of you start to comment, but because we've suffered at the hands of drifting debris on too many occasions, we only use the heavier stuff now. Our current choice of 15lb line is Hutchy's durable Monster Line, but we have used Big Game and Fox's Soft Steel in the past and found both suitable.

The only other thing left to say on the tackle side of things concerns boats. Whenever we are fishing a river, whether it is here or abroad, we go armed with a boat of some description. Boats come in handy for all sorts of things like searching out potential spots, transporting gear or playing and landing fish.

## FIND THOSE FISH

The hardest part to river carping is locating the fish, which in all honesty, isn't any harder than it is on any water. If you use the usual location skills writers refer to in articles, we promise that you won't have any difficulty finding them. We suppose, the difficulty, or should we say, hurdle, that many people will come across is effort. When you walk around a lake you end up back where you started. When you walk a river bank, you don't end up back where you started, unless you turn back. Some rivers run for miles on end, so checking out the water can be a lot more time consuming.

If you don't like walking, there is always the boat. Before we settle into any swim, we always take a boat trip along the river, or get in the inflatable and drift along with the motor on low power. Apart from saving you time and effort, boats also allow you to examine areas close up or even access them (there are plenty of houses or fields alongside rivers that you can't get into without getting shot at! Don't ask Simon about this, just ask his mates about the scars on his arms!). The times we've been up and down the rivers looking for carp is unbelievable. Along

with Rob's good lady Cath, we once walked about 5 miles to find some carp whilst in France. It took us about four hours as we trudged through fields full of cows, over fences as high as ourselves and through bushes and brambles. With a boat it would have been so much easier, especially since we then had to go back and get the gear, and when we finally got everything to the area we fancied, the fish were on the move!

If our experience is anything to go on, we have found there to be two distinct types of carp in the rivers: nomadic ones and ones that live close to one particular feature/area. Dawn and dusk are two very obvious feeding triggers of river fish. As dusk approaches, river carp have been known to move to areas to feed, and at the end of the night, when dawn arrives, they move to their rest areas once again. In France we could name a dozen different places we have fished where this has happened, and over here in England we could name at least half a dozen. Over in France, it is a saying amongst the river regulars that the nights are better than the days, but obviously this is just a generalization.

The other countries where we've

*Look for the features on the rivers and the carp won't be too far away.*

caught river carp, Canada and the USA, we have never even fished a night, but then again, over there it's slightly different. In Canada we fished the St Lawrence River, which is totally ridiculous, and in the USA we fished the Seneca River for less than two hours, which isn't a very good representation.

The sort of places you will tend to find river carp are no different to the spots you would expect to see them in lakes – overhanging bushes, fallen trees, reedbeds, drop-offs, lily beds, weed beds, or anything which you would class as a feature. Some of our best catches have been taken from where two or more rivers meet, as well as close to bridge pillars, weirs or islands. Another good place to look, and one which we think tends to get overlooked, is anywhere close to moored boats, especially marinas, where they are fixed for long periods of time. For some reason, many anglers tend to think that carp will avoid places where humans are regularly present. Whilst this may be true when it comes to anglers, it goes without saying that if the environment isn't too stressed, the carp won't be too far away. Moored boats offer shelter and warmth for carp. They will also, no doubt, offer food, especially if people on the boats throw their scraps over the side. We know plenty of people who've done well in marinas, so trust us when we say that it's worth putting up with a few questions from the curious non-angling fraternity as you sit there with your buzzers and bivvy.

Whilst all of the above examples are visible features of the river, it's not just a case of slinging the baits out when you come across these areas, and reeling them

*A mid-thirty from the St Lawrence River in Canada.*

in. You still have to find the features amongst the features, so to say. An echo sounder attached to the boat comes in really handy here, as does a prodding stick to check out the nature of the bottom. Drop-offs in the margin tend to be good patrol areas for moving carp, or anywhere where you think the sediments/ food particles will come to rest, like slack areas of water. It's all about doing your research really, very much as on any type of water.

We don't know whether this is coincidence, but the majority of times we've fished the rivers, we have located the carp by seeing them leaping or rolling. It's as if river carp really do love to show themselves. At spawning time, especially, they seem to be very active with their 'shows'. This is the sort of thing we tend to be on the lookout for before deciding where to fish. The only thing you've got to be wary of is that the fish may not stay in that particular place. There are a few times we've set up our gear only to have the carp move out within a matter of hours. This is where pot luck comes in, and whether or not you are willing to work for your fish and follow them with your gear.

Another time of the year when we have noticed carp are very active in the rivers is winter. We have even seen carp moving in ice-cold conditions, travelling fairly quickly from one area of water to another. Winter carp, we find, tend to be a lot more active in moving water than they do in lakes. The fish need to be switched on a lot more to hold position, and as a result, need to keep feeding. We are always amazed that we don't pay much attention to the rivers in the winter, but we suppose it comes down to the enjoyment factor when the conditions are

harsh. We're like anyone else, really, in that we need to have company in cold weather as we hate being stuck in the bivvy all by ourselves. Most of our mates prefer the lakes because they have past capture records to work off and know that the carp aren't some three or four miles downstream of their swim!

The only time of the year we'd be very reluctant to fish the rivers is during times of flood, unless that is, the river is siphoning down. The number of times we've fished them in this country and abroad when the flood water is gushing past and we've failed big style is depressing. We've learned our lesson only too well, and these days we will

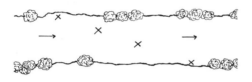

*Situation 1 – A straight section of river.*
*Method – Hookbaits are placed across the river in a diagonal line, hoping to intercept any fish which may pass through. Small groups of bait will work well in this situation, as well as one continuous diagonal line.*

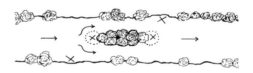

*Situation 2 – An island in the centre of the river.*
*Method – We would pay great attention to the island, and would possibly bait quite heavily around this area. However, don't neglect the margins.*

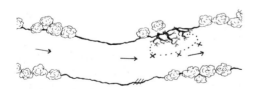

*Situation 3 – Snaggy areas.*
*Method – When fishing to snaggy areas always fish from the opposite bank. Try to fish upstream also, as the flow will usually work to your advantage by forcing hooked fish around in an arc (as long as you keep steady pressure on). Bait heavily on the edge of the snags and place the hookbaits on the edge closest to you.*

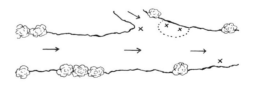

*Situation 4 – A joining river.*
*Method – Place your hookbaits across the river in an arc. Your main baited area should be around the two centre rods close to the opposite bank where the river joins. It is possible that the carp will feed heavily where the river joins, because of deposits left where the two flows meet.*

watch the weather forecast avidly before deciding to fish. One of our mates says that flood water just shuts the carp down completely, but we're not totally convinced by this. We like the thought that it sparks the fish up a bit, a little bit like an energy surge. Because the water is gushing through so fast and disturbing their environment, they end up being more active as they try to keep themselves steady in the flow and in the area they want to be. We think this is connected to the fact that straight after floods, the rivers fish their socks off. The fish are hungry and in need of a repair and refuel.

## BAIT

We rate the location really highly when it comes to the rivers. Bait is important, but we've tried a variety of different baits and have never really come across any favourites for moving water. So long as it catches fish and is a bright colour, we're confident using it on the rivers.

We're currently using Hutchy's Addicted for all of our fishing, and we caught fairly well with this on the Essonne and Seine in summer 2001. In the past, we've done well on Fruit Frenzy ready-mades, Mulberry Florentine ready-mades, Nashy's Squid Mix, as well as Richworth's Tutti-Fruttis and several of our home-made recipes. If we had to select one bait ahead of all others, though, our favourite by far would be particles. We've had such terrific results with maize, tigers, chick peas as well as peanuts that we'd always have a bag of these in the car regardless of which river

we were fishing. We've never found river carp to be very choosy, possibly because they don't tend to get pressured as much as stillwater carp.

The only time we've ever noticed much difference between baits is when we fished the St Lawrence in Canada. We went with a selection of different flavours we were using at the time, but were told by Paul Hunt of Canadian Carping that fruit baits worked best. He was dead right. For some reason the Mainline Fruitella ready-mades or the Hutchy Fruit Frenzies were the only baits we could get consistent action on. Whether this had anything to do with the colour of the two baits we couldn't tell you, but their effectiveness was very noticeable. The Fruitellas were bright orange whilst the Fruit Frenzies were bright yellow.

We do think colour is important on rivers: if the bait is bright, it helps the fish to locate it more easily. We think this is especially important for sections of river that are visited by patrolling/nomadic fish. If a fish is moving from one area to another, usually it isn't going slowly. It knows its intention and needs

*A fabulous 30lb-plus mirror from the river section pictured on the first page of this chapter.*

to be distracted, especially if it has only recently had a feed. Bright baits are one way of doing this, as are big beds of bait, and this is where the particles come in. Particles are cheap and easy to use. A bed of mixed seeds or nuts always seems to work wonders on the rivers, whether it is the Trent, Mayenne or St Lawrence. We also rate the particle pellets like Formula Majic very highly for stopping them. A carpet of pellet is an excellent way of introducing attraction into the swim which lasts for hours. Usually, bits of pellet, once broken down, will drift along with the flow, and come to rest alongside rocks or areas where the carp will root. We always think that if a carp is in the feeding mood, and can taste something it likes, but can't find it, it will eat anything in the nearby vicinity.

The last thing worth noting on bait concerns the water-flow factor. Obviously we should all know that some sections of river are much stronger flowing than others, making accurate, or indeed, any baiting up very difficult. Although carp tend to prefer the slower, meandering type of water, there is no doubt that they also visit the faster flowing areas too. Single hookbaits can be fished effectively in these areas, and they do work well. Glugged pop-ups or bottom baits have produced us a few fish in areas of France, including Simon's biggest river fish to date – 44lb from the Mayenne.

If you aren't keen on the single hookbait thing, then you could always try the method a lot of the French use. This involves attaching an onion sack filled with a load of boilies, tiny particles or pellets to the river bed with a weight or

*A near-thirty common from the centre of Angers in France. You can just about make out some of the street lamps in the background.*

post of some sort. The idea is that this will act as a form of attraction, releasing tiny molecules of food into the area, causing any passing fish to grub around. It works well for the French anglers, but it isn't something we've yet tried ourselves.

## RIGS FOR RIVERS

There isn't a great deal to say about rigs really since we think we all have the common sense to know that where moving water is present, you will need to use a heavy lead to keep your rigs in place. So long as your leads hold bottom, there is no real need for anything fancy. Take a selection of leads with you ranging from an 1–6oz, use a sharp hook, a tough hooklink and you shouldn't be too far off the mark.

To finish off with, we could include a few lines on venues, but because most of us have some sections of river in our local area, we don't think there is any need.

*Two suggested rig set-ups for the rivers.*

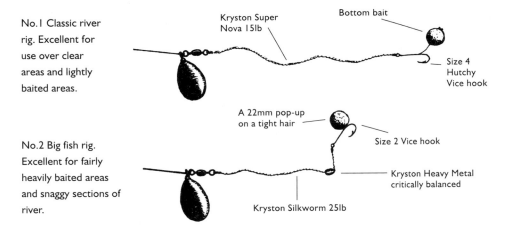

No.1 Classic river rig. Excellent for use over clear areas and lightly baited areas.

Kryston Super Nova 15lb

Bottom bait

Size 4 Hutchy Vice hook

No.2 Big fish rig. Excellent for fairly heavily baited areas and snaggy sections of river.

A 22mm pop-up on a tight hair

Size 2 Vice hook

Kryston Heavy Metal critically balanced

Kryston Silkworm 25lb

The point of fishing the rivers, in our opinion, is to discover the unknown. At the moment there are sections of river both in Britain and abroad that are heavily pressured and well known amongst anglers, leaving miles and miles of yet untapped potential. Some of these previously un-fished sections may well be private, but many are not.

Mark our words, the rivers hold a lot of potential to us all. Our advice is to not let someone else steal the glory first, but instead get yourself out there looking around and try them for yourself!

*Simon cradles a 35lb-plus St Lawrence river common.*

# 12 TACKLING MATCHES

Love 'em or loath 'em, carp matches, otherwise known as enduros, are now an established part of carp angling both in Britain and abroad. Although we've seen it written in one or two of the carp gossip columns that we're big fans of them, to be honest we can take them or leave them. We're not big fans of any one discipline in carp fishing. We just like to enjoy what we're doing and try everything first before we comment on it. Carp matches are not as bad as some anglers would have you believe. They can be a chore at times, but can't all forms of carp fishing? We don't mind nipping down to a lake a few miles down the road and competing in a carp match, even if there is a chance we're going to come last. There's no shame in losing, but we tend to think that some of those anglers who badmouth matches do fear exactly that, which is why matches tend to be on the receiving end of so much criticism.

Simon has fished in twelve carp matches over the years (two World Carp Cups, two Madine Classics, three British Championship eliminators, two British Championship finals plus three Carp Society events). He has got a fairly consistent record in them, which he's proud of, having been part of the wining pair in three of these: the 1996 World Carp Cup (along with Rob), the 1999 British eliminator at Orchid Lake (with Tim Paisley), and the 2000 British eliminator at Tyram Hall (with Tim Paisley). Of the others, he's been in pairings that have come second in a CS regional event, fourth in the British Championship final of 2000, seventh in the 1999 final, eighth in the 2000 World Carp Cup (along with Rob) and part of the six-man Carpworld Team who won the 1999 World Carp Classic team event.

We both enjoy the competitiveness that is an intrinsic part of carp matches. We enjoy the friendly rivalry which comes with them, but most of all, and this is a big plus in our minds, we enjoy the 'after-the-event' feeling, knowing that we have just grafted during the match – a feeling that we probably only experience every three or four angling sessions, but one we get every time we fish in a match. Anyone who has fished in a carp match will tell you the same. When you fish in one, your competitive nature comes through, and you work harder at your fishing. You are always looking for the signs, or the little advantages. How are the fish reacting today? How should I approach them?

*The last fish of the World Carp Cup 1996, when an adaptable approach really paid off.*

Should I do this? Should I do that? We're not going to argue that many of us don't try to read the signs each and every time we are on the bank. We all do. But we guarantee that you'll not do them as often or as thoroughly as you would in a match. There is something about matches that makes you try harder, even if you are unfortunate enough to get a very poor draw in the swim stakes.

## Being Adaptable

We're sure we can all accept that there has to be an element of luck in getting in a 'going swim' in a match, whether it is an out-of-the-bag draw or one which is watercraft. We must say that we much prefer the watercraft draws to the former, though, since there is at least an element of skill involved. We prefer not to fish in out-of-the-bag events, especially overseas. The overseas matches tend to last about a week or so at least; what with all of the travelling, socializing and so on, and when you've returned having spent three days in a swim that you would never have chosen if it was the only one left, you do feel rather let down. It's happened a couple of times to us at Madine, and it takes away a lot of the enjoyment which can be had at matches. At least with a watercraft draw, you get to choose where you want to fish – unless your name comes out last!

Even in a good swim you still have to get your tactics right if you want to be in with a shout of a placing, and this is where being adaptable comes in. There are so many good carp anglers around today that you might only get a very slight advantage from being in a 'going swim' if you are unsure how best to fish it. Too many anglers on today's match scene are capable of pulling out a couple of fish here and there from the most unpromising swim. We can think of several who have done just this: Tim Paisley, Steve Spurgeon, Paul Rayment, Chris Rose, Lee Jackson, Briggsy, Andy Murray, Tim Fromant, Mike Winstone and Ian Poole.

All of these lads are adaptable anglers. They have fished a variety of different venues – waters which are overstocked, understocked, gravel pits, rivers or whatever – learning bits and pieces here and there as they go along. All these types of waters have different patterns and respond better to certain tactics, and being able to draw on previous experiences helps no end, as it will for anyone who is contemplating trying their hand at a carp match for the first time.

## Reading the Signs

For us, the mood of the fish and their location will always be the main factors behind success in carp matches. Being adaptable will give you an armoury of different tactics up your sleeve, as well as a considerable amount

*A carp tops in the far margin. Is it feeding or not?*

of knowledge to go with them. A fish that is feeding will require a different angling approach to one that is not. This is one of the most important points to remember when fishing in matches. You have to think for your fish, and most of all, you have to work for them. The first thoughts that tend to go through our minds after selecting the swim, or being placed in one, are: 'Are there any carp in the swim? If so, how many? Where are they likely to be? What are they doing?'

You always need a different strategy for fish that are feeding, which is a point worth noting because you can mess the whole session up right at the beginning if you decide to approach it wrong. It is a sure thing that the carp will know what is going on around the banks at the start of a match. They will know there are quite a few anglers on the water, and they will be uncertain of a number of things. Perhaps a bit confused. Perhaps a bit on edge. Perhaps neither, but we like to think they are 'a bit more on guard' than normal, which is one of the main reasons we prefer to hang back a bit during the first few hours of an event.

Spods have been widely linked with carp matches and we'll say now what every other carp match angler has said in the past, and that is, a spod is one of the most valuable tools you can have in a match. You should never leave home without one. Use one wisely and you will increase your chances of catching carp. Use one wrongly, though, and you will wreck things big style. We have seen some of the best swims in the world ruined by spods being used wrongly, even at Horseshoe Lake, which is supposed to be the 'home of the spod'. There will be times when you can use a spod straight away, and be able to keep using one, but there will be times when you must hold back. We think the most important time in a carp match is usually at the beginning of the event. If you can sneak out a couple of fish at the off, which is very possible, you can put yourself in a good position immediately. This is one of the reasons why we don't like to plumb around or spod much at the start. We prefer to leave any baiting as late as we can, usually around three hours into an event, but well before dusk starts to set in since the onset of dark is a very good carp-catching time.

### If the Fish Aren't Feeding

At the very start of a carp match the fish have usually switched off altogether since they know something strange is happening around the lake. In these situations we like to use hookbaits only. These are the times when the only way you have any chance of catching is by enticing a fish to sample. Getting an 'on guard' fish to sample can sometimes be very difficult, especially at lightly stocked and well-fished venues, so we can't see any advantages in filling a swim with bait right at the beginning. When a fish isn't in a feeding mood, it isn't going to eat much. It may have a nibble or it might just try one until it feels safer or more hungry, and if it has 200 to choose from rather than one, that is obviously going to decrease the probability of it picking up a hookbait. In a match, you need all the help you can get so you have to bear this in mind, especially if you don't think you're in a top-line swim.

Tempting fish into feeding is very hard

at any stage of a match. Sooner or later, though, the fish will want to feed. It might be in an hour or it might be in a day, which is where things get a bit tricky as you can miss out on a good chance of bagging up if you don't time things right. We usually leave the hookbaits out for the first three hours or so, after which time we start to work a little. We tend to think that if we haven't had a pick-up during the first three hours, the fish either aren't in the swim or we haven't managed to tempt one so they really are on edge.

We will look at the way we tackle swims which we don't think have any fish in later; with regard to tempting the wary ones, if the initial three hours have passed by uneventfully, we generally fire out half a dozen or so freebies or three or four lightly filled spod mixes/pellets in the area of cach hookbait. The theory behind this is that an individual fish is now more likely to see some bait close by. We work on the basis that if a fish isn't interested in feeding, it doesn't do much. It just sits and rests so long as leads aren't landing all around it too often. You have to get your single hookbaits exactly right or the fish in your swim aren't going to find them if they are not moving much. If they do, you may well get lucky. By firing out a few freebies you are at least increasing the chances of them finding some food and tempting them into sampling, which may prompt them to look for a bit more. Remember, this is three or four hours into an event, a time when the fish have usually settled and all of the other anglers have calmed down with their leading/spod disturbances. We are hoping that the fish in our swim will be a little less cautious because of the overall way we have approached things, which in turn may result in them feeding well in the area once they have started to sample. We are trying to create a 'there's another one' syndrome and get them looking. Not only this, but we think that if the bait is lightly spread over a broad area, a fish will approach each bait differently than it would a single pile of bait, such as a stringer or a PVA bag presentation. With a single pile of bait, the location of the hookbait has been found but a fish has to decipher which one it is, something which may take too much effort if it is not in a feeding mood.

We hope we've not lost you with what we've said and that you understand what we're trying to build up to. If we know carp are in the swim, but we're still not getting action, then we will normally sit on this approach for 24 hours. Only then will we start to experiment, for example by baiting fairly heavily in one or two areas. In fact, we might do something completely the opposite of what we've

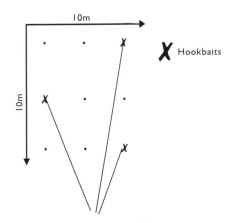

*Spread the hookbaits and freebies about. The theory here is that we are trying to offer an attractive snack to one fish only.*

just said, like trying a PVA bag or something similar. It is all down to the situation, so we can't generalize as they all differ so much. If we start to catch, though, we tend to stick with the 'little and well spread' approach until we think the carp are getting confident, when we'd be wise to get more bait in the area to try to hold them.

### If They Are...

On the other hand, if the fish are obviously feeding when we first arrive in the swim, we will almost always start off with PVA bags or stringers and nothing else. We think if a fish is feeding it is more likely to try a group of baits than one by itself. You can usually knock out a couple of fish with this method if they are feeding, since a lot of the venues used for matches aren't particularly difficult.

We reason that if we catch a couple of fish it's pretty likely that the rest will start to become wary very soon, so we try to bring their confidence back by applying some feed. When this has happened they become almost like children, taking a couple and running away. A couple of spods every hour or so, or a few freebies here and there with the stick is a good strategy. We maintain the bags or stringers alongside them as well, occasionally also applying the same tactics even if we haven't caught. The carp may have singled out the hookbait, which is why no action has occurred, so we would probably try a recast first, then introduce some bait in the same way. You never know, a little bit of bait in the area may lift their confidence.

*Rob with a fabulous-looking Birch Grove mirror during a private carp match between him and Simon.*

### If They Aren't in the Swim

We can only think of one instance during a match situation when we have managed to draw fish into a swim, or entice a take when we didn't think we had many fish there. That was during the British Championships final of 1999 when Simon and partner Tim Paisley had to do something out of the ordinary. Simon and Tim knew they didn't have much to go at so opted to try two different tactics. Tim applied a big baited area out in front of the swim, hoping to attract any passing shoals, whereas Simon focused on the bags and single hookbaits, hoping to attract any roaming individuals. They both knew that Tim was more likely to get a multiple catch, whereas Simon would only get the odd one. As it turned out, Simon ended up catching a 21lb mirror on a bag full of dry groundbait and a 2in pop-up on day two, a deadly method for pulling loners. Before this,

Simon had tried single hookbaits, pellets, glugged baits, zig-rigs, you name it. They came seventh and were the only team to pull a fish from their section of water.

The moral is attract the carp into your swim, or more importantly, to your hookbaits. Cover as many options as you can. Have some roving rods and a baited area. Carp patrol in groups and as individuals. A big bed of bait isn't going to pull you a lone carp unless you are extremely lucky, but a small pile of bait might. The bed is there for the shoal fish, because you never know, they might just pass through – and if they do it is better that the bait is already there. They may not stay for long so you don't want to spook them off by spodding.

## Quality is the Choice

The only other thing we want to look at here is bait. The majority of carp waters of today are pressured throughout the year. Pressured carp react in strange ways during matches, and it is our experience that they tend to prefer the methods that are working well on that water at that time. All waters have 'going' methods and it would be stupid not to get on a going bait or a specific method if the lake is responding very well to a certain approach. We've made that mistake a few times in the past – when we've been told that the fish are on, for example, fishmeals, and we've selected something without any fishmeal in just because we have a lot of confidence in another bait. It's very infuriating

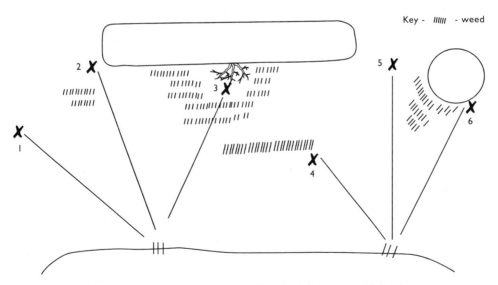

Key - ///// - weed

*Try to cover as large an area of water as possible. This is the best way of finding the fish that aren't showing themselves.*

watching others catch on a bait you haven't got with you but had previously been told was working well on the water. The first piece of advice we can give on the bait front, therefore, is to go well prepared. You'd never see a match (as in float) angler going to an event with just a tin of sweetcorn. He'll have maggots, casters, bloodworm, joker, groundbait and so on. Why so many carp anglers choose to put all their faith in one bait we don't know.

A lot of match anglers tend to use attractive, very visual baits. Ready-mades are very popular, but we think the last few years have proved that quality baits like your Addicteds, MC Mixes, Activ-8s and so on, with low flavour levels, are by far your best choice. When lakes are bombarded with bait during a 48-hour event, the carp can afford to be picky. Quality always prevails, or at least it tends to a lot of the time. That's not to say it's not worth having a bag of bright yellow or orange ready-mades in your bag as well as some pellets, seeds or any particles which can be used. You just never know. We always carry a bag of our old favourite, Fruit Frenzies. During the 2000 World Carp Cup these little beauties pulled us several fish from the chocolate-brown water of Fishabil during a spell when the MC Mix appeared to have dried up on the takes front. It kick-started the action for us once again. We knew the fish were still in the swim, but they had become wise to the MC Mix after 24 hours of pressure.

On the spod front, well, what can we say here. There are hundreds of different ways of making up spod mixes. Our old mate Tim Paisley loves Betaine pellets,

sweetcorn, hemp and chopped boilies, and who's going to argue that it doesn't work? We love tiny seeds like Haiths Red Band, Hinders Parti-Blend or Rod's Formula Majic. There are hundreds of different ways of making up a spod mix, and the emphasis should be on designing something capable of holding the carp in your swim. The smaller the fragments of bait the better, because this gets the carp rooting around almost to the point that they are preoccupied. Pellets are probably the greatest carp bait for doing this. They pull so many fish without causing that scenario we all fear, over-baiting. We don't think it's possible to over-bait with pellets since they are attractive to all manner of different fish species. Some anglers may not like bream in the swim, but you can guarantee that if they are there, the carp won't be too far away.

We could write just as much again on match fishing because it is one of those

*Seventh in the British Championships final of 1999.*

topics you can't wrap up in half a dozen pages. There are so many scenarios out there that you may be presented with, it is so difficult to generalize. We hope that you can pick up a few bits and pieces from what we've said and put it to good use. Just don't get winning too many events, though, because a few of us writers want to be in with a shout as well!

*Fourth place in the BCAC final of 2000 with partner Tim Paisley. This one was our third of the match and weighed almost 28lb.*

# 13 BIG-FISH HUNTING AT BIG OVERSEAS WATERS

How do you go about tackling a large lake? Where do you start and what gear should you use? Where will the fish be and what is the best way to find them? The first thing to do is consider exactly what is a big lake. If you fish small waters like many of the ones in England then anything over 35 acres (15ha) is a big lake. However, if you fancy targeting some of the inland seas like those in France, as many seem to be doing these days, you may not think that your lake is big until it is 2,500 acres (1,000ha) in size.

Carp fishing in large lakes requires a very different approach to fishing smaller ones. For a start your tackle needs to be capable of fishing at very long distance and there are factors that will have a very great effect on where the fish will be. Fish location is one of the most important aspects of big water carping, and when the target is big carp, as it tends to be, it becomes all the more difficult.

## LOCATE THE FISH

There is no point whatsoever in sitting at one end of the water when all of the fish are at the other end. Too many anglers choose where they are going to fish before they actually get to the lake and catch nothing as a result. On a large lake this can be much more obvious than on a smaller one. If you sit in the wrong place on a large venue the carp might be miles away from you and so you will have very little chance of catching.

*Lac de Madine. A big water with some big carp.*

*Our first trip to Chantecoq in 1990. We were caught night fishing!*

## Carp Behaviour in Big Waters

As with rivers, there are two types of carp in big waters. There will always be fish stationary in localized areas for long periods, and there will always be fish shoaled up and on the move. Most of the time, the localized fish will be attracted to features and it is these areas that we both prefer to target first. Past capture records are a major tool for any angler wishing to catch big fish on the big waters. We only have to look at the famous common known as the Bulldozer, which lives in French mecca Fôret d'Orient. This fish almost always gets caught from the same area each year. Or how about the world record mirror in Raduta as another example? This fish, to date, has only been caught three times, and on each occasion from the same swim.

## Finding Nomadic Fish

However, it isn't always easy getting into the 'known' swims because you can almost always guarantee that if you know about them, other anglers will too! This is where having a bit of courage to target the moving/nomadic fish comes in handy

because you can always find a lump or too amongst these as well. Here's a look at a few tips on locating them.

## Head and Shouldering Fish

If we see fish 'head and shouldering' in the same place more than once we would confidently expect that fish to feed in the area where it had shown itself. However, a fish that 'head and shoulders' in two different places is more likely to be a moving fish and is not necessarily going to feed in the place where you have seen it. It sounds obvious that if a fish shows itself in more than one place it is moving, but we would say that if it jumps within 15ft (5m) of the place it showed the last time, then it is likely to feed in that area. If it jumps more than 15ft away from the last spot you saw it then it is likely to be moving to feed somewhere else. In that situation, the best thing to do would be to watch the water to see in which direction the fish is moving. Once you have decided this, it would be stupid to not put a bait in front of it, as hopefully it will come across it and feed.

*Our great friend Steve Briggs with a Madine forty.*

## Listen Out for Movement

It is not just a case of spotting carp jumping, however. You will also be able to hear the bigger ones jumping out, so keep your ears open as well as your eyes. Night time is one of the best times to locate carp on big waters as sound travels much better over water during the night, when things are quiet. Spend a few hours listening for fish and get in the area where you heard them moving.

## Water Temperature Changes

All waters, especially the bigger reservoirs and those deeper than 100ft (30m) or so, undergo a number of environmental changes during the twelve months of a year. In the deeper waters, it is possible for what is known as a thermocline to occur. This is a zone of rapid temperature change, a layer of water between the water below, which is very anaerobic and constant in temperature, and the water above, which is generally warmer due to the penetration of the suns rays. The thermocline usually sits in the upper half of the water, with warmer water resting on top. If there is one at your water, it is likely that most of the food will be in the upper regions of the water, and thus the fish will be feeding in the shallower margins or upper layers. Thermoclines are present in most deep lakes, but will not occur when strong winds are present, especially where there is an undercurrent.

## What If You Can't Find Them?

There is a very good chance that there will be at least a few carp around the visible features of a large lake. Some prefer to hang around the same area for years, and this is why features such as fallen trees are so good. Not only do such areas offer shelter and safety for the carp, but they also house plenty of food such as mussels and snails.

On some of the larger waters, though, especially reservoirs, the bottom of the lake may be very flat and there will not be too many features to attract the carp. If this is what your target lake is like then you will have to make your own feature using bait. We will take a look at this strategy later, as there are a number of things to think about, such as the amount of bait and the style of the baiting pattern, and these points are a subject in themselves.

If you cannot find any fish, and the lake has very few features, then a good strategy is to follow the wind. Carp love to follow the wind, especially if it is a new one, and you cannot go far wrong moving to the windiest end of the lake and fishing with your face into it. Very often the water at the windward end of a lake will have more oxygen in it, and

*One of three forties in 24 hours for Simon from Madine.*

there will also be food items brought down on the wind (such as zooplankton and floating debris). In the margins the bottom will be stirred up with a possible scum on it, and the carp may be found really close in searching for food in these areas.

## BAITING STRATEGIES

There is a good chance that some of you reading this are simply hoping to catch carp from big waters, whatever their size, so we have decided to give you a few pointers on ways to catch both big carp and carp from the main shoals of fish. We will begin with catching carp of any size, and then move onto a few methods which we adopt for selecting bigger fish. You may even find that some of these methods work not only on big reservoirs, but also rivers and smaller waters.

### Catching Fish when Size is Irrelevant

We have found that the main bulk of fish in bigger lakes tend to move around a lot more than in smaller ones, for obvious reasons. They can travel many miles in one trip, but it is possible to stop and hold them in one place if you use the correct strategy. Normally we would do this by making a large feeding area in the carp's predicted path, so if you see moving fish, go a little ahead of them and set a trap that they will come across and stop at, instead of casting or boating directly into the area where you spotted them. You have much more chance of stopping moving fish with an ambush trap that is

set before they arrive rather than by throwing bait directly onto their heads. It is also worth noting that lightly baited areas, using a few pounds of bait, is usually not sufficient to hold a shoal of carp in a swim for very long. One of the ways that you can successfully present bait in this way is to place a large bed of bait, either particles or boilies, in a long diagonal line out across an area you think the fish will move through. Two anglers fishing three or four rods each should be able to cover this area quite well, and by using a diagonal line you will pick up fish swimming in either direction, as well as at different distances. We have found that they will follow the trail of bait to where your hookbait is presented and you should then catch them.

Another of our favourite methods to ambush moving fish is to fish a large bed of bait in a circle with hookbaits positioned behind, in front, and in the middle of the baited area. In this situation we are trying to offer an intense food situation similar to the way that natural food is found in the water (for example bloodworm beds are very concentrated). The idea here is that we will catch the

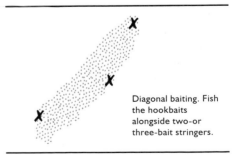

Diagonal baiting. Fish the hookbaits alongside two-or three-bait stringers.

*Bait a long strip in the area you think moving carp are likely to pass.*

fish that are feeding confidently in the area, and also the ones that are just hanging around off the bed of bait deciding whether to feed or just pick the odd one or two baits. This method usually selects one or two of the bigger fish, similar to the baiting pyramid mentioned below.

Another strategy that we have used in the past is to find an area about 15ft (5m) deep near to snags or weed. Crayfish feel very comfortable at this depth in the dark, and we use two different baits in the swim. The first is a soft, smelly bait that we think the crayfish will like. The other is bigger and harder, which the crayfish will find more difficult to eat. Hopefully the crays will happily feed on the soft boilies, and when they do move in to feed, they will attract the carp. This method is a very good strategy if the carp on your lake are put under great angler pressure. The fish should not be as scared by feeding crayfish so they will lower their guard.

## Big-Fish Strategies

Many of the big waters around France contain some of the bigger fish, simply because the fish have places to hide away from anglers and a plentiful    supply of food. All anglers love to catch big carp and one question we are often asked is what tactics to use to target the biggest, or at least bigger, fish in a  water. Unfortunately there is no answer to this question as only luck will allow you to catch the biggest fish time and time again. There are, however, tactics that will help you to cut out some of the smaller fish and thus improve your chances of catching the bigger fish in a water.

All fish in a lake are on the lookout for an easy meal, so it is quite often the case that the fish that are in the majority, usually the smaller ones, will beat the bigger ones to the bait. Do not be too disheartened by this, as the bigger fish did not get to the size they are by watching the other fish feed. Their size dictates that they will have to eat more food than smaller fish simply to maintain their body mass. Large fish are quite

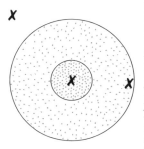

Inner circle = 400 boilies in a 1m radius. Single hookbait as free-offerings. Outer circle = 200 boilies in a 2m radius. Hookbait as free offerings. Third rod = A four-bait stringer 2m past the outer ring. Make the hookbait stand out.

*Intense baiting. Fish the hookbaits in the centre, on the edge of the bait, and outside the area. The outside rod is likely to produce the bigger fish regularly.*

*A long and very powerful fish of 35lb for Rob.*

often loners or stick with at most one or two other fish of a similar size, so once they have been located, they can sometimes be quite easy to catch.

All the following methods are effective strategies for selecting the bigger fish from your water and have a proven track record.

## Selection through Large Bait Rigs

This is a method used by most anglers when trying to avoid the smaller occupants of the lake, on the principle that if the bait is too big for the fish to get into its mouth, it will be left until the big one turns up. This method is quite often successful for selecting bigger fish, but remember that if you are going to use big hookbaits, you will need to increase the size of your hook also. We use size 2s with anything over 20mm, as smaller hooks can be masked by bigger baits very easily if using a long hair rig.

## Selection through Multiple Bait Rigs

Another popular method for big carp is the use of multiple baits on the hair rig. Most people use just single baits on hair rigs, but if the method has not been used on your water before, try using two or three baits instead. The principle is very similar to the one mentioned above, in that the smaller carp will only be able to mouth the set-up and not get hooked. The bigger fish, on the other hand, will be able to pass the multiple baits deeper into the mouth and at the same time get hooked. Whilst we have found this

method to be quite effective for bigger fish, it does present an awful lot of false indications when the smaller fish have picked up the hookbaits and not become hooked. In this case, you will often find yourself striking at nothing when a take occurs. We prefer using bigger single baits rather than multiple baits, but multiples can be effective if the carp have become wise to big baits.

*Big fish angler and great friend Steve Briggs with a big St Cassien common.*

*You can catch them in the margins as well!*

### Baiting Principles

A good method of fishing large baits is to feed the swim with large amounts of smaller baits, say 14mm boilies. Now fish a larger hookbait of 30mm at the side of this baited area. The action of the smaller fish in the swim will quite often attract the larger ones in, but we have found that they frequently hang around on the edge of the baited area picking up a few baits here and there before feeding confidently.

Conversely, on another water we found that it was the kiss of death to bait the swim at all, as all this achieved was to bring hordes of smaller fish into the area of your hookbait. A single bait cast into a known producing area will be less conspicuous than a baited area, and a larger fish will have just as much of a chance of finding the bait as a smaller one.

One final method we will mention in this section is the baiting pyramid. This involves developing a swim over a period of time. The theory is that when the bait is introduced into a swim, the first fish that come into contact with it are the smaller ones. These smaller fish, in turn, attract bigger ones into the area

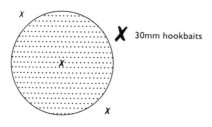

30mm hookbaits

*A circular zone is baited with 1,000 14mm boilies. The small fish will normally be attracted to the baits first, usually feeding all over the area, whilst the big wily fish will hang about on the edge.*

by their feeding behaviour and, eventually, the largest fish will arrive and feed. Whilst we haven't always found it to work, this is an interesting theory and worthy of putting to the test every now and again.

## BAIT FOR BIG-WATER CARP

There isn't really much to say about bait choice for big carp in big waters other than one important point – use top quality! Let us exlain ...

It is very likely that a large part of the diet of the fish in big waters will be natural food, and so bait selection is very often an important factor behind success; especially if the water has seen a lot of angling pressure over the years, as most have these days. The big carp in a lake have usually been around for many years and will have encountered numerous different types of artificial baits. In some cases, most of the big fish will have been caught on such baits and thus developed an awareness of danger from those used over a long period. Carp learn through association and the matter of baits 'blowing' (becoming worse over a long period) has been proved time and time again on some of the pressured waters around Europe. Instead of wasting time and effort with the cheap 50/50 mixes that used to be all the craze for visitors to big waters because they were cheap and easy to obtain in large quantities, most successful anglers nowadays prefer to opt for high-quality baits, such as those marketed by the top bait firms like Hutchy, Mainline, Nash, Nutrabaits and

*Not a big fish on a global scale, but certainly a biggie for the target lake. Rob with a Fishabil mid-thirty.*

Carp fishing at big waters is not that difficult. The fish are more often than not easy to catch once you have found them, and the capture of a big fish from a large water can be a very satisfying feeling indeed. Just bear in mind, not only all we have mentioned above, but also everything which we have considered in earlier chapters – and in the next, Chapter 14. 'Cutting down the angles' is possibly the next most important topic to consider behind location when tackling big waters. This involves making sure your tackle is capable of detecting a pick-up on the rig, something which we are sure you will agree is vitally important when fishing at a range of 300yd.

so on. You can guarantee that the main baits by these companies will be geared towards catching big fish at all types of venue. The chemists and bait buffs working for these companies will know which ingredients have a habit of pulling big carp and which have a proven track record. Such baits include Addicted, Grange, NRG, MC Mix, Squid Mix, Trigga, Formula One, and a host of others, all with their own little touches which help to make a bait special.

In short, if big fish is your target on big waters, then go top quality and pay that little bit extra – we promise you won't regret it. Big carp in big waters don't always need to sample anglers' baits. All sizes of carp will like quality bait. Choose a cheap alternative and you can almost forget catching a biggie if it has been out a few times in the past. Put the odds in your favour, because if you don't then luck is all that you will have on your side.

*Christian Finkelde with a Chantecoq mirror caught 300 metres from the bank.*

# 14 CUTTING DOWN THE ANGLES

We think it's fairly safe to say that no one is totally sure of what is going on under the water whilst carp are gorging at our baits. OK, recent videos have shown us what can happen on certain waters, but all carp feed differently – some are confident, some are not; some run when hooked, some do not.

One thing we are sure of, though, is that carp frequently mouth and eject our hookbaits without the slightest indication at our end. With the vast amount of rigs available to us today, one would have thought that this mouthing and ejecting of baits would be a thing of the past, but, unfortunately (or fortunately, depending on how you look at it) it is a part of carp fishing that will stay with us for many years to come.

Great time and effort must go into the designing of these rigs and it is obvious that many people have different opinions and reasons for their rig design. This can easily be seen in the latest magazines or books that are around. We bet there is one article per issue on this topic. Confusing? We know!

One area that does not get as much coverage is that of the rod set-up. Once you've got your new super-rig into position, it is no good if you are not getting as sensitive indication as possible at your end of the tackle. Too many anglers today neglect the importance of the set-up of the rods. By this, we do not mean how good it looks, we mean how sensitive the set-up is between us and the business end. Many anglers fall into the habit of setting up their rods in the same way every time they are on the bank, whatever the situation. In some cases, it has become common for the angler to practise what he/she reads without considering as to why and when the author uses such tactics. If Joe Bloggs fishes with his tips in the air and is catching fish, then Joe Bloggs may have reason for setting up as such. Anglers should never be all too quick to copy what others are doing without considering why they are using

*It is sometimes necessary to fish with the rod tips up in the air to avoid obstructions, but try to keep the angles in the line to a minimum or you will suffer bite registration problems.*

it first. If you jump in without thought, your fishing could be affected for the worse.

We once approached an angler on a water renowned for line-shy fish and asked him why he was fishing with his rod tips in the air with backleads under the tips of his rods. He replied that he felt confident fishing that way as looking at his set-up gave him confidence. In other words, he felt good because he thought it looked good. This same man, later on in the day, had a take that screamed off and when he connected with the fish it was somewhere in the region of 10–20yd away from the original position of the hookbait. This happened to the chap on numerous other occasions, and he swore at the time that some of the fish were on the same steroids as Ben Johnson because of the distance they had moved in such a short space of time.

Now, what we think was happening, and this has been proven to us following many hours of testing set-ups in Simon's pool and from the garage roof, is that the more angles you have in your set-up, the less sensitive it can be, and the greater the angles are the worse it is.

Many times we have watched anglers fishing with backleads right under their tips, with an angle present between rod tips and line, only to receive a couple of bleeps on the alarm. The rod has been left and the indication put down to line bites or something else, such as bream knocking the lead. In some cases this may be so, but in many we believe it is not and we are sure that if the set-up was made as sensitive as possible, many of these indications would be turned into confident takes that could result in

personal best sessions, especially when fishing at long range.

From our tests we discovered that when using a set-up with many angles in it, a fish that picks up your hookbait and bolts off to the side can often result in a delayed indication. One reason for this is that in such a set-up an angle is created to the side, to which the fish may move without it registering immediately. If this occurs, only when the fish starts to move away from the angle will it register fully, and by then the fish may be 10yd or more away from the original position of the hookbait. If a fish has a chance to move more than 10yd to the side without registering on the indicator, then something is surely drastically wrong.

Using the same set-up, a fish that picks up your hookbait and does not bolt off but moves the lead a short distance can

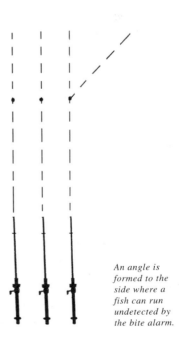

An angle is formed to the side where a fish can run undetected by the bite alarm.

result in no indication at all. During our tests, we could actually play about with the lead without it registering immediately. Not always, but often enough to make a difference between fish or no fish on the bank.

To enhance your set-up's sensitivity to an indication of a fish moving the lead or the hookbait, it is better to cut down the angles along the path of the line. We use monkey climbers, bobbins or swingers because they create an angle in the line so that a pull from the terminal tackle can be registered. The sooner this indication is registered, the better, but if there are angles in the line before the indicators, this signal can often be delayed. In our tests we found that when there are more than two angles in the set-up, the initial pull on the line is registered at the first angle before any other. The reason this happens is that the pull from

the terminal tackle forces the line to straighten between the lead and the rod tip. To prevent this from happening, point the rod directly down the line towards the backlead to cut out the angle between the rod tip and the line. This, we believe, is the best way of fishing backleads as almost maximum sensitivity is obtained.

When using backleads, we prefer to use one as light as possible, but we have found that the weight of the backlead needs to be adaptable to the indicator being used. If it is not, there is again a chance that it may move first. What happens is that it tends to lift off the floor as the line tries to straighten, often resulting in no indication until it is at its highest point. The use of a heavier backlead would be better for indication, but this is impractical as, on a take, the

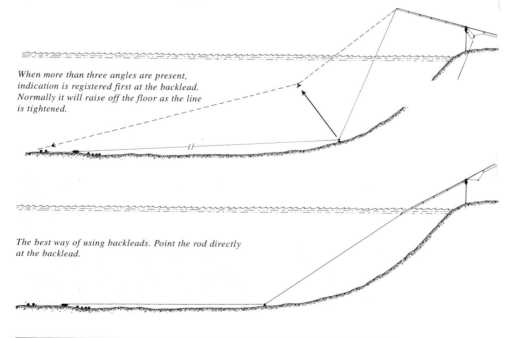

*When more than three angles are present, indication is registered first at the backlead. Normally it will raise off the floor as the line is tightened.*

*The best way of using backleads. Point the rod directly at the backlead.*

power of the strike at the terminal end would be used to lift the backlead. The closer the backlead is to the tip, the more power is required to lift it. We have seen people fishing at 150yd or more with heavy backleads only to lose fish because of the backlead pulling the line down. The reason we keep our rods up whilst playing fish is to pull the hook upwards. If a backlead is weighing the line down, then this height is obviously reduced. The best weight of backlead to use would be one that could just hold bottom and allow the indicator to move freely. This weight will vary depending on the weight of your indicator, so you will need to carry out tests to perfect it.

Backleads are an essential part of our tackle, but always try to minimize the angles in the line that they create and try to use the best weight suited to the indicators you are using.

Another angle-creating method that is widely used and copied is fishing with rod tips in the air. Many people today fish like this even when they have no reason for doing so. The angle which is created between the rod tip and the line has a detrimental effect on the sensitivity of the set-up. Often a pick-up is only indicated by the twitching of the tip, with no register on the bite indicator itself. This is fine if you are fishing for rod knocks, but many people prefer to fish for an indication on the bite alarm rather than sit looking at rod tips for ages on end.

We have both caught fish that have only registered at the rod end by twitching the tip. Had we not been alert at these times, we believe that the fish may have had enough time to have shed the hook without the slightest indication.

Again, we are not intending to criticize this method. It is an invaluable way of fishing over gravel bars, snags or pads without causing damage to the line, but the message here is, do not fish like it without good reason for doing so because it does have drawbacks.

The indication of drop-backs when there are angles in the line is no real problem. This type of indication works in the opposite direction. Instead of pulling against an angle, the initial indication is at the area where weight is pulling the line down. This is usually at the bobbin, but if the backlead is left hanging from the line in mid-water whilst the rod is not pointing straight down the line, it may be registered at this point first.

We are not saying that everyone should change their set-ups to remove all the angles as, although this would enhance the sensitivity of the set-up enormously, it would be impractical in certain cases. What we are saying is, more thought should go into rod positioning before casting out.

*Rob with a cracking mirror that registered just two bleeps on the alarm.*

# 15 PIONEERING

Discovering new waters that contain sizeable carp that have never been fished for before has to be one of the most interesting as well as adventurous forms of carp fishing. Unfortunately, pioneering is an area of fishing which very few have the chance to partake in and is becoming increasingly difficult. Carp waters are being snapped up very quickly, and in the modern era anglers have nowhere left to turn to for the unknown in their home countries. This is certainly the case in Europe where our beloved sport is most popular, but there are still plenty of waters in far-off lands, such as South Africa, which almost certainly contain previously uncaught fish.

The mid-1980s were a historical time for carp fishing in that the discovery of big carp in the south of France at Lac de St Cassien unearthed possibly the most famous carp water of all. The water contained big carp, many of which had never been caught before, and started the boom in European carp anglers looking for previously unfished waters.

One of the most famous carp waters to have been discovered in recent years is Lake Raduta (Sarulesti) in Romania. In May 1998 the lake produced a new world record carp of 82lb 3oz, and it is fast becoming the mecca of world carp fishing, a far cry from when the lake's carp were first discovered by Austrian carp anglers Helmut Zaderer and Thomas Angerer in 1997 following the advice of a friend.

Since that first trip, the lake has been visited by anglers from all over the world, and has been responsible for numerous big fish. We first visited the water in May 1998, as members of a party of five anglers from the Rod Hutchinson and Carp-Talk stable which also included Rod Hutchinson, Kevin Clifford and Mally Roberts. Although the group were not the first anglers to ever fish for carp there, we were the first British anglers to do so, which in itself is a form of pioneering as a real picture of the lake can never be gained from articles and conversations in another language.

In this, the final chapter of this book, we wish to share the story of our first visit to this historical water. Hopefully it will give you an insight into what we consider to be the ultimate form of carp fishing – that of chasing big carp at a water which you know very little about.

## ROMANIAN ADVENTURE – FIFTEEN DAYS IN MAY

It is every angler's dream to be one of the first to fish a water that contains monster carp. Between the dates of the 2 and 17 May 1998 we were both fortunate to be members of a team of five British anglers who visited the Romanian superwater known as Lake Raduta – the venue which is fast becoming famous amongst carp anglers world-wide for the capture of the infamous 1998 world record carp, as well as having produced five different fish over 70lb up until the start of 2000.

Following four or five months of solid preparation, the trip began on Saturday 2 May when 'Captain' Kev Clifford, Rod Hutchinson, Mally Roberts and Simon set out from Humberside airport to meet up with Rob at Schiphol Airport in Amsterdam. From here, we were to fly direct to Bucharest where we would arrive in the early afternoon. If we were lucky, we'd be in our swims and fishing for the evening that day.

We were full of anticipation when we arrived at Schiphol and met Rob without problems. He found us all sitting on the floor in the departure lounge singing songs and dreaming about what was in store for the two weeks ahead. For Hutchy, arriving at Schiphol was a great relief, as it meant that the first of our four flights had been a safe one. Anyone who knows Rod will know that he absolutely dreads flying and that he is never happy until the plane comes to a standstill at the terminal.

We were travelling with twelve French lads who were fishing the lake as members of a Media Carpe team, and included with the bunch was our long-time friend, Ludovic Dyevre, who was going to be fishing the lake for a week. He would pair off with either Simon or Rob during the first week so that our group could spread out around the lake in three pairs.

The trip to the lake via car was as rough as you could have ever imagined. We all had an idea that Romania was not going to be as well developed as the western side of Europe, and we were right. The roads were awful. Every 200yd or so there was a whacking great pothole. We would just

about get up some speed when the van had to slow down again. Secondly, there were broken-down cars everywhere. It was as if Romanians simply abandoned their cars if they broke down, never bothering to return. The journey to the lake would probably have taken less than 30 minutes on a British road, but in Romania it took us over an hour.

## ARRIVAL AT THE LAKE

When we arrived at the lake we were met by Robert Raduta, the lake owner, after a short wait. He'd been around in his speedboat, eyeing up some of the potential spots. According to him it had not been fishing well the previous week. There'd been only a handful of fish out to fifteen Belgian anglers, the biggest weighing in at 45lb.

Following the greetings and the introductions, he invited us into the hotel, which lay on the banks of the water. It was here where he was to give the group an introduction to the lake and where he thought we should fish. It was an impressive building compared to the surroundings. We couldn't see most of the lake from here, though there were at

*The fabulous Raduta hotel. Our first sight of the venue.*

least three villages lining the otherwise barren and open banks that we could see.

Pictured on the walls inside the hotel were some impressive-looking fish, but the main attraction was a stuffed 78lb mirror. It was enormous. The fish was caught in April 1997 and at the time was the second biggest carp ever caught on rod and line. Robert Raduta told us he had caught the monster whilst fishing from the bank near the hotel. He was stunned when the beast took off with his maize hookbait. The enormous king carp in the lake were known by Robert and the locals who fished there, but none of them had any idea what would follow after this historic capture. Robert told us later that since the biggie was caught, he has received faxes and letters from all over the world about fishing for the carp.

We were in the hotel for somewhere close to an hour when, along with our gear, we were driven to the dam end of the lake. It was here, we were told, that many carp had been seen the previous week. According to our hosts, we would be in a cracking spot and likely to catch. We had mixed feelings about the advice because we wanted to have a good look around the lake before choosing where to fish. Instead, we were being driven to an area without applying what we considered to be our full effort. None of us argued, preferring to follow the advice and then take it from there; after all, we had two weeks ahead of us.

## SLOW BEGINNING

The area of water by the dam probably covered 300 acres (120ha). It was barren and there were no trees whatsoever on the banks. It looked featureless as well as lifeless. There were a couple of French lads already bivvied up along the south bank so the first thing we did was pay them a visit and try to decipher what was what. During the two days they'd been fishing they had lost one fish in some snags, but not seen a thing. We found it hard to believe that no fish had been showing as the weather was fairly warm. We had also been informed that the water contained a massive head of grass carp: 2 million, we were later to find out.

It was the grass carp we were to see moving first. Simon noticed a huge splash out of the corner of his eye, some 300yd away near the opposite bank. At first the lads didn't believe him, but then they all witnessed fish coming up all over the area of water. The place looked alive with fish and we were soon setting up our gear at intervals around the lake. Rod and Mally chose to fish a beach-type area averaging 6ft (2m) deep about 100yd out. The echo sounder revealed it to be completely featureless. Rob teamed up with Ludo and opted for a point 400yd to the left of Rod, whilst Kev and Simon

*What's that in the swim Ludo?*

decided to try an uncomfortable, muddy area on the opposite bank where loads of fish were showing. It was a strange sight watching the fish show in this area, as all you could see was a massive splash on the surface and nothing else. We later found out that this was the grass carp feeding in the upper layers. Amongst the grassies, there were one or two proper carp head and shouldering, decent-sized ones as well.

The night passed uneventfully for us all apart from Rod, who'd had a couple of aborted takes. None of us had caught, and there had only been one take on the lake: a 22lb common.

As the morning moved on, we all met up for a meeting. Rod and Mally were happy with their spot for another night, but the rest of us decided to have a good look around neighbouring parts of the lake. We covered about a quarter of the lake with an echo sounder, and discovered that whatever you saw on the surrounding land, you would find in the water. If you saw bare land, the lake next to it would be featureless. If you saw trees on the land, there would be trees in the water, and if you saw buildings, there would be buildings in the water. It became obvious that the lake was exactly as Robert had told us, simply a flooded valley.

After half a day of rowing about, four of us decided to cover some nice-looking areas close to one of the villages. Ludovic and Simon would try off a point which had a lovely 9ft (2.5m)-deep clear plateau running out 100yd, surrounded by sunken houses in 20ft (6m) of water. Rob and the 'Captain' went opposite, near to a pylon where we'd seen a very big carp

*View from the opposite bank to the hotel.*

top earlier in the morning. The plan was to cover as many features as possible and search out the areas where the fish would pick up hookbaits. The hardest thing about being one of the first anglers to fish a lake is that you have very little information to go on. The fish could change at any time as there was no fixed pattern of their behaviour.

It was hard graft those first few days, and we were forming the impression that the lake did not contain a vast head of carp. We knew that once we'd found the fish there would be no problem in catching them. It was just a matter of getting it right.

We hadn't got it right yet, though. Over the next two days none of us caught, and we found ourselves scratching our heads. It was only when Ludovic banked the first fish at 15lb that we thought things may be on the up. Following this capture, Rob and Kev moved in next to Simon and Ludo, opting for a small bay that was filled with an incredible assortment of features. Mally and Rod also opted for the same bank, but favoured an area where the 22-pounder had been caught on the first night.

The weather had been fairly mild to

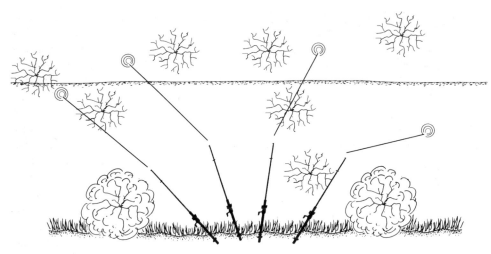

*A view of Simon and Ludovic's swim.*

this point. Day four, however, brought our first taste of Romanian wind and rain. The heavens opened and white-capped waves appeared all over the lake. There was the odd bit of lightning mixed in as well. Thankfully the bad weather didn't last long, but the fishing didn't improve either. By this time, Ludo and Simon had moved a mile or two around the corner to an area opposite the hotel, where there were plenty of sunken trees present. This was a bit different to the area they'd been fishing, which had underwater houses and cars. That was a horrid place to fish and the group were surprised that Ludo had landed his solitary fish. Both Ludo and Simon were getting cut off on the retrieve by the hundreds of sharp bits of metal which were coated with mussels and scattered all around. Rob and Kev were also suffering with the snags and over the next couple of days surrendered three fish to them. The group had all started off on 32lb braided line, but ended up using 40lb and 60lb mono with a 90lb

Tortue sea braid shock leader. It was heavy stuff, but the rigs were safe since we were squashing the barbs down on the hooks, and we subsequently found out that it did the job.

## FIRST CATCH

The change of gear was like a breath of fresh air, and day six brought an historic moment for the group. The 'Captain' banked the first Lake Raduta carp to a British angler. The common picked up a Rod Hutchinson Monster Crab hookbait which had been fished just short of some snags at 50yd range and put up a good account of itself. It turned the scales to 28¾lb and was the start of better things to come for the Hutchinson/Carp-Talk team.

Over the next three days, Rob and Kev banked another couple of fish to upper twenties, whilst Ludo and Simon located a shoal of commons in some snags just

*An historic Raduta fish. Kev Clifford with the first ever carp to a British angler from the lake.*

in front of the hotel. At first they'd tried fishing for these fish from a point to the side of the snags, but to no avail. They had success, however, when they moved right in the middle of the snags where they could get a direct line on the fish. The area was absolutely stuffed full of carp. They'd found them during a hot spell when the water went flat calm. Drifting amongst the snags in a boat, they could see the large shapes amongst the trees. The area had obviously been a wood at one time, but the flooding of the valley had turned it into a haven for the carp. The snags looked a bit daunting, though, as in areas the trees were top to bottom in 25ft (7.5m) of water. They were also closely packed, so it was going to have to be 'hook and hold' tactics for Ludo and Simon.

The location of the fish in front of the hotel brought Ludo and Simon ten takes during the next twenty-four hours. Ludo was due to leave on the Saturday morning, and his last twelve hours brought him six fish to 37lb. He also lost a couple of fish on the snags, but the heavy gear was holding firm. All of his fish weighed over 20lb, with a brace of thirties coming in less than half an hour. His face prior to this little spell had looked dejected. We think he'd expected to be going home with a couple of seventies under his belt. Thankfully, the water rewarded him well for his efforts over the last day, and he left a happy man at midday on the Saturday. All of his fish fell to maize, popped-up an inch or two off the bottom, and presented over a couple of pouchfuls of feed. The two takes Simon had during those twelve hours resulted in a common of 23lb and a lost fish, which he'd estimated at near 40lb. Needless to say, Simon stayed put for the immediate future and continued to catch well on the Saturday, which

*Ludo with one of two commons in excess of 15kg on his last night.*

really was warm.

Over the next twenty-four hours Simon banked three fish, all over 20lb, the biggest a grotesquely deformed and spawn-bound common over 40lb. The group felt a little bad for Ludo at this point. He knew that Simon would continue to catch well from the spot after he'd left.

## DETERIORATING WEATHER

The start of the second week brought a change in the weather conditions. The Saturday had been very mild with sunny spells all day, but the start of the   Sunday brought cloud and rain. After banking the 40lb common just after Ludovic left, Simon proceeded to lose the next three takes due to the snags. He wasn't fishing very far out, and each take that he received saw him running down the left-hand margin to a clearing, trying to prevent the fish from reaching a horrendous snag between him and where he was placing the hookbaits. It was a horrid snag which angled 45 degrees facing forward. Any fish which went round it were almost certainly lost, so he had to run as fast as he could to the left whilst at the same time keeping the line as tight aspossible. The strategy worked a couple of times on the Saturday, as after losing the three fish on the trot, he managed to squeeze a 24¼lb common out to back up the forty.

The change in the weather on the Sunday saw the 'Captain' and Rob on the lookout for a new swim. The previous forty-eight hours had brought them no

*What a monster! Not Simon, the fish!*

joy apart from lost fish. They were getting a bit fed up with the hazards and decided that they'd be better off somewhere else. Besides, the wind had turned to a strong blow from the Black Sea which, according to Robert Raduta, was the warm wind that usually turned the fish on the feed. The area they chose was an open area of water which had been fished by some of the French lads the previous week. On that occasion, no fish had been caught, but the two Brits were confident of a fish because a local angler had accounted for a 35lb common from the same spot the night before. Like many of the swims on the water, it was packed with snags approximately 80yd out. These were mainly old buildings with horrendous metal structures lined with sharp mussels. Hookbaits would have to be placed just in front of the snags if they were to have any chance of landing fish. This proved to be a bit of a problem, though, as the wind really was blowing and creating a huge bow in the line which was effecting the sensitivity of their set-

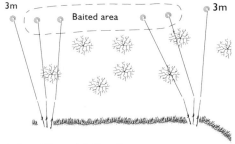

*A view of Kev and Rob's swim.*

ups. So strong was the wind, that the 5oz Korda Flat Pear leads they were using were being dragged into the margins after an hour or so in the water.

It was at this point that 'Captain' Kev was dragged off by Robert for a spot of zander fishing. All week he'd been told about the quality of the zander in the venue, with Robert promising to take him on the Sunday afternoon. He disappeared for about two hours, only to return with a very, very impressive catch. The biggest of the short session weighed in at 8lb, with the catch totalling over forty fish, most of which were killed for food.

By this time, Rod and Mally were hard at it on the point, but to no avail. Simon was still in front of the hotel, where the rain from the afternoon had turned the banks to mud. The cooler weather had turned the fish off also. He'd had no action since the early hours of the morning, when he lost two further fish to the dreaded snag.

At five o'clock that afternoon, Robert, along with French angler Guy de Restrapo, came speeding into Simon's swim with the boat. He wondered what was going on, as they appeared to be in an excited mood. It turned out that Robert

had been speaking to an English guy on the walkie-talkie system which each angler was issued with, and had been informed that he'd been amongst the fish. They obviously thought it was Simon, which it wasn't, so as soon as Simon had reeled in, he grabbed a lift from them and headed off in the direction of Rob and Kev's swim. Upon  arrival at their post, which took all of four minutes in Roberts high-powered boat, the group could see the smiling face of Rob. As soon as Simon was out of the boat, Rob came bouncing over to him full of confidence.

'What you had?' Simon shouted to him. It was difficult to hear one another due to the strength of the wind. It  really was hacking into our faces. Rob replied by shouting: 'I was sitting there looking out of the bivvy in a really fed up mood. Nothing was happening and I was thinking to myself how bored I was. The weather's crap, and so's the fishing. Suddenly, one of the rods burst into life and I was playing a 44½lb common. I

*Rob with his first chunk at 44lb.*

*His second one which weighed in at mid-thirties.*

sacked it up and less than a minute later I was into another fish of 34lb. One of Kev's rods went at the same time as well. That turned out to be a 32lb common. A shoal of fish must have moved into the swim and just mopped everything up. It was mad.'

All of the fish had fallen to Mulberry Florentine bottom baits that had been baited at 60yd range. The group took the pictures and some video footage for the library and returned the fish. It was nice to see that the fish were coming on the feed where they were. It was equally as

nice to see that they'd had no problems with the snags in this new spot either. Both Kev and Rob looked a lot happier now. The group just hoped that Mally and Rod were catching as well. Both Rob and Simon couldn't contact them on the radio, as they hadn't got one, and there was no way that they could get round to their area of the lake in the boat because the waves were too rough. If they weren't amongst the fish, then Robert's objective was to move them next to Rob and Kev. The fish were obviously in the area, and he was trying his hardest to make sure everyone was in a decent swim.

Simon arrived back in his swim about an hour later after a brew with the lads. The wind had calmed down a bit by then. This was good news because it meant that he could place his baits in the correct positions easily. The Korda leads were holding bottom well for him. He was only fishing 10–20yd out, on the edge of a steep slope in 6ft (2m) of water, and the leads were exactly what he needed. It took him about ten minutes to get the rigs back into position. Although he had six rods with him, the tight space he was in

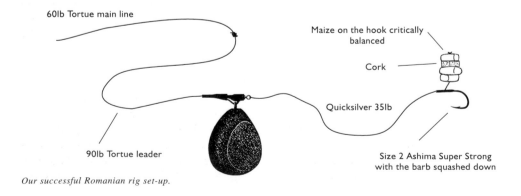

60lb Tortue main line

Maize on the hook critically balanced

Cork

Quicksilver 35lb

90lb Tortue leader

Size 2 Ashima Super Strong with the barb squashed down

*Our successful Romanian rig set-up.*

could only accommodate four rods maximum. Two of these were cast to the left, where Ludo had been getting most of the action, with the other two over to the right. Three rods were baited with popped-up maize which was critically balanced by the hook. He was using cork to pop the baits up and simply trimming bits off to make it critical. The other rod was baited with a 20mm Chocolate Malt bottom bait.

So far, most of the action in Simon's swim had come to maize, with only one or two takes occurring on the boilie. It's worth pointing out here that the takes on the maize had been very twitchy whereas the two on the boilie had been violent whacks on the rod tip followed by a screaming run. We later found out that Robert pre-baits all over the lake with maize and has been doing so for some time. The fish were obviously far more confident of the maize than the boilie. Nevertheless, fish had been caught from the water on the boilie, but it was obviously in its early stages. The whole group concluded that a year of introducing the boilie would improve catches on this bait. The modern carp angler has to bear in mind that when pioneering, modern baits and rigs are not always needed: uncaught carp are not educated and therefore you don't need the most sophisticated gear to catch them.

## MONSTER CATCH

Simon was settled in his swim with the rods cast out for about 7pm and was starting to tuck into his evening meal. Out of the corner of his eye, he watched one of his swingers drop slowly by an inch and then rise slowly by an inch. There had been no sound on the indicator as he'd got them on the lowest sensitivity due to the strong wind of the afternoon. He put his cup down still unsure of what was happening. The strong wind of the afternoon had frequently caused the indicators to move in such a fashion due to the bow in the line caused by using so much braided line. As he put the cup down and leant out of the bivvy he saw the tip start to bounce. At this point the buzzer started to sound. It was a take.

He leapt up, grabbed the rod and legged it to the left, where he knew it was possible to land the fish successfully. He was now well prepared as he'd placed one of his two landing nets in the area to the left. He kept a tight line on the fish and gave it everything he could. The fish was boiling on the surface and he could see its scaling – a common. It was trying hard to gain control of its senses. As it realized what was happening, it surged off to the right. Knowing that it was heading for the snag, Simon ran into the water where the snag lay to try and spook it out. It worked a treat and the fish bolted to the left. He kept its head up with the Dream Maker rod well past its test curve. It was now coming towards the landing net which he was holding in place. In she went head first ...

The nose of the fish was touching the spreader block, with its tail still hanging over the back. It was obviously a big fish, he could see that. However, he wasn't able to lift the net quickly enough through the water and it went bolting off as it panicked. It didn't get very far though, and Simon bullied it back towards the net, which this time he wrapped all around it. 'What a relief', he thought to himself. He'd have been gutted if he'd lost this. As he pulled the net towards himself he knew instantly that it was bigger than everything that he'd ever caught before.

On his Nashy scales, the immaculate common went 52½lb exactly. It was pristine and he was very happy with his prize. It was at this point when he thought about the fish which he'd lost. If he'd landed four fish, two of which were over 40lb, what were the six or seven fish which he'd lost? Robert had seen the commotion with the fish and immediately came over to see what Simon had caught. The light was fading fast as it was nearly 8.30pm, so he went off in his boat to inform the

*A proud Simon with his memorable biggie from that first trip.*

others of what he had so that Simon could have some pictures taken. Simon didn't want to sack the fish as it was very shallow and warm where he was fishing. He made sure that plenty of pictures were taken, and Rob even filmed a short piece on the video camera. In total, we think there were about ten people in Simon's swim firing off pictures. He definitely won't forget that day in a hurry.

Simon was amazed to find that there were still fish in his swim shortly after everyone had left. To the right of the marker where the biggie had come from, a huge vortex appeared in the flat calm water, and a massive (there's no other way of describing it) fish rolled on the surface. Five minutes later Simon's left hand rod went belting off, but he lost the fish on a snag. His mind then started to wonder what he'd just lost as another whacker came clean out of the water in the same spot. It sounded like an elephant had just been chuckcd in! The night, however, went by uneventfully but he wasn't too bothered as he was still on cloud nine with his 52lb common.

For the others, the night had been fairly hectic. Kev led the way with a brace of twenties and a lost fish, whilst Rob landed one just into twenty. Rod and Mally spent the night in the same area as the previous few nights. They were a bit upset at this as they couldn't move swim due to the wind. Thankfully it had calmed down by now and they were able to move near to Rob and Kev. They jumped in to the left of the lads, and were full of confidence as the wind was still hacking into their faces, albeit not as strong as the night before. The only problem was that most of the other anglers on the lake

were also heading to this very spot also. They'd all got wind of where the fish were coming from. None of them wanted to fish near Simon because of the uncomfortable conditions with the mud, so they opted for the grassy banks and the facing wind near to Rob and Kev. Looking back, the lads wished they'd kept details of their catches quiet, especially as they knew the fish were still there.

## LAST FEW DAYS

The proceeding few days turned out to be lot better on the weather. It soon started to warm up again. Kev managed another fish of 20lb-plus whilst Rod banked his first Romanian carp at 28lb. The fish of Kev's was a bit of a surprise really, as we'd been informed on numerous occasions that should one of us catch a mirror, it would certainly be

*Was it that rough over there Kev?*

*The Master. Rod with his first Romanian carp.*

over 50lb. This obviously wasn't the case because he'd banked a low-twenty mirror. Rod's fish had come during the evening and was a well deserved fish. It put up a good account of itself, but the big man soon had the better of it. It had fallen for a Monster Crab bottom bait fished at 60yd.

The following evening Mally had a taste of the Raduta snags when he hooked into a fast take which quickly went slack. It had been a long time coming for Mal, but the poor fella had not been fishing for the first week as his gear had got lost at the airport. His pride wouldn't allow him to take a fish on somebody else's rods. The whole group felt for the old boy as none of us would have liked to have been in the same situation. We suppose we're greedy anglers in that we would have borrowed somebody else's gear, but for Mal, he just wouldn't have any of it. That's the difference between the old school and many of the newcomers, we suppose.

Over the last few days, Simon managed another couple of fish in the low

twenty region, as well as continuing to lose a few, whilst Kev and Rob banked another one each (both twenties). By day thirteen, we think the whole group was worn out. The weather hadn't been on our side and we were basically fatigued by the hard work we'd applied to our Romanian adventure. Neither of us are long-session anglers and this was the longest session either of us had ever fished, and looking back at it, we have to take our hats off to some of the full-time anglers who fish the likes of Yateley. It really is hard work and we think you have to be mentally prepared for what lies ahead. We're a bit impatient, and so decided to end our trip on the Saturday simply so that we could do something different. Simon needed a break from the dreadful swim that he'd been fishing as well as from the loneliness of being by himself over the last week.

It had been a great experience, and we

*Only a small one, but they all count.*

*The daunting snags on that first trip.*

had enjoyed it thoroughly. The rest of the group had also had enough by this time, and they opted to spend the last day fishing in front of the hotel ready for an easy departure on the Sunday.

Despite the fact that we knew what the lake contained, we spent the final night having a bit of a social in front of the hotel. We were the only anglers on the whole lake that last night, and weren't too bothered about singing our hearts out and simply letting our hair down. We think that the locals may have been a bit put out by our singing though, as every one of the villagers owned a dog. As we sang, so did the dogs! It was a hell of a row, but we didn't care.

For anyone contemplating visiting this lake in the near future, take it from us, it is a water that is quite different. It is also one that certainly does contain some massive fish as well as snags. Indeed, the hype is all true, but don't expect to reel in the whackers as though you were fishing your local day-ticket water. Raduta is Raduta, and the biggies really do have to be worked for.

*Chilling out on that last night.*

*We came. We saw. We caught. It was hard graft for two weeks! Now we're off back home. Yesss!*

# Index